BUYING · OWNING · ENJOYING

KU-707-425

Caravanning
handbook

SECOND EDITION

JOHN WICKERSHAM

CONTENTS

CHAPTER ONE

THE FIRST
STEPS

The adventures start here! But you're not in this on your own. It is claimed that in Britain, over 500,000 caravans are in regular, active service. Some make an annual appearance in summer whereas others are used every month of the year. Without doubt, modern caravans provide comfort irrespective of weather or season. Interested in finding out more? This book will help you to learn what's involved.

Caravanning can take you to countryside venues.

My father wasn't prepared to tow a caravan behind his 1939 'Flying Standard'. On reflection, he was probably right, because caravans built in the post-war years were very much heavier than the types built today. As an alternative, he hired his cousin's pre-sited caravan for a week every Whitsun and I've never forgotten the pleasures we had. I even took photographs with the Standard 10 reversed up to its tow hitch to pretend we had towed it ourselves.

Whether it is the smell of leaking gas that I remember most or collecting fresh water in a white enamel jug, memories of holidays in the 1950s remain clear to this day. With a caravan providing a base for our trips I became keen on outdoor pursuits.

TENTS AND TRAILERS

Ten years later I built a sailing boat, and its trailer was easy to tow, even behind a Mini. After that, I bought a frame tent and built a camping trailer that also towed well with equipment on board.

When carefully loaded, a trailer stays stable and

faithfully follows its tow-vehicle with dependable ease. On the other hand, the prospect of towing a caravan was rather more daunting, even though I'd purchased a much better tow car. Come to that, there weren't sufficient funds in the family savings to consider a caravan in place of our tent.

However, it was in the late 1960s when the family's frame tent developed incurable leaks. So the 'caravan idea' resurfaced once more.

THE CARAVAN ALTERNATIVE

There was another issue, too, which added an attraction to buying a caravan. It revolved around tax – or rather the lack of it. For some inexplicable reason 'purchase tax', as it was called in pre-VAT days, didn't apply to caravans. Both new and second-hand models, therefore, were quite reasonably priced.

In consequence, when a work colleague advertised a small but carefully maintained Cygnet caravan, I decided to scrap our sieve that had once served as a tent. A cheque was presented, and the deal was complete. I then spent some time learning levelling procedures, and getting the hang of its hitch.

Simple though this model's amenities were, a couple of seasons in the Cygnet were sufficient to confirm that caravans are fun. Then the Government made an unexpected announcement: new caravans sold after 1972 would be subject to purchase tax, like pretty well everything else.

Convinced that caravanning was the answer to our young family's travel needs, we joined hundreds of others who bought a new model before caravan tax came into force. So we purchased a 1972 Lynton Javelin – and the number of new caravans sold that year hit an all-time high. In fact 1972's remarkable sales figures have never been equalled.

Many towing miles later, I still recommend a newcomer to start with a pre-owned model. It's a less costly way to find out whether caravan holidays are something you like. Then, if you look at new caravans with a purchase in mind, you'll compare different models with a more critical eye.

LEARNING PROCEDURES

I know what he meant but I don't entirely agree with Rousseau, an educational philosopher, who said,

'Learn by doing whenever you can, and only resort to books when "doing" is out of the question.' In my early moments of caravanning need, I would have paid a king's ransom for a book to explain how to do this and do that. Problems began when I realised that the instruction manual unfolding the mysteries of my Cygnet had been lost by its earlier owner. Things didn't improve much with the purchase of a brand new caravan either. Its owner's manual was a parsimonious assembly of stapled pages which didn't even give information about the tyre pressures needed.

So I blundered on and when problems occurred I was ever-grateful for the helpful advice, willingly given by more experienced owners. Bit by bit I learnt the ropes, and adventure experiences were gaining momentum. But that's enough of the personal snapshots, though I suspect many readers will have had similar experiences to the ones I've recalled.

Towing techniques are easy to learn.

MODERN CARAVANS

Caravans nowadays – like the cars which tow them – are truly remarkable products. Safety standards have led to the creation of new practices, and appliances proliferate when you look round inside. Put all these things together and there's an awful lot more for a newcomer to learn.

A modern caravan provides you with all kinds of comforts.

This purpose-built site near Rutland Water is tidy, clean and well laid out.

In fact, anyone new to caravanning clearly needs an illustrated book to guide them. So here it is, and the 17 chapters cover a wide range of topics. However, a few things are missing and that's with good reason. Guidance on Continental travel is an example, because this book is just one in a group of caravan-related titles. For instance, a comprehensive book called *Driving Abroad: skills, advice, safety and laws* was published recently. Equally, if it's caravan repair work that interests you, *The Caravan Manual* (4th Edition) should also be on your shopping list. Its sister volume, *The Motorcaravan Manual*, is another key source book, especially if you later decide that a towed caravan isn't your preferred choice of leisure vehicle.

SELECTING SITES

If you subsequently decide that you want to use top-quality caravan sites, *The Alan Rogers' Good Camps Guides* are unique. Whether you're planning to take a caravan to the Western Highlands, Portugal or Poland, these guides list venues that have passed the stringent biennial inspections of experienced site assessors. Their concise reports give clear information about all the sites recommended. Of course, there are other useful guides on the market, but few of their compilers check the sites they've included.

This kind of site at Pencelli, near Brecon, lets you escape from the crowds.

TAKE TO THE ROAD

In summary, there are many ways to arrange a memorable holiday. Inexpensive flights, package tours and Internet booking systems have certainly extended our horizons. Recently, however, airport delays, international problems, currency issues and concerns about environmental damage have started to change our holiday habits.

Issues like these have undoubtedly prompted a growing number of people to look at alternative arrangements and caravanning is attracting new interest. In fact, many newcomers are rather shocked to find that a modern caravan has hot and cold running water, a shower, a flushing toilet, central heating, mains electricity, television, and so on. It certainly doesn't have the austerity of the 1950s caravan that I remember with such warm affection.

Home comforts aside, don't be worried by the prospect of towing. In fact there are excellent practical training courses using off-road locations, as described in Chapter Five.

Also, use the advice given later when comparing the models on sale. Consider joining one of the national clubs too; the benefits of membership are legion. And don't forget to read the caravan magazines, which report on recent developments.

Now let's get down to detail. Your travelling adventures start here.

Comfortable living is a feature of modern caravans.

CHAPTER TWO

CHECK POINTS **FOR PURCHASING**

If you decide to buy a second-hand caravan, what precautionary measures should be taken? For example, how can you establish that a caravan being offered for sale privately is owned by the vendor and not subject to a hire-purchase agreement? Alternatively, if you're in the fortunate position of being able to buy a brand-new model, what points should be borne in mind? Issues like these are discussed in this chapter.

Whether you buy new or second-hand, there are many points to consider when buying a caravan.

BUYING A CARAVAN

Not surprisingly, buying a caravan is not the same as buying a car. For instance, a caravan doesn't have a mandatory registration document. This means that if you're looking at a second-hand model, its date of manufacture is often hard to establish. Moreover, there is no official MoT test to confirm the integrity of a caravan. You must also be absolutely sure that a pre-owned 'van is being offered for sale by its rightful owner.

These issues don't arise, of course, if you intend to purchase a brand new caravan from a dealer. However, choosing a dealer isn't quite as simple a task as you might imagine. For example, an impressive discount from a caravan specialist whose headquarters are a long way from your home carries a problem that doesn't arise when you're buying a car. If a warranty repair is needed at a later date, you will usually have to take the caravan all the way back to its original supplier. It's not the same with a car, where warranty work can be done at any franchise dealership. Also be aware that factory warranties differ from one manufacturer to another.

Matters like these are discussed in this chapter. In addition, the purchase of a new or a pre-owned model is considered in detail.

NEW OR SECOND-HAND?

In the previous chapter, the merits of buying new or second-hand were discussed briefly. Further considerations are also described in Chapter Three, where changes in manufacturing methods are explained. For instance, improvements in thermal insulation need to be borne in mind. Similarly, when looking at an older caravan you should be aware that obtaining spare parts

Most dealers tend to specialise in a particular marque – although some retail new caravans from two or three manufacturers.

may not be straightforward. That's particularly true if its manufacturer has ceased trading.

Problems obtaining spare parts shouldn't be an issue if you're in the fortunate position of being able to purchase a brand new model. On the other hand, there are several points to note before placing your order.

BUYING NEW

Choosing a dealer

Most dealers specialise in a particular brand of caravan, although this often extends to include products from two or three manufacturers or importers. In other words, if you merely call at your nearest supplier, you're only going to see a small selection of caravans currently on the market.

In fact if you look at a 'Buyer's Guide' in one of the monthly caravan magazines you'll see there are around 18 different marques made in Britain and nearly ten imported brands. To be strictly accurate, it's true that in recent years the Swift Group has manufactured caravans bearing the brand names of Abbey, Ace, Bessacarr, Sterling and Swift, just as the Explorer Group has been manufacturing models under the brand names of Buccaneer, Compass, Crown and Elddis. However, there's plenty of choice even if there are less manufacturers today than 20 years ago.

Moreover, these two major manufacturing groups retain individuality in different models, just as British Leyland did when major takeovers brought cars like Austin, Morris, MG, Rover and Triumph into a major conglomerate. Notice, too, that if a caravan dealer is franchised to sell Explorer Caravans, this doesn't mean the dealership will retail all the 'badged models' coming from this North-Eastern manufacturer.

So to see what's on offer, a good way to gain a broad picture is to purchase several of the major monthly magazines. For instance, *Caravan Magazine*, *Practical Caravan* and *Which Caravan?* all publish monthly test reports and there are back-issue departments so that you can catch-up on reviews that you've missed.

In other words, if you're prepared to get hold of sales literature and to read test reports in magazines, a 'phone call to the manufacturers or importers will reveal where different dealers are located. Alternatively this information is normally given on manufacturers' websites. This enables you to see a product 'for real'. However, there's another approach to consider, namely a visit to one of the major indoor exhibitions or outdoor shows.

Buying new
- Choosing a dealer
- Buying at an exhibition
- Delivery calendar
- Dealer 'specials'
- Warranty terms and conditions

15

Getting model details and the addresses of manufacturers

Most monthly magazines include 'Buyers' Guides' in which key information is laid out in tabular form. This allows you to single out models which meet your particular needs using criteria such as weight, size, bed accommodation and so on. These magazines also include the addresses of manufacturers, thereby enabling you to send away for brochures. In addition, the majority of manufacturers run websites giving details of models as well.

Where are caravans built? Most monthly caravan magazines include an address list of manufacturers.

Name change

At the close of 2009, the Explorer group announced that it would change its name to ELDDIS and the Compass range would not be included in its 2010 models.

A large selection of caravans are on show at indoor exhibitions such as The Boat & Caravan Show held at the NEC, Birmingham in February.

Buying at an exhibition

The two largest caravan exhibitions are currently:

1 The International Caravan and Motorhome Show, which is held at the National Exhibition Centre (NEC), Birmingham, in October.
2 The Boat & Caravan Show, which is held at the National Exhibition Centre, Birmingham, in February.

In addition, there are regional shows held in cities like Cardiff, Glasgow and Manchester, although these are organised on a smaller scale. There are also several outdoor shows where caravans are on sale and details of venues and dates are given in caravan magazines. Typically these are held at agricultural show grounds or racecourses so there's plenty of room to show the exhibits.

By visiting a large event you can look closely at products and make your assessments. You'll also find that on caravan manufacturers' stands there are sales people from several approved dealers together with staff from the factory as well. You can also place an order at a caravan show, which is different from arrangements at motor shows where dealer representatives are seldom in attendance.

Sometimes there are special prices or 'add-on' accessories when orders are taken for caravans at an exhibition.

Sales strategies

Not surprisingly, if you appear to be interested in a caravan displayed on a stand, a dealer is likely to approach and strike up a conversation. He or she will often enquire if you are already a caravan owner, and for anyone visiting a show as a potential purchaser, here is a good opportunity to conduct business. There may also be 'show discounts', either in the form of a price reduction or the inclusion of additional accessories as a buying incentive. Overall it's a good way to compare prices and products, but there are important words of warning.

Dealer location

First, you should establish where a sales person's base is located, because that is usually where you'll have to visit in order to collect the 'van you've ordered. Equally, you will usually have to return to the dealer conducting the sale if warranty work is needed at a later date. So if you get the best selling price from a dealer situated 200 miles from your home, the cost of travel to and from the base can quickly eliminate the apparent benefit of an attractive price.

Delivery

Secondly, you should appreciate that when purchases are 'signed and sealed', it is often many months before a caravan is built, supplied to the dealer, given its pre-delivery inspection (PDI) and made ready for collection. Orders taken at shows held early in the New Year are not always ready for use in time for Easter. Delivery is certainly a point to discuss with the dealer.

Technical issues

Lastly, you should check all the technical points raised in the accompanying chapters before placing an order. Some sales specialists are well-versed in details about their products and a few might own a caravan themselves. On the other hand, there are others whose understanding of technical detail is woefully limited. At a show, this need not be a serious handicap because there's usually a technical member of staff in attendance from the factory. So don't be reticent to pose important questions; a less-knowledgeable salesperson should be able to provide answers by consulting the manufacturer's representative.

Delivery calendar

The fact that most new caravans are ordered rather than purchased directly from a dealer's forecourt inevitably means there is usually a waiting period.

Furthermore, the caravan industry calendar means that new models are usually launched every year. As it often turns out, changes might be cosmetic rather than radical but there are yearly changes nonetheless.

Many manufacturers finish making the prototypes of models to appear the following year as early as June or July. These are then unveiled to members of the caravan Press in July and August.

After this, one of the first trade shows falls in September; public exhibitions follow in late autumn.

Models held in stock
Occasionally a dealer might have an example of the model you want back at his or her base. However, in reality that is often unlikely because to stock every model with all the different permutations of internal layout and equipment would take a large amount of space on a dealer's forecourt.

Annual post-season sales
With the advent of new models not far away, there are typically late autumn sales where dealers make strenuous efforts to clear stock in readiness for new models. Some of the mark-down prices are notable, although for most people the summer has passed and the idea of caravanning with winter approaching acts as a purchasing disincentive. But there are usually bargains at the close of each season.

Dealers and members of the Caravanning Press are shown the following year's models in July or August.

Buyer's Tip

Timing a purchase
When planning to purchase a new model, be mindful of the caravan industry's annual roundabout. Arrange the dates with care so that your intended purchase will arrive well before your first planned trip. Unexpected delivery delays are not unusual.

Without doubt, the annual late autumn exhibition held at the NEC, Birmingham, in October is one of the best times to order a new caravan if you want to ensure delivery early next spring. Orders placed here set the manufacturing pattern over the winter period, even though many caravan factories have a traditional extended shut-down at Christmas/ New Year.

Then there are the spring shows accompanied by spells of frenetic energy on the production lines. Some deliveries can get delayed quite considerably – partly because many manufacturers produce caravans in batches according to model. Hence all the twin-axle models might take the production line for a week, thereby putting on 'hold' the manufacture of single-axle models.

Spring is always busy both at the factories and dealerships. Even caravan workshops are stretched to the limits as customers arrange annual pre-season servicing.

Dealer 'specials'

As a way of boosting sales, several large retailers make arrangements with a manufacturer to produce a model specific to their dealership. Typically this is a model already in the line-up, albeit with the addition of a new name, different external decals and a package of extras like a gas barbecue point on the side, an additional chest of drawers inside, and so on.

Similar techniques are employed, of course, by car dealers – particularly with high-volume hatchback models. The offer of something 'special' which includes 'complimentary' accessory items acts as a buying incentive.

How this strategy affects a resale at a later date is a little less clear. In truth, the benefits bestowed by a few 'add-ons' is unlikely to enhance a trade-in price. Moreover, a model associated with a particular dealer might not be so favourably viewed when offered as a trade-in to a rival supplier. Apart from that, there's little against buying a dealer special, especially if you like some of the extra items being thrown-in as part of the package.

Warranty terms and conditions

When considering new models for a shortlist, don't forget to compare manufacturers' warranties too. These differ in various ways, especially with regard to the period over which the external fabric of a caravan is covered against leaks arising from faults in construction. This particular affliction is often referred to as 'water ingress'.

Over the years, some workmanship has been disappointing, especially if it has led to damage caused by water ingress. When a survey undertaken in 1999 by The Caravan Club produced disturbing findings, manufacturers responded and standards improved. Moreover, the confidence of some constructors led to warranties against water ingress through manufacturing faults being extended from three to six years. One manufacturer, Bailey of Bristol, is now offering a ten-year warranty on some of its 2010 models. Furthermore, a monocoque GRP caravan called the Voyager Vector carried a 25-year warranty before production ceased.

BUYING SECOND-HAND

Private purchases

Specialist magazines and local newspapers usually contain a classified advertisement section devoted to caravans. Purchasing via the internet is becoming more popular, too. There are certainly some very good caravans on sale privately – as well as plenty of poorer products. The term *caveat emptor*, or buyer beware, is particularly relevant here.

Warranty conditions
You should take note what has to be done in order for a warranty to remain valid. As a rule there's a stipulation that the 'van has to have a full service at regular calendar intervals at an approved workshop. Overlook this at your peril. Equally, you should establish what is deemed to be an 'approved workshop' in the eyes of the manufacturer.

19

Buying second-hand
- Private purchases
- Dealer pre-owned models
- Caravan auctions
- Obsolete models
- Owners' clubs
- Imported models
- Pre- and post-1980 models
- Caravan Registration Identification Scheme

When purchasing a pre-owned caravan, ask to see the results of its last damp check conducted at a service centre.

In truth, every transaction has to be evaluated individually and it is quite impossible to give more than a few guidelines. Suggestions include these points:

☐ If you are not familiar with caravan construction, read Chapter Three with care. This identifies some of the features to check.
☐ Establish when a caravan was last serviced and ask to see the signed service schedule to establish the extent of the work undertaken.
☐ Ask to see approval certificates that the gas and electrical systems have been checked and deemed safe.
☐ Ask when the last professional damp check was carried out using an electrically operated damp meter and ask to see the certificate.
☐ Where possible, follow up the CRiS registration check described on pages 26 and 27.

In practice these recommendations are easy to list but you'll soon find that many caravans are *never* serviced professionally. Others have been given a cursory service but the 'van is returned without any documentation showing the extent of the work carried out. Equally, there are thousands of caravans that have never been damp-checked with a meter. Nor for that matter are many pre-owned models sold with certificates from appropriately qualified gas and electrical engineers to verify that their supply systems are in safe working order.

In acknowledgement of this, a cautionary purchaser might wisely decide to avoid anything not supported by this kind of documentation. On the other hand, if the price is attractive and you are prepared to get this work done as soon as you take ownership, you might decide to proceed. There are certainly some cared-for caravans on sale that have been lovingly cherished and kept immaculately clean by fastidious owners. Many pre-owned examples like this have also brought much pleasure to their subsequent owners. Conversely there are also appalling purchases that have proved to be disastrous. So all I can add is: look closely, compare critically – and *caveat emptor*.

Dealer pre-owned models

Obviously there are inherent risks when purchasing privately, whereas buying a pre-owned caravan from a dealer generally provides some post-purchase support if a subsequent problem arises. Admittedly, the degree of cover offered by a warranty on a second-hand caravan varies from dealer to

Checking a caravan's credentials
A particular worry is establishing whether a caravan being offered for sale is wholly owned by its vendor. On the one hand it might still be the subject of a hire purchase or loan agreement; on the other, it might be a 'van that has been stolen. This is where the CRiS scheme is helpful, for an explanation of which see pages 26 and 27.

Inclusion of accessories
Most dealers sell their pre-owned stock empty of accessories. Not surprisingly, a dealer will willingly direct you towards the accessory shop when you realise you need cutlery, crockery, a leisure battery, water containers and costly items like an awning. In contrast, private sellers often include these accessories as part of the sale. Admittedly some items might not be included where the private seller is purchasing another caravan in its place, but things like awnings might not fit the new model, so they tend to be included in the transaction.

dealer but there's far more likelihood of after-sale support. Needless to say, that's one reason why the asking price is usually higher than it is on private transactions.

A further benefit of purchasing from a dealer is the fact that a caravan offered for sale is likely to have been serviced and fully checked over. In addition a post-1992 CRiS registration transfer of ownership would normally be carried out on your behalf – a topic dealt with in the CRiS section later in this chapter. However, don't expect to find accessory equipment like an awning or water containers included in the package. They might be included in private sales, but at a dealers you normally get directed to the on-site accessory shop.

All in all, many purchasers prefer the support that accompanies a dealer sale; it's just that you normally have to pay slightly more to secure the additional peace of mind.

Caravan auctions

Broadly speaking, caravan auctions are on two levels. On the one hand there are small-town affairs conducted by a local auctioneer and estate agent. Though comparatively unusual, these are sometimes staged at a caravan storage centre, near a factory or a dealership that has gone into liquidation.

Dealer prices might be higher than private sales, but you can insist that the caravan is sold fully serviced before collection.

Small auctions are sometimes conducted by local auctioneers and estate agents at venues such as storage centres.

Thorough inspection is most important before placing a bid at a local auction.

British Car Auctions

At present, you would expect to find around 60 to 70 caravans and motorhomes at a Measham Centre auction, and there are guidance leaflets produced by BCA on bidding procedures.

For more information and dates of sales, contact: The General Manager, British Car Auctions (Measham Branch), *Tel* 01530 270322.

If you buy a really old caravan – as kept at the back of a dealer's forecourt – you might have difficulty buying spare parts.

The Caravan Club can supply members with a list of caravan breakers around the country.

More easy to track down are sales conducted by a specialist like British Car Auctions (BCA). This company's occasional 'Leisure and Caravan' auctions have taken place at several of the 23 or so BCA centres around the country but nowadays most are held at the Measham branch in the Midlands. Caravan sales are timetabled on a fairly regular basis.

While the popular image of auctions depicts a situation where there's little purchaser protection, this is not necessarily accurate. Legislation affords more support than is often appreciated and there's plenty of opportunity at Measham for a purchaser to scrutinise caravans thoroughly prior to the sale itself. Occasionally there are even brand new caravans included in the sale as a result of company liquidations. Not surprisingly, purchase prices are often attractive.

Obsolete models

In the last 20 to 30 years many caravan manufacturers have ceased trading. Some have been taken over by larger conglomerates while other factories have closed down completely.

When it comes to obtaining spare parts, this can present a problem, but components for post-1980 chassis are usually easy to obtain. Many appliances

(*eg* refrigerators, hobs, water systems and so on) can usually be repaired as well.

However, it is items like matching furniture, unusual catches, window glazing, and upholstery products that are often impossible to replace with identical units. This is where owners' clubs (see next section) can be helpful points of contact. So, too, are caravan breakers, and a list of yards is available to members of The Caravan Club from its head office in East Grinstead.

After the proposed 2009 Avondale range was shown to dealers and the Press in June 2008, the company ceased trading.

Models no longer in production

There are many familiar names among the caravans that are no longer in production. These include the

Known for its range of ultra narrow caravans, Silverline finished production in 1992.

The Forest was produced for several years in Nottingham before its demise in 1977.

High quality woodwork, a glass-fibre body and rainwater downpipes with a hopper head were features of this 1950s Cheltenham – a marque that finished production in 1974.

The Lynton ranges from Manchester were often lively in style; production ceased, however, in 1986.

Berkeley made innovative caravans using GRP bodies, but the Biggleswade company ceased production in the early 1960s.

The famous Sprite range was made in Newmarket but the factory ceased manufacturing in the early 1980s.

Caravans like this Eccles from the 1920s are still in use by collectors and can often be seen at outdoor shows.

following, although there are many more lesser-known brands:

A-Line, Astral, Avondale, Berkeley, Buzzard, Castleton, Cavalier, Cheltenham, Coronet, Cygnet, Deanline, Europa, Fisher, Fleetwind, Forest, Knowsley, Lynton, Mardon, Mustang, Panther, Robin, Royale, Safari, Silverline, Sprite, Sovereign, Sunseeker, Thomson, Trophy, Viking Fibreline and Windrush.

Old and even older

Some Owners' Clubs are concerned with caravans that went out of production in the last few years, whereas others support models of much greater heritage. There are even two clubs catering for the owners of very early caravans, and these charming products – usually towed by a car of the correct vintage – are often seen on display at outdoor caravan rallies.

Owners' clubs

There are currently around 45 clubs devoted to particular brands of caravan and the addresses of their secretaries are published regularly in magazines like *Caravan Magazine* and *Practical Caravan*.

Committee members of those clubs concerned with models still in manufacture often attend major exhibitions, like The Boat & Caravan Show held at the National Exhibition Centre. Furthermore, a section is usually provided for them on the stand of the host manufacturer.

Many clubs concerned with obsolete models are also surprisingly active; interest in old caravans is not dissimilar from the enthusiasm shown by owners of classic cars. Club members can often provide advice if a model you've purchased needs attention.

Imported models

With caravans being built in several European countries, some potential owners enquire whether they can import a model independently. While this is certainly possible there are a number of disadvantages to bear in mind.

Firstly, the caravan door is normally situated on the opposite side to suit right-hand driving. When parked by the roadside in Britain, this presents a possible danger when you step from the 'van. However, there are exceptions, as the photo above reveals.

In addition, an imported caravan might not comply with British Standards. For instance, all UK-manufactured caravans now have to comply with the Furniture and Furnishings Fire (Safety) Regulations 1988 – which means that any foam in mattresses has to be fire-retardant. This requirement is not obligatory in all European countries.

As regards the gas supply system, some foreign models used to be fitted with different gas jets in appliances. That was because these caravans operated on a different operating pressure and were fitted with a gas regulator to achieve that setting. However, since 2003 there has been greater standardisation in respect of European gas systems, as described in Chapter Fourteen.

In practice, Continental caravans imported into

This imported Knaus caravan has been purpose-built for the UK market, as the position of its door confirms.

Imported caravans

Whereas some imported caravans have much to commend them, they are seldom fitted with a grill. Our friends from overseas seem not to have discovered the pleasure of toast. Equally, many imported models lack carpet, and while a vinyl floor covering is distinctly practical many British caravanners prefer a carpeted floor. And not surprisingly, a mains installation will have different switches, sockets and control units, unless the importing dealer has arranged for these to be replaced to suit British owners.

On the other hand, some caravans, especially Scandinavian models, are fitted with a greater level of thermal insulation to suit lower winter temperatures.

Since its inception, the CRiS registration scheme has involved etching an identification number on a caravan's windows.

the UK by specialist companies are often fitted with items that British caravanners usually want. So whereas the door position is unlikely to be changed, if you like a particular model built abroad it is better to buy through a specialist who carries out modifications such as changing a cooker and altering mains electricity fittings.

Pre- and post-1980 models

When buying an older caravan, it is important to recognise that many radical changes in construction took effect around 1980. Externally, these features are not very obvious to the layperson, but 'below the skin' the revised building techniques are very difficult.

To find out more about these developments and their implications for ownership, refer to the following chapter.

Caravan Registration Identification Scheme (CRiS)

Unlike cars and other motor-driven vehicles, caravans had no registration document until the CRiS initiative was launched in 1992. This scheme was created by HPI Ltd working in partnership with the National Caravan Council (NCC). There is no mandatory registration but all new caravans launched with National Caravan Council badge accreditation were included from 1992 onwards.

The visible evidence of CRiS registration is given on each window, where the caravan's identification number is etched. Other features which developed later were:

1997   from July of that year, all new caravans from NCC member-manufacturers were fitted with a hidden electronic tag that carries the VIN (Vehicle Identification Number).

1999   from October of that year, owners of pre-1992 caravans and owners of imported models could also register them on the scheme. Points about this are as follows:

☐ There is a small registration fee.
☐ A VIN is allocated.
☐ A DIY etching kit is supplied for marking the 17-digit code on the windows.
☐ At the time of initial registration, a DIY electronic tag can be supplied for an additional charge.

The benefits of CRiS are especially evident to anyone purchasing a pre-owned caravan; these are explained in the panel below. Information is available on the HPI website at www.hpicheck.com or by telephoning 01722 411430. Lines are currently open seven days a week; on Monday–Friday from 8:00am to 8:00pm; Saturday 9:00am to 5:00pm; Sunday 10:00am to 5:00pm.

CRiS benefits for buyers and owners

Through the CRiS scheme, caravan keepers have 'access to a vital register that can help protect the security of their caravans and help the police in returning stolen caravans to their rightful owners'.

Alternatively, if you want to purchase a second-hand model, you can verify that it hasn't been stolen, or can find out if any hire purchase payments are still outstanding. As a potential purchaser you can pay a small fee for a history check. All you have to do is to submit the caravan's 17-digit VIN code, a description of the 'van, and the name and address of the seller. This will then be checked with the database to see that everything matches.

But note: CRiS won't give away confidential information about the owner – merely whether your information and theirs matches.

You will also be able to establish if the caravan is:
• Currently recorded as stolen.
• Officially written-off by an insurance company.
• Still the subject of a loan from a finance house.

Finally, when purchasing a CRiS-registered caravan, change of ownership procedures are as follows:

a) A private seller has to complete the Notification of Sale section on the registration document and send it to CRiS.
b) The private seller should pass the rest of the document to the purchaser.
c) You, as purchaser, must then fill out the Notification of Change section on the document and send it to CRiS. A small charge is payable.

CHAPTER THREE

DESIGN AND
CONSTRUCTION

Not surprisingly, most people buy a caravan on the basis of its appearance, layout and suitability for towing. It is not until much later that the qualities relating to its overall design and construction become apparent. This chapter takes you beneath the surface and explains building details and their implications. With this knowledge, you'll be able to make a more informed judgement when buying a new or second-hand caravan.

Body panels are usually pre-formed and then assembled on the production line.

A discerning and knowledgeable purchaser pays particular attention to details like these when comparing caravans:

- ☐ The materials used for the roof, side walls, front and rear panels.
- ☐ Type of windows fitted.
- ☐ A-frame fairings.
- ☐ External lockers for gas cylinders, battery and leisure equipment.
- ☐ The chassis and running gear.
- ☐ Installation of appliances such as the cooker, heater and refrigerator.
- ☐ Body trims and panel assembly.

To evaluate these elements when comparing caravans, you need to know what you're looking for – and that's where this chapter can help. Unfortunately many prospective purchasers only make their buying decisions on the basis of the internal layout, sleeping capacity, soft furnishings, and price. The wider implications of a caravan's design, construction and possible weaknesses only become apparent when something goes wrong.

CARAVAN BODYWORK AND EXTERNAL ELEMENTS

At first sight, caravans look much the same regardless of model. But the differences are more than skin deep. The construction of a caravan's body, for example, can differ significantly and this has implications if a repair has to be carried out.

Whilst there are some excellent caravans around, there's no doubt that a few models are poorly built and hard to repair. So here are some points you'd be wise to check.

Structure of the shell

If you are buying a low price, older caravan, it's important to realise that around 1980, the way that most caravans were built underwent a radical change. This change led to reductions in weight and improvements in insulation. New constructional strategies also speeded up manufacture, so building costs were lower as well.

Prior to 1980, caravans were built using a skeleton of timber struts which was subsequently clad on the outside with aluminium sheet. On the inside, a thin

Technical Tip

A few manufacturers were still using traditional coachbuilding methods in the late 1990s, particularly companies specialising in high quality, low volume products. A Carlight caravan, noted for its high level of craftsmanship, was one example. Buccaneer caravans were also built traditionally until the brand was taken over by the Explorer Group. Buccaneer bodies were then assembled using pre-fabricated sandwich panels.

ply lining was fixed to the struts. As a rule, the void between these cladding materials was filled with glass-fibre quilt; this provides thermal insulation, but it often slumps down over time, and that's when cold spots appear.

Floors were heavy structures consisting of thick plywood panels fixed to timber joists that in turn were supported by the steel chassis members. No form of thermal insulation was included in the floor itself, and on winter trips many caravanners found their feet got quite cold.

The major structural changes that subsequently took place involved the introduction of prefabricated panels which include block insulation in the core. The accompanying photographs highlight key features.

☐ Instead of being formed with heavy joists and thick plywood, a modern floor is created using a core of block insulation (usually Styrofoam™) and timber battens. This is then bonded on either side with specially treated 5mm plywood.

☐ The composite wall panels start with a core of block insulation (usually polystyrene) which is later bonded to an outside skin of sheet aluminium and an interior layer of 3mm decoratively faced plywood.

☐ A caravan's front panels – and sometimes the rear sections – are generally built using a plastic moulding supported by a timber framework. Only budget models are constructed with the same flat panels used for the side walls.

☐ Behind a front or rear moulded panel, the manufacturer uses a supporting timber framework to provide rigidity and employs either a block or quilt-type insulant.

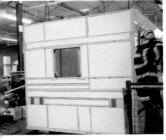

The bonded sandwich panel used for side walls has a core of polystyrene insulation.

☐ Roofs structures are sometimes built in situ using traditional methods or, as shown here, a prefabricated bonded panel is prepared away from the assembly line.

Naturally there are variations on this approach to construction. For example, some caravans have been manufactured using flat sheets of glass-reinforced plastic (GRP) on the external side walls instead of aluminium sheet. This alternative cladding first appeared in 1996 on the Abbey Domino and a benefit is the fact that a skilled 'fibre-glass' repairer can sometimes repair a damaged GRP skin. In contrast, if an aluminium sheet panel gets dented the whole side section usually has to be clad with a new layer bonded on top of the old one.

When the techniques for producing bonded wall panels were first developed at the close of the 1970s, this coincided with new thinking about the design of caravan chassis as well. In fact the radical changes that took place went hand-in-hand, because both the prefabricated floor panel and the chassis interact to produce a strong but light supporting structure.

Note: *With these constructional points in mind, if you're planning to purchase a second-hand 'starter' caravan, bear in mind that around 1980 many constructional features were changing.*

Today, caravan floors are built using a prefabricated sandwich panel; this one has blue Styrofoam in the core for insulation.

 Buyer's Tip

Delamination

Caravan floors and walls are prefabricated using three relatively weak materials in a 'sandwich'. Their strength, however, is achieved because they are bonded together. Indeed, the whole success of the system depends on the effectiveness of the bonding adhesive. If the adhesive fails, rigidity is lost, and it's common knowledge that a polystyrene or Styrofoam™ panel used in the core is as brittle as a biscuit. So delamination – as the problem of bond failure is called – mustn't be taken lightly.

Fortunately you don't often find the aluminium skin on side walls bubbling and losing its bond with the insulating core; nonetheless, it *can* happen so it's something you should check if looking at pre-owned caravans. Floors, however, are more likely to fail and this occurs when the ply in the living area loses its bond with the block foam below.

Not only does the floor then start to flex; the overall strength achieved by the combined bracing effect of the floor, the axle tube and the chassis is going to be reduced. As stated in the later section on lightweight chassis, a rigid floor panel is one of the important elements that contributes to the overall effectiveness of chassis members.

So look out for delamination as follows:

- Make sure the corner steadies are lowered, then enter the 'van.

- Walk around inside and listen for pronounced, tell-tale creaking sounds.

- You might see slight rises in parts of the floor that in essence are blisters where the plywood has flexed upwards away from the foam.

- Check for a feeling of movement and floor flexion when you walk around.

- Particularly check areas that occupants use often. Classic weak spots are just inside the door where everyone steps on entry. Look around the kitchen units too, because a lot of time is often spent here.

Note: *Delaminated sections can usually be repaired, and a service specialist re-bonds a faulty area by injecting a liquid adhesive into the damaged zone to recreate adhesion. This aside, it's obviously wise to avoid buying a caravan with the problem in the first place.*

If the floor ply does break away from the foam core, a delamination repair involves drilling holes and injecting a special adhesive.

Sealant under the central cover strip of a 'boat-style' roof may need to be renewed periodically.

Variations in roof design and construction

Irrespective of the age of a caravan that you're planning to purchase, have a look at its roof design. Most are built using a framework of timber that is subsequently skinned in a traditional manner. However, several manufacturers are now starting to use pre-formed sandwich-insulated panels instead.

Flat roofs are the least effective for discharging rainwater, and that can be detrimental as far as weather-proofing's concerned. On the other hand, if you plan to fit a roof-mounted TV aerial, a solar panel or an air conditioner, these undoubtedly fit more successfully when the surface is flat.

In contrast, boat-style roofs have a raised ridge that runs from end to end. Separate aluminium sheets are mounted on either side of this ridge and a trim-strip bedded on sealant covers the join. In this design, some surface water drains off at the sides.

You may also come across the old-style 'lantern roof', where a central raised section is fitted with narrow windows on either side. Caravans like the Safari adopted this pattern and the style later became a patent design of Carlight Caravans. It's a distinctive feature on craftsman-built models.

Lastly you'll find that some roofs are built using a one-piece glass-reinforced plastic (GRP) moulding. Avondale was a company that often used this type of roof. For example, the moulded roof fitted to later Avondale Landrangers was truly impressive. Its design ensured that rainwater was discharged efficiently and its lack of seams gave it a weather-proof performance second to none.

Avondale has been noted for single-piece GRP roofs which are fitted on models such as this Landranger.

Is the front panel on this Fleetwood made from GRP or acrylic-capped ABS plastic? An inspection soon shows that it's made from the latter.

Moulded front and rear panels

All but the least expensive caravans now have moulded panels at the front and rear. However, when purchasing a caravan, whether new or old, it's helpful to know if moulded sections are made from GRP or acrylic-capped ABS. There's a good reason for this and the accompanying box explains how you can tell the difference.

The reason why it's helpful to establish which material has been used is related to repair work. Although a GRP panel is usually heavier and more expensive, it is often easy to repair. Boat builders, car body specialists and others familiar with GRP products can effect neat repairs, even when panels are damaged quite badly.

In the last few years, procedures have been developed to repair ABS panels as well. However, not many staff at caravan service centres are familiar with the special repair compounds needed. There are exceptions, of course, but the majority of repairers prefer to replace an entire unit that has been damaged. In other words, if you brush against

This 1990 Compass Rallye is built with GRP panels on both the front and rear walls.

Technical Tip

Checking for GRP and acrylic-capped ABS moulded panels

The key feature of GRP is that it has a shiny side and a reverse side that's usually quite rough to the touch. This roughness is not a problem, though, especially when the reverse face of a panel is largely unseen. However, on expensive caravans items like GRP locker lids often have a secondary inner skin of GRP to hide the rough texture.

In contrast, acrylic-capped ABS (acrylonitrile-butadiene-styrene) has a natural shine on both faces. Admittedly, a textured surface is sometimes created on one of the sides – as it is on many car bumpers made from ABS. But when you rub your hand over the reverse face, you'll see how ABS differs from GRP. In fact, many A-frame fairings at the front and items like wheel spats are now made in ABS plastic.

Running a hand over the rear of the front skirt on this Compass Rallye immediately reveals that it's made from GRP.

Fairings which cover a caravan's A-frame are often made of ABS plastic.

The wheel arch extension here is made from ABS plastic and it might be hard to obtain a replacement for this 1990 model.

a kerbstone and crack a small part of a front or rear ABS panel, many dealers will want to replace the whole section. Fitting a new 'front end' can result in a four-figure bill.

So until repair work on ABS panels is practised more widely, there's good reason for preferring caravans built with GRP mouldings. Unfortunately, this material is being used less and less on most recent models.

Moulded fairings and fittings

Caravans are built with moulded wheel arch extensions (usually called 'wheel spats'), and road lights are mounted in housings as well.

As regards the chassis extension at the front, referred to as the A-frame, this remains exposed on earlier caravans. However, on more recent models a cosmetic moulded fairing is usually added to hide the projecting chassis members. Unfortunately this plastic cover is usually too fragile to stand on should you want to wash flies away from the upper sections of your caravan's front. When the author pointed this out to UK manufacturers, Bailey responded by creating two small reinforced steps in its fairings.

The fairing on recent Bailey caravans has two steps that are useful when cleaning the front.

This bestows practical use on a component that is largely a cosmetic appendage.

In summary, wheel spats, moulded road-lamp housings and fairings are made in either ABS or GRP, most of which can get easily damaged. In consequence, if you own a caravan whose manufacturer has ceased trading, replacement body mouldings are often unobtainable. However, a few specialists have addressed this problem as the accompanying panel explains.

Technical Tip

Replica panels and parts

Two specialists are able to create replacement mouldings in GRP provided you can supply broken parts. For instance, if you have a damaged gas locker lid in either ABS or GRP, these experts can piece together the broken fragments, add filling compounds, and then create a replica mould. From this new mould, it is then possible to create copies of the original damaged component.

The contact details for GFL Panels near Preston, and V&G near Peterborough, are given in the Appendix.

When the locker door had broken on an old Lunar caravan, V&G made a perfect copy.

Many moulds to make fairings have been produced by GFL Panels.

Windows

In November 1977 it became mandatory for caravans to be fitted with safety glass. At this point,

Prior to 1980, a caravan window was glass which was mounted in an aluminium frame.

If a stone cracks a window on the front of your caravan, a small unit is not too expensive to replace.

manufacturers decided to move away from glass units set within an aluminium frame; frameless, moulded acrylic plastic units were then used instead. To begin with, most plastic windows were single-glazed, although double-glazed versions were fitted on several top-of-the-range models. But that soon changed. During the 1980s, double-glazed units

Caravans built with a single window on the front are going to cost the owner a considerable amount of money if a flying stone causes damage.

Windows

Windows fitted to pre-November 1977 caravans consist of glass held in an aluminium frame; spare units are hard both to trace and to replace.

- Replacement double-glazed plastic windows are surprisingly expensive; they need to be ordered from a dealer and delivery can take a long time.
- Products are sometimes available from caravan breakers; members of The Caravan Club can obtain an address list from the Club's head office.
- Surplus stocks of new products bought from caravan manufacturers – including windows – can be purchased from Magnum Caravan Surplus (Grimsby). *Tel* 01472 353520.
- Stones can get thrown up when you're towing and windows on the front occasionally get cracked. When it comes to buying a replacement, the cost will be considerably less if it's one of the three small windows fitted at the front as opposed to a large single unit.
- Sometimes condensation forms inside double-glazed windows so replacements are needed. A short-term cure is to remove one of the small plastic plugs in the panel and to leave the unit in an airing cupboard for a day or more. The plug is subsequently glued back in place before the window is then re-installed.
- If you really cannot find a replacement plastic window – for instance, if your caravan's manufacturer has ceased trading – EECO (near Halifax) makes one-off windows with a reasonably fast turn-around time. *Tel* 01274 679524.

On a Carlight caravan, the gas cylinder is easily accessed by sliding its support tray forward out of the locker.

became standard and the higher level of thermal insulation was clearly beneficial. So windows should be checked if you're buying a second-hand caravan from around this period.

The centrally located gas locker on this Avondale means that the weight of the cylinders is close to the axle.

39

External lockers

Lockers often didn't exist on caravans made 30 years ago and gas cylinders were merely mounted on an exposed rack fitted to the A-frame near the coupling. Today, it's standard practice to have a purpose-made gas locker and you should check that its lid fits well and isn't damaged. Most lockers are located at the front, although on Avondale caravans the locker is usually situated on a side wall instead. This offers benefits in respect of a caravan's weight distribution.

Check that access to the cylinders is easy; apart from Carlight, few manufacturers have fitted a sliding base to facilitate cylinder replacement.

As regards a caravan's leisure battery, this should have its own separate locker. A few caravans built in the 1980s had a cage to house a battery installed alongside the gas cylinders. This is bad practice because gas can seep from a faulty cylinder valve and sparks are not unusual when coupling up a battery terminal. To avoid any likelihood of an explosion, gas and battery lockers are now kept completely separate.

Beyond this, check to see if there are any external lockers built to house outdoor leisure gear. Regrettably, only a few caravans include this provision.

The imported Knaus 'Sport & Fun' is one of the few caravans which has large locker accommodation for outdoor activity gear.

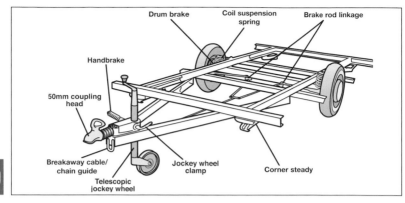

Drum brake   Coil suspension   Brake rod linkage
              spring

Handbrake

50mm coupling
head

Breakaway cable/   Jockey wheel
chain guide   clamp   Corner steady

Telescopic
jockey wheel

*The B&B (Bird &
Billington) chassis used
prior to1983 was a
popular design.*

Chassis

Caravans built before 1980 featured a heavy chassis
that was usually painted; products from Peak
Chassis and B&B (Bird & Billington) were especially
well-known.

Then it was discovered that by using a sandwich-
bonded floor panel, its inherent strength could
be used to contribute a bracing effect to the steel
chassis members. The result? A new breed of
notably lighter, computer-designed chassis where
the overall strength was derived from the interplay
between a bonded floor, the axle tube and purpose-
designed lightweight steel chassis sections.

Lightweight chassis made by AL-KO or BPW are
fitted on virtually all caravans currently in production.
However, that hasn't always been the case. For
instance, Sprite caravans were built using a traditional
and comparatively heavy steel chassis until the early
1990s. Lunar caravans were built on an aluminium
chassis made in Lancashire until the mid-1990s. Swift
used an aluminium Syspal chassis on the Silhouette
model too. Carlight Caravans was the last major
manufacturer to use a robustly constructed British steel
chassis until production ceased a few years ago.

*Older chassis are
comparatively heavy in
structure and the steel
sections have to be
painted periodically.*

*A galvanised axle tube,
light chassis members
and floor panel combine
to provide a sound
foundation.*

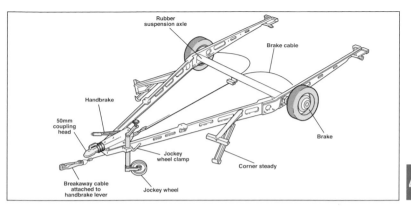

Rubber
suspension axle

Brake cable

Handbrake

50mm
coupling
head

Brake

Jockey
wheel clamp

Corner steady

Breakaway cable
attached to
handbrake lever

Jockey wheel

If you buy a 'van with an older steel chassis, it will be heavy. It will also need painting occasionally when it gets chipped because very few were ever galvanised. Even some of the lightweight chassis from AL-KO were painted in the early 1980s; examples of non-galvanised AL-KO products were used on some Elddis caravans of that period. Nowadays all AL-KO and BPW chassis and axle tubes are galvanised; provided these do not suffer from any abrasion damage, they are maintenance-free products.

Running gear
This term includes items like the suspension and the braking system. Again you should note two differences between the older type of chassis and the lightweight versions that replaced them in the post-1980 period.

On older chassis, the suspension usually employs coil springs together with telescopic shock absorbers. If you purchase one of these models, crawl underneath and check that no oil is seeping out of the shock absorber casing. Although a shock absorber can be replaced, it's not an easy job and the labour charge can be surprisingly high.

On modern lightweight types of chassis, the ride is cushioned by rubber installed in the axle tube instead of a coil spring. This is maintenance-free and on most 'rubber-in-compression' systems there's not usually a need for shock absorbers. This is because rubber doesn't create the bouncing effect that you get with a coil spring.

The other difference on old and new chassis designs relates to the brakes. Apart from minor differences in the operating rod arrangement, there is also an inconvenient feature in older models. Before you can use your tow car to reverse a 1960s

On a lightweight chassis, the main members are in direct alignment between the coupling head and the outermost ends of the axle tube. This shows an AL-KO two-piece chassis, bolted together forward of the axle.

This Swift Silhouette was built on an aluminium Syspal chassis.

or '70s caravan, a brake-disabling lever near the coupling has to be engaged. It's so much simpler on an AL-KO or BPW lightweight chassis because an automatic release mechanism is built into the brake drums. This senses when a caravan is being reversed and it automatically prevents the brakes from engaging during the manoeuvre.

Overall, there's no doubt that the running gear on models made in the last three decades embodies many improvements.

INTERNAL FIXTURES

Appliances

In a modern caravan, the gas-operated space heater will be a sealed unit. This means its gas burners are fitted inside an enclosure and combustion air is drawn from outside via ducting and not from the living space. Similarly there will be a flue that takes exhaust fumes directly outside. This arrangement is for safety reasons.

If you purchase an older caravan which has an open-burner gas fire, this should be removed and scrapped. Liquefied petroleum gas (LPG) gives off moisture when it burns – which aggravates condensation problems. Moreover, open-burners are no longer considered safe and combustion fumes should not be permitted to discharge into the living area.

Turning to refrigerators, it is a matter of concern that some caravan manufacturers have not fitted

This Carver appliance is a heater with sealed burners and separate intake and outlet air ducts.

these units in accordance with the Electrolux (now Dometic) installation instructions. When correctly installed, the whole of the rear section of the casing on which the cooling unit is mounted should be completely enclosed and shielded from the living quarters. If the caravan manufacturer has failed to construct a proper enclosure around the cooling unit and gas burner assembly, three problems arise:

1. Draughts blowing towards the outside wall vents are then able to enter the living area.
2. In hot spells, the refrigerator will not run efficiently and you won't be able to obtain the level of cooling of which the appliance is capable.
3. When a refrigerator is running on gas, some of the fumes from its burner can then discharge into the living area.

So when comparing new or second-hand caravans, peer through the outside wall vents and make sure that you cannot see into the living space. Alternatively remove a kitchen drawer near the fridge to check if you can see light through one of the outside ventilators. If the vents are visible from inside, the appliance is not fitted with the rear shielding that the refrigerator manufacturer specifies.

Finally, have a close look at the condition of the washbasin and shower tray (if fitted). These plastic components *can* get damaged and cracks on shower trays are a common failing. If replacements are no longer available, contact either GFL panels or V&G, whose contact details are given in the Appendix.

After removing a cutlery drawer it was easy to see through the upper vent in the side wall; so this fridge wasn't properly sealed off at the rear.

43

At GFL panels, this damaged shower tray will be used to make a mould so that a new tray can then be produced.

Work starts with the assembly of an AL-KO or BPW chassis.

A prefabricated floor panel is mounted on the chassis and fitters can then install several appliances simultaneously.

ASSEMBLING CARAVANS

Now that you are aware of the many elements used in the construction of modern caravans, it is useful to know how the structure is assembled. The photographs alongside show a typical assembly sequence.

The cooker, fridge and space heater are often pre-installed in a bench-assembled furniture unit.

Access from all four sides has permitted speedy assembly of all main fixtures and fittings.

Bonded wall panels with pre-formed window apertures are often late additions to the structure.

This part-bonded roof panel is fixed to the sides; quilt insulation is added at the forward part of the roof.

An acrylic-capped ABS moulding is offered-up at the back and fitted to an insulated support framework.

Note

Manufacturers adopt different procedures but most high-volume caravan builders adopt production-line strategies using modules preassembled at independent work stations.

The moulded front panel, also made in acrylic-capped ABS plastic, is fixed in place.

There are rather a lot of aluminium trim strips on this caravan; the screws which hold them in place can become points where rainwater enters.

Trim strips on a caravan often need rebedding on a strip of fresh sealant to ensure that leaks don't develop.

All the screws which attach trim strips can act as an entry point for rain when the sealant fails.

Trim strips and awning rail

Once body panels have been assembled, the usual procedure is to cover the junctions between adjoining panels using aluminium trim strips or awning rails.

Sometimes these strips are added for cosmetic reasons and I make no secret of the fact that where embellishment is concerned, I'd rather see a painted stripe or an adhesive transfer. This is because an aluminium strip is usually held in place using screws and a bedding of mastic. When the mastic goes brittle, each screw hole becomes a potential entry point for rainwater. And damp in caravans is something to look out for with great care when planning a purchase, as mentioned in Chapter Two.

Alu-Tech construction

Without doubt many caravans fail prematurely because of water ingress. A structure is placed at risk as soon as bedding sealants lose their flexibility and start to crack. At this point, the many screws used to fasten aluminium extrusions (like body trim strips) offer points where water seepage can easily develop. In response to the obvious shortcomings in the present method of assembling external body panels, Bailey of Bristol has now developed an entirely new process for sealing key joints between adjacent sections.

Known as Alu-Tech construction, this new process will undoubtedly revolutionise caravan assembly in future and will help to create products that are not affected prematurely by leaks. Caravans built using this new technique will be supported by a ten-year warranty against water ingress problems arising from faulty workmanship. This is clearly a big step forward that will have a major influence on the caravan industry at home and abroad. The first caravan built in this manner was named the Pegasus, and went on sale in October 2009.

A Pegasus front wall and roof are made from a single bonded panel to eliminate a join. Overall, the lack of screws used in assembly is a great benefit.

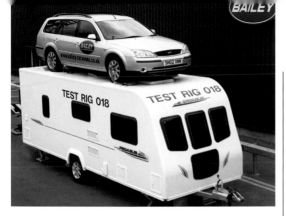

The remarkable strength of a Pegasus built using Alu-Tech construction was shown at the factory and on track tests.

Establishing the age of a caravan

Whereas cars have a Vehicle Registration Document, there is no obligatory form of registration to accompany a caravan. It can therefore be quite difficult to establish a caravan's age. Chassis plates, for example, are not always helpful, and there's no doubt that some second-hand models on sale are older than their sellers suggest. The notes that follow record some of the changes that have occurred, which provide helpful clues for anyone trying to establish when a caravan was manufactured.

Though normally hidden, internal clamp plates hold all external panels in place.

1970s caravans:

☐ Caravans of this period are heavy and were built very differently from post 1980 models.

☐ Bargain buys for around £500–£800 certainly exist and sometimes provide a pleasant introduction to caravanning. But be careful if you're not prepared to carry out repairs or improvements yourself.

☐ Spares can be difficult to obtain for earlier models – particularly spare parts for appliances, fittings for furniture, chassis items and coupling components.

☐ Locker boxes to house gas cylinders - previously clamped to the draw-bar and open to the weather – became common after 1971.

☐ Refrigerators like the Morphy Richards models of the early 1970s had to be lit using a match and often failed to provide cooling because of an air lock.

☐ Chassis made by firms like B&B, Peak, and CI need periodic painting.

☐ The running gear of the period employed spring suspension and shock absorbers; damaged items may be difficult to replace.

☐ To reverse a 1970s caravan, you usually need to operate an override catch on the coupling head before starting the manoeuvre. This is an annoying chore.

The shaped Alu-Tech moulded sections are used along the junctions of the walls and the single-piece bonded roof panel.

Before the 1980s windows were single glazed and the glass was mounted in an aluminium frame.

- [ ] In the early 1970s, fluorescent lights became popular but gas lamps were often fitted, too, in order to provide back-up lighting.
- [ ] In the early 1970s, water pumps were usually foot or hand-operated devices.
- [ ] Bodywork construction comprised a framework made of wood. This skeleton structure was clad with aluminium sheet on the outside and coated hardboard or plywood on the inside.
- [ ] Insulation was poor on most 1970s 'vans. Usually fibre glass wool was placed in the void between the wall panels – but this slumps down in time leaving cold spots.
- [ ] Floors were made from plywood with supporting joints underneath and seldom had any form of insulation.
- [ ] Windows were single glazed and glass was used. However, in November 1977 it became obligatory for new caravans to be fitted with safety glass.
- [ ] In response to legislation, the industry introduced acrylic single-glazed windows comprising a frame-less moulded pane. Aluminium frames were discontinued overnight.
- [ ] Not long afterwards, double glazed versions of these 'plastic' windows became the standard fitting.
- [ ] After 1st October 1979, it became mandatory for new caravans to have a rear fog lamp. Absence of a fog lamp suggests a 'van is an earlier model.
- [ ] From October 1979, a double plug system was used – the 12N plug for caravan road lights; the 12S plug was reserved for internal supplies.

1980s caravans:
- [ ] A new approach to building was introduced using pre-manufactured bonded sandwich floors and wall panels; most manufacturers soon adopted the system.
- [ ] New computer-designed lightweight chassis were introduced around 1980.
- [ ] On lightweight chassis, coil springs hitherto fitted with shock absorbers were replaced by a rubber-in-compression suspension system.
- [ ] A few chassis as late as 1984 were still painted, but galvanising was more usual now as a standard finish.
- [ ] In April 1989, all caravans manufactured had to have auto-reverse brakes; a manually operated lever fitted to the coupling head became obsolete. Automatic brake disengagement mechanisms were now built into the drums.
- [ ] More and more low voltage appliances appear in

Before reversing, a lever was used to disable the brakes on older types of over-run system such as this B&B Beta IV unit.

caravans including electric pumps, reading lights, fans and stereo systems. Now a separate "leisure battery" becomes an essential item.

☐ Fused distribution panels were introduced so that 12V appliances could be operated on separate supply branches and fused independently.

☐ In the mid 1980s, caravans lost their symmetry and became wedge shaped using sloping fronts to achieve better fuel economy.

☐ After 1986, virtually all gas storage lockers were built into the body itself. A separate locker box mounted on the draw bar was not often fitted.

☐ From the mid 1980s many caravans were equipped with water heaters; the Carver Cascade storage heater was particularly popular.

☐ Around 1987, the 'built-in' cassette toilet arrived, revolutionising bathroom design and vastly improving emptying arrangements.

☐ From 1st May 1989 smoke alarms had to be fitted to all new caravans *and* all pre-owned 'vans sold by a dealer.

1990s caravans:

☐ Road lights set high on the sides – called marker lights - became obligatory on caravans over 2.1m wide and manufactured after 1st October 1990.

☐ Combustion Modified High Resilience foam (CMHR) became mandatory in caravan upholstery supplied after 1st March 1990.

☐ From April 1991, all fabrics have to be a fire-resistant type.

☐ The first AL-KO Kober side-lift jack was introduced in the early 1990s

☐ Hardly any caravans were sold in the 1990s without a 230V supply system as standard.

☐ In 1992, AL-KO Kober announced that their latest lightweight chassis must *not* be drilled – even for mounting a stabiliser bracket on the draw bar.

☐ CRiS (Caravan Registration and Identification Scheme) was introduced in 1992 and UK-manufactured caravans were issued with a Vehicle Identification Number (VIN). This is supplied with the owner-information pack, recorded at CRiS headquarters and etched on windows.

☐ Around 1992, the running gear on BPW chassis used maintenance-free sealed bearings.

☐ The AL-KO Euro-axle with sealed bearings appeared in 1994 models. The bearings are well engineered, but after a brake assembly has been cleaned an expensive torque wrench is needed to tighten the nuts securing the drums.

In the late 1980s, some caravans were fitted with built-in 'bench-type' cassette toilets.

49

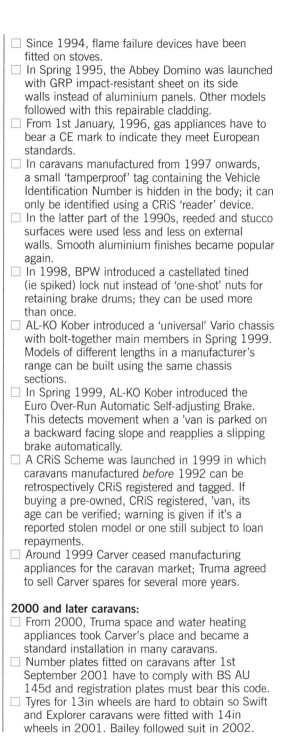

In the late 1990s, this type of decorative aluminium panel was used less often on external walls.

☐ Since 1994, flame failure devices have been fitted on stoves.

☐ In Spring 1995, the Abbey Domino was launched with GRP impact-resistant sheet on its side walls instead of aluminium panels. Other models followed with this repairable cladding.

☐ From 1st January, 1996, gas appliances have to bear a CE mark to indicate they meet European standards.

☐ In caravans manufactured from 1997 onwards, a small 'tamperproof' tag containing the Vehicle Identification Number is hidden in the body; it can only be identified using a CRiS 'reader' device.

☐ In the latter part of the 1990s, reeded and stucco surfaces were used less and less on external walls. Smooth aluminium finishes became popular again.

☐ In 1998, BPW introduced a castellated tined (ie spiked) lock nut instead of 'one-shot' nuts for retaining brake drums; they can be used more than once.

☐ AL-KO Kober introduced a 'universal' Vario chassis with bolt-together main members in Spring 1999. Models of different lengths in a manufacturer's range can be built using the same chassis sections.

☐ In Spring 1999, AL-KO Kober introduced the Euro Over-Run Automatic Self-adjusting Brake. This detects movement when a 'van is parked on a backward facing slope and reapplies a slipping brake automatically.

☐ A CRiS Scheme was launched in 1999 in which caravans manufactured *before* 1992 can be retrospectively CRiS registered and tagged. If buying a pre-owned, CRiS registered, 'van, its age can be verified; warning is given if it's a reported stolen model or one still subject to loan repayments.

☐ Around 1999 Carver ceased manufacturing appliances for the caravan market; Truma agreed to sell Carver spares for several more years.

2000 and later caravans:

☐ From 2000, Truma space and water heating appliances took Carver's place and became a standard installation in many caravans.

☐ Number plates fitted on caravans after 1st September 2001 have to comply with BS AU 145d and registration plates must bear this code.

☐ Tyres for 13in wheels are hard to obtain so Swift and Explorer caravans were fitted with 14in wheels in 2001. Bailey followed suit in 2002.

The Powrtorch electric motor mover was one of the many moving devices fitted since the late 1990s.

- [ ] From 1st September 2003, manufacturers supplied caravans with a wall-mounted 30mbar gas regulator instead of requiring owners to purchase cylinder-mounted 28m bar butane or 37m bar propane regulators.
- [ ] Electrically driven, fixed moving devices gained popularity. Carver's Caravan Mover, introduced in the 1990s, set a standard; many other makes have followed.
- [ ] After a slow start in the 1990s, Thetford's swivel bowl cassette toilets which take up minimal floor space became more popular than bench-type models.
- [ ] Around 2003 Thetford introduced Norcold absorption refrigerators into its range of products; several manufacturers started to fit these appliances.
- [ ] AL-KO Kober AKS coupling head stabilisers were being fitted to more and more caravans as a basic equipment item. Models built on a BPW chassis have a dark blue WS3000 stabiliser manufactured by Winterhoff.
- [ ] In 2005, some wall-mounted 30mbar gas regulators were reported as being contaminated with an oily substance. Dealers then remounted regulators higher in the gas locker and fitted a 90° elbow at the top.
- [ ] Around 2006, several caravans built on AL-KO Kober chassis were equipped with a locking plate to prevent wheel rotation on parked 'xsvans.
- [ ] In 2007 AL-KO introduced the ATC, a safety device which identifies excessive lateral instability in a caravan and applies its brakes to help bring it back into line.

Summary

Using the advice provided, now have a critical look at some caravans being offered for sale. While it's true that caravans look broadly similar to an uninitiated observer, you'll soon recognise many of the features described in this chapter.

CHAPTER FOUR

STORING
YOUR CARAVAN

A point that often worries potential purchasers is where to keep their caravan. In practice this isn't the problem that many people imagine and seven suggestions are proposed in this chapter. There's certainly more scope than you might have thought.

53

On farm sites, arrangements can sometimes be made to leave your caravan in a barn.

A caravan usually takes up more space than the car that tows it, so storing it between holiday trips is a matter that needs some thought. Here are a few ideas you might like to consider:

- ☐ On hard standing alongside your house.
- ☐ In a commercial compound specifically designed for caravan storage.
- ☐ At an indoor facility intended for storing caravans.
- ☐ In a storage compound at a privately owned caravan site or a club site.
- ☐ On a short-term seasonal pitch on a club or privately owned site.
- ☐ On a farm, either inside a barn or outdoors.
- ☐ At a storage facility abroad near a venue you return to on a regular basis.

Don't let storage put you off buying a caravan. There are caravanners who live in high-rise flats, in split-level houses on the side of a steep hill, or in properties where there's a dreadfully tight chicane in the driveway. Some own a house that offers sufficient parking space but they cannot contemplate reversing a caravan into the allotted position. A number of caravanners solve this by installing a manual or electric winch so that their 'van can be pulled over a kerb and along difficult terrain to its parking place.

Others purchase a battery-driven pulling device or have an electrically driven motorised mover fitted. Where there's a will there's a way.

So let's look at the plus and minus points about different storage solutions.

54

To draw a caravan up a drive when parking alongside their home, some owners install a manual or electric winch.

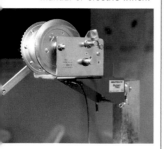

Motorised movers like this Powr Wheel model are indispensable for some owners.

Most recent 12V motorised movers are operated using a cord-free hand control.

ALONGSIDE YOUR HOUSE

Of the seven alternative storage possibilities, parking a caravan alongside your house is the only one that doesn't involve a fee. On the other hand, this isn't always permissible. For instance, there's sometimes a covenant that a property developer imposed when your house was originally built. Covenants occasionally forbid the storage of a caravan, and these restrictions are often established on open-plan estates where front gardens are unfenced to give an overall impression of space.

Notwithstanding the existence of covenants, there are instances where stored caravans are screened from sight alongside a house, and when this is done discreetly neighbours seldom raise an objection. Common sense usually prevails, although there's no doubt that a conspicuously parked caravan can occasionally spoil the views of other residents.

On a compact housing estate, a large parked caravan can spoil the views of neighbours.

With a motorised mover, a caravan can be placed alongside your home with considerable precision.

In addition to covenant restrictions, it is equally likely that a Local Authority's permission will be required to park a caravan on Council-owned property. And be aware that in both these examples of possible restrictions, the references relate to an empty caravan; it stands to reason that using a caravan for additional permanent accommodation would not meet with approval.

With these points in mind, it should also be pointed out that several Acts of Parliament do permit a homeowner to store a caravan on his or her driveway in certain circumstances. The legal departments of both the Camping and Caravanning Club and The Caravan Club are able to provide members with more information about rights and restrictions.

When restrictions are absent, there are both advantages and disadvantages to storage at your place of residence. These are:

Advantages
☐ You can keep an eye on your caravan.
☐ It's easy to keep it clean on a regular basis and you can also heat the interior periodically when winter temperatures plummet or damp weather arrives.
☐ Within reason a caravan can provide useful storage space for summer chairs, a picnic table and your patio sunshade.
☐ If fitted with an electric moving device, a caravan can be positioned alongside your home with impressive precision.

Disadvantages
☐ When screening is difficult or if there's no access to the side or rear of your house, a caravan stuck in the front garden is not an asset to your home's appearance.
☐ If you take a holiday in your caravan, everyone in the area knows you're not at home. Indeed, a caravan can become a conspicuous landmark and

you don't have to be a professional housebreaker to spot that a 'van is missing from its normal resting place.

So there might be better storage strategies.

COMMERCIAL STORAGE COMPOUNDS

If you look at the entry entitled 'Caravan Storage' in the *Yellow Pages* covering your area, you're likely to see addresses of commercial storage compounds. Furthermore, if you're a member of The Caravan Club a list of storage specialists is available free from the club headquarters.

Outdoor storage centres vary a great deal in respect of security, service and price. It's no secret that caravan theft has been a growing problem

When a caravan that is normally parked outside a house is being used, it could signal that the property's unoccupied.

Security at many high-quality commercial storage venues includes CCTV camera systems.

Caravan Storage Site Owners' Association

Recognising the security problem, a professional trade body was instituted in 1999 to represent caravan storage owners. Known as CaSSOA (Caravan Storage Site Owners' Association), this specialist organisation demands a high level of security at member storage facilities, and the growing national chain of approved centres is now in excess of 500 members.

An inspector checks all storage sites that apply for membership and if the venue meets the Association's criteria, a gold, silver or bronze badge is allocated depending on the level of security. This takes note of the site's location, protection from the elements, security, safety and control of access. An item like a sound, secure perimeter fence, for example, is deemed essential.

The scheme is currently supported by 13 specialist caravan insurers and in some instances policy-holders are given a discount if their caravan is stored at one of the Association's accredited sites.

On the CaSSOA website there's a search facility to find your nearest approved storage centre(s), either by carrying out a countywide search or by using your post code. For information visit www.cassoa.co.uk or telephone 0115 349 826.

58

Storing caravans in a compound merely protected by a padlock and gates is not going to present a thief with much of a challenge.

and some commercial storage centres have security fences, alarms, closed-circuit cameras and a resident warden living on site. That's one extreme. At the other end of the spectrum you'll find a few compounds merely protected by a five-bar gate and a tractor.

Not surprisingly, insurance companies ask for detailed information about the place where clients park their caravan, and some storage specialists fall far short of the minimum level of security that the insurers specify. So check this point most carefully before towing your 'van to a compound and parting with money.

And one more point. Not all owners using a storage facility choose one that's close to their home. Owners who particularly like to return to the same area year after year sometimes prefer to select a storage site near their holiday venue in order to reduce towing distances.

Once again, there are advantages and disadvantages to this storage option:

Advantages
☐ Your caravan is not taking up precious garden space at home.
☐ The level of security on a high-quality storage facility is likely to be much higher than it is at your home.
☐ Some storage specialists offer additional services like caravan cleaning. A few can carry out servicing work as well.

Disadvantages
☐ Out of sight, out of mind. Once the 'van is sited, some owners completely forget to remove their battery for winter charging. Equally, end-of-season jobs like the water drain-down are overlooked.
☐ If you want to collect something left in your caravan, or perhaps you've got repairs to carry out, it isn't always easy to gain access to a storage compound at short notice.

Addresses of commercial storage compounds are often listed in Yellow Pages.

Indoor storage ensures that a caravan is kept out of inclement weather.

COMMERCIAL INDOOR STORAGE

Specialists offering indoor storage for caravans and motorhomes are relatively uncommon. However, there are a few in Britain and one of the largest is Calvers Caravan Storage in Bedfordshire. Not only are there caravans here owned by UK residents from all over the country; there are also clients from as far away as South Africa and the United States of America. These are people who enjoy touring the United Kingdom and other European countries but who prefer the versatility and flexibility of a caravan rather than stopping at hotels.

Taking this particular storage centre as an example, caravans are closely packed inside darkened and thermally insulated storage buildings. Items like the upholstery or curtains are thus unlikely to fade and the caravan is not exposed to the extremes of weather.

The intricate task of manoeuvring a caravan into or out of its bay is undertaken by personnel at the storage centre and clients simply drive up to a parking area near the entrance to collect or return their caravan. During a six- or twelve-month storage period there are no restrictions on the number of times you request the use of the 'van.

Whereas a layer of dust will inevitably accumulate on a caravan stored under cover, there is no likelihood of leaks, algae deposits or bird droppings leaving their unwelcome marks.

At this indoor storage centre, caravans are skilfully parked and retrieved whenever the client requires.

Advantages

☐ There's greater security when a caravan is locked away and packed tightly amongst many others in a storage building.

☐ A caravan remains cleaner when kept indoors and any model afflicted by occasional leaks in very bad weather will benefit from indoor storage pending repair work.

This storage facility is one of several offered at sites owned by The Camping and Caravanning Club.

Disadvantages
☐ The fees charged for under-cover storage are usually quite high.
☐ There are not many covered storage centres in Britain.

STORAGE AT CARAVAN SITES

Both The Camping and Caravanning Club and The Caravan Club offer storage facilities at some of the sites they own. Appropriately the compounds are not always conspicuous and it's a useful service for members that often passes unnoticed.

In practice, storage is only available on selected club sites although you don't have to choose a venue close to home. Equally, many other caravan sites and holiday parks also get involved in storage as a sideline. Take Highfield Farm Park near Cambridge, for example. This is a privately owned site that is in membership of the Best of British Holiday Park group. Manicured lawns and screened sections are part of the charm and it is not unusual for visitors to be wholly unaware that there's a small storage compound at the site. This is because it is appropriately shielded by trees and has strong steel posts to provide security at the entrance.

Another discreetly located compound can be found on a site with landscaped, reseeded and rolling hills that was once a coal mine at Oakdale, not far from Newport in South Wales. Again, you may not see the fenced compound and it certainly doesn't detract from the site in any way.

These are just two of the hundreds of caravan sites around the country which also offer a discreet storage service. So if you stop at a caravan park in an area you find particularly pleasing, you might like to enquire about storage. But be aware of the advantages and disadvantages of this arrangement.

Entry to Caravan Club sites sometimes requires either a swipe card or a security code.

Advantages

☐ You can easily return to an area you enjoy with the knowledge that your caravan can quickly be transferred from the compound to a pitch.

☐ Towing – which for some owners is a chore – is reduced, and for a quick weekend getaway that's especially beneficial when fighting Friday traffic.

Disadvantages

☐ Don't be surprised to find a dusty and streaky caravan on your arrival. And remember to make arrangements for its transferral from the locked compound.

☐ Levels of security vary and some sites don't have the sophisticated surveillance equipment found on many purpose-built commercial storage centres.

☐ There's a discouragement to having a caravan regularly serviced when it's stored some way from home. And most site owners do not allow you to wash or repair a caravan once it's transferred to a pitch.

SHORT-TERM SEASONAL PITCHES

On both club and privately owned sites it is often permitted to leave your caravan on one of the pitches for an extended period. This is not strictly storage in the normal sense of the word, but it enables you to have a base away from home. The term 'seasonal pitch' is used for this facility.

From a site owner's point of view it is always a gamble knowing how many pitches to allocate for long-term use. On occasions, caravans with drawn, faded curtains and a fair share of long grass around their perimeter can detract from a site's appearance. Equally they effectively curb the chance of more lucrative pitch lettings if the season is blessed with long spells of summer sunshine. But, of course, it's a guaranteed income for a pre-agreed period of time.

As far as the co-ordinating staff of the club sites are concerned, they constantly review the position, knowing that touring members will not be pleased if they find pitch availability much reduced on account of 'sitting tenants'. So the position is reviewed regularly and venues offering seasonal pitches are intentionally changed from year to year.

As far as a caravan owner is concerned, this is a splendid way to establish a 'second home' and a place of escape. You can even keep an eye on the

Seasonal pitches are organised both at Club and privately owned sites.

At some Club sites, the level of security is especially good.

If you leave a clamped caravan on a seasonal pitch, make certain you can be easily contacted by the warden, especially if it's near a watercourse.

weather and defer an away-weekend until the last minute. However, the booking conditions relating to seasonal pitches are strict. For instance, the sub-letting of a touring caravan is normally not permitted and you would need to read the 'small print' carefully.

Also, be aware that a caravan kept on a pitch in the main part of a site is unlikely to be as secure as it would be in a locked and fenced compound. On the other hand, at some Club sites, entry for all visitors is via a security barrier for which you need a card or key number. This is certainly a praiseworthy provision.

As a postscript, it is also crucial that you keep in close touch with the site proprietor, particularly at times of severe weather. The photograph alongside shows a situation during extreme wet weather in 2001 when the owner of a wheel-clamped caravan on a seasonal pitch couldn't be contacted by the warden. Anxious 'phone calls went unanswered and floodwater from the nearby River Trent kept rising. Unclamped 'vans, meanwhile, were pulled to safe ground by tractor.

Advantages
☐ During the caravanning season, you can have a leisure base properly established and ready for occupation.
☐ Home storage inconvenience is eliminated for extended periods during the year.

Disadvantages
☐ Being 'locked-in' to one site discourages you from travelling more widely.
☐ Security on a pitch in the main part of a site doesn't match the level of anti-theft provision achievable when a caravan is locked in a fenced compound.
☐ Seasonal pitches can be costly, and if circumstances prevent you from using the caravan on a regular basis this strategy is hardly cost-effective.
☐ Wardens cannot crop the grass close to a caravan parked for a long period, so you may need to take some shears to keep your caravan's perimeter tidy.

STORING ON A FARM

If you visit some of the small location sites that both The Camping and Caravanning Club and The Caravan Club list in their Members' Site Book, you'll find that many are farms. Bearing in mind that farmers have been experiencing tough times in recent years, it's hardly surprising that a number are willing to store your caravan in a barn or within the farmyard itself for an appropriate fee.

You might like to take up this opportunity, but don't overlook the realities of rural life. Farm animals sometimes break through a fence and it's always amazing what they decide to eat. You might also find that manure which is so beneficial on the land is less welcome on a caravan's drawbar.

So whereas you might decide to leave an inexpensive elderly caravan on a farm, I'd seriously doubt the wisdom of adopting this arrangement for an expensive and almost new model.

Advantages
☐ Points made earlier in respect of seasonal pitch arrangements and storage away from home all apply once again.
☐ Farms which take no more than five caravans under special exemption arrangements described in the adjacent panel can be enchanting places to visit.
☐ The fee to leave your 'van on a farm is often extremely reasonable and sometimes there's space in a barn which provides weather protection.

Disadvantages
☐ Security is often open to question.
☐ Movement around a farmyard – both of livestock and agricultural implements – can easily lead to a brush with your paintwork.
☐ Be prepared to find a dirty caravan on every visit.

Both major clubs list 'five-van only' sites in their directories. These are known as Certificated Locations (CLs) with The Caravan Club (around 3,000) or 'Certificated Sites' (CSs) with The Camping and Caravanning Club (around 1,500). These venues obtain a special exemption under the 1960 Caravan Sites and Control of Development Act and a large proportion are based on farms. A number are able to offer small-scale storage as well – sometimes under cover in outbuildings.

63

This old orchard is a Caravan Club Certificated Location near Ludlow and some storage is available at the adjacent farm.

STORING ABROAD

Caravanners who embark on long trips to Southern France, Spain and other more distant European venues will often see advertisements for caravan storage. Signs announcing *Gardiennage Caravanes* are often seen in France and a number of farmers advertise storage opportunities on roadside notice boards. In addition, you'll often find a leaflet left on the door of your caravan when stopping at a large holiday site. Recognising that journeys to these warm venues are costly on fuel, costly on ferry tickets and often rather tiring, it is no surprise that local entrepreneurs offer to store your caravan.

But the position is not straightforward. Current EU Law appears to allow these storage arrangements provided your caravan is strictly used for pleasure purposes. However, the legal responsibilities, insurance and security situation are complex. For instance, your roof light might get blown off in a gale-force wind, striking a neighbouring caravan in the process. This raises Third Party considerations, not to mention the damage to your own caravan, which will now get wet inside whenever it rains.

Similarly it is normal for storage specialists to want to move caravans around to achieve access, so your request to fit a robust wheel clamp as a security measure will probably be refused.

On a practical note, it is also likely that the higher temperatures in more southerly countries will hasten the drying out of the sealant along your caravan's seams. Similarly, direct sunlight won't be kind to the sidewalls of your tyres. And, if you leave a caravan at a distant venue for several seasons, when will it be serviced and by whom? This is likely to be a problem when you finally decide to tow it back to the United Kingdom.

Add to this the fact that you'll need to take an awful lot of caravanning clobber in your car

In rural France, you often find Gardiennage Caravanes signs announcing the storage of caravans.

whenever heading for the distant venue, and you begin to see why this is a very questionable strategy.

In reality, the savings on a ferry and fuel are counterbalanced by a number of disadvantages. In fact when a friend of the author was rather slow to renew storage payment on his elderly caravan that he left at a site in Spain, he subsequently found that the impatient proprietor had destroyed it.

Advantages
☐ You will save on ferry costs, fuel costs and avoid the aggravation of towing over large distances.

Disadvantages
☐ Insurance problems, security doubts and damage to the fabric of the 'van from heat are just a few of many imponderables that place a big question mark over this idea.
☐ When and by whom will the caravan be serviced?
☐ A touring caravan left hundreds of miles away cannot provide the pleasure of travelling around closer to home.
☐ A lot of caravan equipment needs stowing in your car when travelling to and from the venue.

INSURANCE

These seven alternative approaches to storage provide a number of possibilities. However, it is most important to emphasise that all caravan insurance companies will want to know where your caravan is kept. This is clearly stated in their literature, and if you contravene the agreed arrangement it is likely that a claim will not be met.

Furthermore, if you check the insurance position with storage proprietors, they normally point out that insurance is your responsibility. Some storage centres are as secure as the Tower of London and have a blemish-free record. Others are less impressive.

With this in mind, it's a matter of considerable concern that caravan theft has grown considerably in recent years and determined thieves go to great lengths to secure certain models. Whereas some storage specialists happily take your caravan off your hands, they sometimes make it all too easy for thieves to take the 'van off your hands in a way you didn't anticipate. Even though there might be a high fence and an alarm system, you are urged to fit security devices as well.

So be especially careful, even if you park a caravan outside your home. Wheel clamps and other security products need to be considered too, and these are discussed in Chapter Six.

Provided a storage site owner doesn't insist that your caravan should be easy to move, fitting it with a security device is much to be commended.

65

CHAPTER FIVE

TOW CARS
AND TOWING

Most people planning to purchase a caravan are constrained in their choice by the suitability of their car for towing. A few go about things the other way round. They become so eager to own a particular type of caravan that they're fully prepared to buy a more powerful car if it's needed. Either way, a well-matched partnership is essential, so what attributes does a car need in order to tow efficiently, economically and safely? And how can you acquire the skills of towing a caravan on today's busy roads?

Guidance on tow cars and towing is provided at the practical manoeuvring courses run by the two national caravanning clubs.

If the letters sent by readers to caravan magazines are anything to go by, there are a surprising number of potential owners who find it difficult to work out what size and weight of caravan their car is able to tow. To create a well-matched 'outfit', several factors are involved and this chapter looks at some of the key points. (Note: The term 'outfit' is used to describe a coupled car and caravan.)

FUNDAMENTAL REQUIREMENTS

☐ **Pulling power** The engine of a towing vehicle has to be sufficiently powerful to pull the chosen caravan when it has been fully loaded up.

☐ **Weight issues** A packed caravan must not be heavier than the fully laden tow car. Moreover, the weight limits relating to a car, a caravan or the complete outfit must *not* be exceeded.

☐ **Brakes and suspension** A tow car's brakes need to be powerful enough to slow down the outfit. Similarly, a car's rear suspension needs to be robust enough to withstand the extra downforce of a caravan's tow hitch. In reality, most modern cars fulfil these braking and suspension expectations, although some vehicles derive benefit from an add-on suspension aid.

As a general rule the best cars for towing are:

1. Equipped with a powerful engine
2. Fairly heavy

Though not an essential requirement for caravanning, it certainly helps if a tow car is fairly heavy and has a suitable engine.

Without doubt, a heavy tow car is better placed to help the stability of a combined outfit as explained later, but its engine has to be up to the task of pulling a substantial weight too.

MANUFACTURERS' LIMITS

Car manufacturers normally publish the maximum overall weight of a fully-packed trailer that a vehicle is able to tow; their 'trailer' includes caravans as well. This is referred to as the 'towing load limit'. However, there are a few cars that are not built to perform *any* kind of towing, as shown in the adjacent panel.

CAR WEIGHTS

As regards the weight of a car as specified by its manufacturer, this is correctly referred to nowadays as the 'Mass (of vehicle) in running order' (MRO). However, the older terms 'kerbside weight' and 'kerbweight' are also still in use. These and other terms are defined in the panels on pages 70 and 71.

The data section in your vehicle's owner's handbook should provide the all-important figures that you need to know. Alternatively a Type-Approved vehicle will have elements like the maximum towing weight stamped on its VIN plate; this is usually mounted in the engine compartment. Incidentally, the term 'mass' is preferred by physicists; for our purposes and in this context we'll regard this as 'weight'.

CAR AND CARAVAN WEIGHT RELATIONSHIP

As the panels overleaf indicate, there are several weight limits that influence the type of caravan that your car will be able to tow. There are other legal constraints too. For example, a vehicle whose Maximum Authorised Mass (see panel for definition) is no greater than 3,500kg is only permitted to tow a caravan whose:

☐ Maximum technically permissible laden mass does not exceed 3,500kg.
☐ Overall width does not exceed 2.3m.
☐ Overall body length excluding the drawbar and coupling head does not exceed 7m.

If you want to tow a caravan that exceeds these limits, such as an imported American model, you need a heavier type of vehicle which is typically a commercial product.

Manufacturers' towing information

A few cars cannot be used to tow at all. Examples include:

Aston Martin DB7
Audi A2 (model launched in 2001)
Ford Ka
Some Mazda MX5 models
MGF
Vauxhall Tigra

In reality these are hardly the kind of vehicles you'd choose to tow a caravan. There are also others whose manufacturer's towing limit is so low that it would exclude caravans. For example, some Ford Fiestas have a very modest towing limit. The Zetec 1,250cc, for example, had a maximum of 250kg – which hardly covers a camping trailer.

Note

Large trailers and caravans which form part of a travelling circus or fair are subject to different laws in respect of towing.

WEIGHT (MASS) TERMINOLOGY – The towing vehicle

MASS OF VEHICLE IN RUNNING ORDER (MRO): Also referred to as 'kerbside weight' or 'kerbweight'. Defined by the vehicle manufacturer, this normally –
Includes:
A 90% full tank of fuel.
Other liquids forming part of the vehicle's operating systems.
The driver.
Excludes:
The weight of passengers.
Any load apart from essential tools such as a wheel brace and jack.
The weight of towing add-ons like a bracket, 12V sockets, mirrors, etc.

Note:
Add 25kg as a typical figure for towbar, towball and other 'add-ons'.
Some manufacturers do not include a driver's weight in the quoted MRO figure.

MAXIMUM AUTHORISED MASS (MAM): Also referred to as Maximum Permissible Weight (MPW) or Gross Vehicle Weight (GVW). This is the total weight of a vehicle that must *not* be exceeded. It includes the driver, passengers, all carried luggage, and the imposed downthrust (noseweight) of a caravan's coupling head when the outfit is stationary.

MAXIMUM PERMISSIBLE TOWING MASS (MPTM): The manufacturer's stated weight limit of any caravan or trailer that is towed. Also note:

TOWING LOAD LIMIT: Sometimes specified by a car manufacturer and often based on the maximum towing weight that a car's restart ability can handle on a 1:8 (12.5%) uphill gradient.

GROSS TRAIN WEIGHT (GTW): Also referred to as Maximum Train Weight. Defined by the vehicle manufacturer as the maximum permissible combined weight of both the laden tow car and the laden caravan. GTW is the total sum of the coupled outfit, which includes the weight of the occupants, the weight of all loaded items in the car and the weight of all contents in the caravan.

TOWBAR LOAD LIMIT: A trailer or caravan should be towed with a certain amount of 'noseweight', which has to be supported by the towball. The maximum permitted vertical load when a tow car is stationary will be given by the towbar manufacturer. On recent products this is known as the 'S' value and it is stated on a plate normally affixed to the towbar.

The 'S' value marked on this towbar plate as its 'noseload' must not exceed 50kg.

70

Tip

WEIGHT (MASS) TERMINOLOGY – The caravan

The terms below are defined in the European standards for caravans (EN 1645 Pt 2). Terms used before these definitions were adopted are also given.

MAXIMUM TECHNICALLY PERMISSIBLE LADEN MASS (MTPLM): Formerly Maximum Authorised Mass, Maximum Allowable Mass or Maximum Technical Permissible Weight. Stated by the manufacturer and displayed on a plate. The factors on which a caravan's MTPLM are based include elements like tyre ratings, suspension weight limits, material rigidity etc. This represents the absolute weight limit of a caravan when it is fully laden, and includes any accessories that have been fitted retrospectively, liquids, fuel (eg gas cylinders) and all personal belongings. To exceed this figure would not only be an offence, it could also represent a serious danger to road-users.

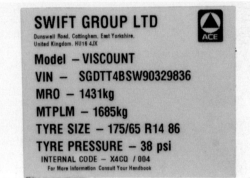

The MTPLM shown on the plate affixed to this Swift Ace Viscount Caravan is 1,685kg.

MASS IN RUNNING ORDER (MRO): Formerly Ex-works Weight or Unladen Weight. Weight of the caravan with factory-supplied equipment as defined by the manufacturer and shown on its plate.

USER PAYLOAD: Formerly Caravan Allowable Payload. This figure is calculated by subtracting the MRO from the MTPLM. The user payload is made up of three elements:
Personal effects payload: items you take including clothing, food, drink, cutlery, crockery, cooking utensils, bedding, hobby equipment etc. A formula sometimes used to confirm if the available payload is appropriate for a particular model is: (10 x number of berths) + (10 x length of body in metres excluding draw bar) + 30 = minimum recommended allowance in kg for personal effect payload.
Essential habitation equipment: any items, including fluids, deemed by the manufacturer as essential for the safe and proper function of equipment for habitation – including toilet fluids, fuel, drinking water etc.
Optional equipment: the weight of optional items like a cycle rack, an air-conditioning unit, and an extra bunk must now be itemised by caravan manufacturers, and figures usually appear in their brochures. The weight of items subsequently installed by the owner, eg a solar panel, also fall within the optional equipment total.

ACTUAL LADEN WEIGHT (ALW): This is what your caravan actually weighs when it is loaded up with the essential habitation equipment and personal possessions. The ALW can be established by taking your 'van to a weighbridge. When this weight is known, you can verify that you are not exceeding the caravan's MTPLM. The figure also enables you to compare its weight relationship with the car and to calculate the 'van's ideal noseweight.

In addition to complying with these legal issues, you will also want your coupled car and caravan to form a stable 'twosome'. Not surprisingly, stability is strongly influenced by the car's weight and the weight of its fully laden caravan. It was stated at the beginning of this chapter that the best cars for towing are usually fairly heavy, especially when compared with the weight of a coupled and fully laden caravan. However, this doesn't mean that lighter vehicles don't make good tow cars. Some perform very well, as long as the towed caravan is appropriately light too. In a marriage, it's the relationship that makes a good or bad match.

Experienced caravanners are well aware that the weight relationship or car/caravan weight 'ratio' is one of the key contributors to stability when towing. In this regard, the caravan clubs both strongly advise that **the weight of a loaded caravan should not be greater than 85% of the tow car's Mass in Running Order.**

This is a useful ratio to remember, but if a tow car is capable of pulling a heavier caravan whose weight is much closer to its own weight, experienced caravanners often exceed the 85% relationship. Of course, the outfit may be more likely to suffer from instability, and it's important to remember that **a caravan or trailer must *never* weigh more than the towing vehicle itself.** If you totally ignore this crucial element, there's a great likelihood that the 'tail' (*ie* the caravan) might start to wag the 'dog' (*ie* the tow car). It is at this point that the stability of a towed caravan is under severe threat.

Recognising the importance of having a stable outfit, striving to achieve an 85% or lower ratio is a good starting point, especially for drivers who are towing for the first time. Of course, the car/caravan weight ratio is not the only issue at stake where stability is concerned. Two further matters of importance are:

1 Achieving the ideal noseweight at the coupling head (*ie* 'hitch') of your particular caravan.
2 Making sure that you position heavy items being carried in your caravan as close to the axle (or axles) as possible.

Both 'noseweight' and 'load distribution' issues are explained in Chapter Eight. For the moment, let's look more closely at the 85% recommendation and carry out a typical calculation to show the procedures involved. The panel alongside is your step-by-step guide.

Typical calculation exercise

What caravan could I purchase that, when fully loaded, weighs no more than 85% of my present vehicle's Mass in Running Order (MRO)?

Let's imagine the following situation. You want to tow with a Citroën 1.8-litre car and have your eyes set on purchasing a new or pre-owned caravan. The Citroën has already been fitted with a towbar and associated electrical items.

Objective: To find a caravan whose maximum technically permitted laden mass (MTPLM) is 85% of your tow car's MRO. For this example it is presumed that you own a Citroën Xantia 1.8-litre Dimension which is in good condition. (All weight terms used in this example have been defined in the earlier panels.)

Your Citroën's owner's manual lists the vehicle as having an MRO of 1,264kg. Add 25kg to this figure to account for the towbar and associated electrical items that you have since had fitted. The amended MRO is now 1,289kg.

The manufacturer also lists a Maximum Permissible Towing Mass/Towing Load Limit of 1,500kg, but in this pairing exercise you won't be considering a caravan anywhere near that weight. It's good to know that the engine is pleasingly powerful, but stability could be seriously compromised by towing a caravan that is heavier than its tow car.

With the help of a calculator, work to this formula:

$$\frac{\text{Car MRO} \times 85}{100} = \text{Weight of caravan to achieve an 85\% ratio.}$$

1,289kg x 85 = 10,9565kg, and divided by 100 = 1,095.65kg.

The calculation reveals that if this Citroën owner were to tow a caravan that is loaded up to its permitted maximum (MTPLM) of 1,095kg, it would represent 85% the weight of his or her Citroën tow car.

As stated already, an 85% car/caravan ratio is widely recommended. However, a driver with extensive towing experience who drives with great vigilance, and whose towing vehicle is suitably powerful, may choose to extend the tow car/caravan weight relationship up to (but *not* greater than) 100%.

This strategy is permissible as long as the caravan exceeds neither the car's MRO, nor the car manufacturer's stated Maximum Permissible Towing Mass/Towing Load Limit. In the case of the Citroën 1.8-litre described above, an experienced owner might therefore use this model to tow a caravan whose MTPLM is 1,289kg.

USING A WEIGHBRIDGE

Unfortunately, a surprising number of owners overload their caravans with no regard for safety. In consequence, the Police are carrying out an increasing number of roadside weight checks. Not only does towing an excessive weight present a greater likelihood of stability problems, but overloading a caravan or trailer can also lead to prosecution and may render an insurance policy null and void.

Without doubt, the best way to get accurate information regarding your caravan's Actual Laden Weight (see panel for definition) is to take it to a public

The stability of an outfit is potentially dangerous if a loaded trailer or caravan is heavier than the car that's doing the towing.

weighbridge. These are often listed in *Yellow Pages* but you can also contact your Local Authority's Trading Standards Department (Weights & Measures Section) for addresses of weighbridges near your home. A visit to a weighbridge enables you to verify the weight of your loaded car and the Gross Train Weight of the car and caravan when coupled together.

Once you've obtained these figures, you can then calculate the ideal downforce or 'noseweight' imposed on the car's towball by your caravan's coupling head (*ie* 'hitch'). This matter is explained in Chapter Eight.

Incidentally, it is not being suggested that every time you plan a trip away in your caravan you need to load up and head for a weighbridge. However, you should check important weights at an early stage of ownership and it is most regrettable that many caravanners never bother to do this. It is therefore hardly surprising that roadside checks find such dreadful examples of overloading. For example, in summer 2009 a Police inspection conducted at Strensham Service Station on the M5 found that the driver of a BMW tow car was pulling a twin axle caravan which was 400kg (around 880lb) over its specified Maximum Technically Permissible Laden Mass. Action has to be taken when there is such a blatant disregard for the welfare of road-users.

So let's go through a preliminary trip to a weighbridge to confirm that your car, caravan and combined 'outfit' is fit for the road. This 'case-history' trip explains how to get three weights, each of which will be recorded on a dated printout issued by the weighbridge operator. Normally a report also includes the date, the tow car's registration number and the caravan's identification number. Fees vary, but at the time of writing each recorded weight at my local weighbridge cost £8.00.

Typical calculation exercise
OBTAINING THE WEIGHTS OF A LOADED CARAVAN, LOADED CAR AND COMPLETE OUTFIT
Pre-arrival preparations

☐ Load your car for a 'dummy run' using all the gear you normally take on board for a typical holiday. Let's imagine that you have also stowed in the car a lightweight universal awning that fits your caravan. Four lightweight camping chairs have also have been tied to its roof rack.

☐ Your reliable bathroom scales have revealed that your partner, yourself and your two young children weigh 190kg when you're clad in holiday clothes.

☐ Take note of the caravan manufacturer's stated Mass in Running Order (empty weight) and then load the 'van with caution. If you normally include heavy items like a large crate of bottled drinks or a crate full of tinned food, you might be wise to check these on the bathroom scales. That's because you need a rough indication that the loaded weight isn't going to exceed the caravan's Maximum Technically Permissible Laden Mass (MTPLM) when towing it to a weighbridge for the first time.

☐ Telephone the weighbridge to confirm its opening hours and to enquire if there are busy periods which are best avoided. Check the tariff of charges.

☐ Just before reaching the weighbridge, fill your vehicle to the brim with fuel at a service station – just as you might when genuinely travelling to a holiday destination.

Typical procedures
At some weighbridges there are certain procedures that have to be followed, such as the approach on to and off the weighing plate. Seek advice about the arrangements. Note, too, that a car's weight is not normally taken until its driver and passenger(s) have disembarked and left the weighing plate.

☐ Provided it fulfils the weighbridge station's procedures, start by taking the total weight of the

Having driven the coupled car and caravan onto a weighbridge plate, you can now find out its laden Gross Train Weight, albeit without the occupants.

This holiday-laden caravan has been put on to a weighbridge to measure its Actual Laden Weight.

car and caravan while coupled. This produces the Gross Train Weight (GTW).

☐ Uncouple the outfit and drive the car away to a suitable parking spot. The Actual Laden Weight (ALW) of the loaded caravan is now taken.

☐ At a later date, the subtraction of a caravan's ALW from the GTW reveals what the tow car itself weighs. However, to obtain a more accurate reading, take a separate weight check of the car in its solo state. It then won't be saddled with a caravan's noseweight bearing down on its towball.

☐ Settle up and make sure that the issued certificates for each weight check show all the information you require, including the date, car reg number, caravan VIN or chassis number and recorded weight.

Post-visit conclusions

☐ On your return home, compile a list of all the key items that were loaded into the car and caravan at the time of the weight check. For example, jot down if one or two gas cylinders were being carried in the caravan's gas locker. Also record the capacity of the cylinder(s); if they are already part-used, you could weigh them on some bathroom scales. Since this trip provides your benchmark for the future, the more detail regarding the contents the better.

☐ Add to the recorded gross train weight the combined weights of the driver and passengers. Also add this element to the tow car's reading if the weighbridge recording was completed without occupants in the car.

☐ Compare all the weighbridge readings with limits stated by the respective manufacturers. If your caravan's recorded weight exceeded its listed MTPLM, decide what items to leave at home in future.

☐ When you know the Actual Laden Weight of your caravan in a typical holiday state you can subtract this figure from the MTPLM to find how much scope remains to add more gear and extra accessories. That figure is most important to know, especially if you're planning to fit an electric motor mover or a refrigerative air conditioner at a later date. Both are especially heavy accessories, and some people fit them without bothering to check if their caravan can accommodate them and still remain within its MTPLM.

☐ Once you know a caravan's Actual Laden Weight, you are then able to calculate the ideal noseweight needed for towing. This is described in Chapter Eight, *Hitch-up and Go*.

OTHER TOWING CONSIDERATIONS

Let's now consider the subject of engine power and that time-honoured phrase about 'horses for courses'.

Engine characteristics and torque

A fast, powerful horse likely to win a flat race at Newmarket might seem an impressive equine performer, but if required to pull a cart laden with beer crates it would be pretty ineffective. Conversely a large shire horse which displays stunning strength when required to pull a heavy farm cart would hardly feel at home running in the Cheltenham Gold Cup.

Cars are much the same. In fact many of the 'GT' types of 'sports' cars are swift performers but achieve their peak power characteristics (or 'torque', as it's usually called) when the engine is running at high revs. One of these cars being driven in top gear and at high revs would easily achieve an illegal speed of 130mph or more. That's fine on a private track but of no interest whatsoever to a caravanner, who in the UK is not permitted to exceed 50mph on single-

Weight and a powerful engine are important – but you don't need the latest model to achieve safe and certain towing performance.

Vehicles with an automatic gearbox usually make good tow cars, as long as the transmission fluid doesn't overheat in extreme temperatures.

carriage roads (where there is not a lower enforced restriction in place), or 60mph on dual carriageways and motorways.

What the caravanner wants is a car which achieves its best pulling power when it's in top gear and the engine is running at low revs. Hence you'll hear technically-minded caravan specialists saying that it's best to own a car which achieves its maximum torque at a low engine speed.

It's worth commenting that diesel engines are especially noted for achieving their best pulling power when the engine is turning over quite slowly, but there are plenty of petrol-driven cars which achieve good torque at low revs as well. Although diesel vehicles often make good tow cars, you certainly don't have to buy a diesel car to tow a caravan.

Most of the caravanning magazines publish tow car test reports, and in a thorough appraisal, issues relating to torque peaks and gearing will be discussed.

Automatic versus manual models

In recent years it has been claimed with increasing frequency that a vehicle with automatic transmission often makes a good tow car. That used not to be the view held by car enthusiasts, but it is now recognised more and more that an automatic affords relaxing driving, especially when progressing with stop-start irregularity in a traffic jam. It is also easier if you're required to drive a caravan up a steep slope from a standing start, because automatic transmissions provide maximum torque at very low revs.

Notwithstanding these points, many caravanners still prefer manual gearboxes so it's mainly a matter of personal choice. Transmissions continue to improve as well. For instance, most automatics now have at least four 'gears' and manual cars are often equipped with five- or six-speed gearboxes.

That said, it's important to point out that serious problems can still occur with an automatic transmission if the fluid in its torque converter starts

5-SYSTEM

mad

Many suspension aids are available, but check if the type you plan to purchase is deemed suitable by the vehicle manufacturer.

to overheat. This condition sometimes develops when outside temperatures are high and the towing task is a tough one. To combat this it is often recommended to have an additional oil cooler fitted in the system. If you need advice on this matter, consult a main dealer and also make contact with The Federation of Automatic Transmission Engineers (FATE), either by telephoning 07885 228 595 or visiting their website at www.fedauto.co.uk. There's a particularly helpful page on the website about overheating. By calling the phone number or sending an email you can also find where your nearest FATE-approved automatic transmission specialist is located.

Suspension

The suspension of a towing vehicle faces extra load when a caravan coupling head (or 'hitch') is bearing down on the towball. Caravan noseweight, as it's called, is an important contributor to stability as explained in Chapter Eight.

Moreover, when a vehicle has a long overhang rearwards of the back axle, a downward thrust on a towball (which is borne by the suspension) is then magnified. In some cases, the rear of the tow car will then start to sag excessively. This condition causes headlight beams to lift to an unacceptable level and also has the effect of reducing the load on the front tyres. On front-wheel-drive cars, this can also cause a loss of traction between the tyre tread and the road.

It's true that many vehicles have a stiff enough suspension to cope with noseweight but others need reinforcing products to assist the standard springs. Seek advice on this subject – especially from the customer service department of the car manufacturer. The technical departments of the caravan clubs also have useful free literature on this subject available for members.

The trouble with some remedial devices is that by stiffening-up the suspension for towing there's a hardened ride when the car is being driven solo.

However, there are other devices on the market that offer progressive resistance; that means they only harden the suspension when a caravan or trailer is coupled-up.

Tyres

Good stability is also dependent on having car and caravan tyres of the appropriate type, in good condition and correctly inflated. Some car handbooks suggest that tyre pressures are increased when the vehicle is heavily laden and this usually relates to towing as well. It's not unusual, for example, to increase the rear tyre pressure by 4psi to 7psi (0.3–0.5 bar) prior to towing – but to avoid false readings, only alter pressures when the tyres are cold.

If your tow car is not supplied with a standard spare wheel, check with a main dealer what procedure should be followed if you sustain a puncture when you're towing a caravan.

Off-road 4x4 vehicles

Some owners presume that the 'ultimate' tow car for caravans is a 4x4 all-terrain vehicle. That's not entirely true.

Certainly, on a campsite in muddy conditions this type of vehicle is ideal for hauling a large caravan from a slippery pitch; and on the road, the weight of this type of vehicle also helps in the vehicle/caravan weight relationship. But there are other elements that are less advantageous including the tendency of 4x4s to have a poor turning circle.

Moreover, the chassis rigidity of a true all-terrain vehicle can place a relatively light chassis on a modern caravan under surprising stress. In contrast, a conventional monocoque car has more resilience in its body construction.

To ease the unyielding nature of true chassis-based 4x4 vehicles, some owners fit proprietary 'cushioning' devices between a bolt-on towball and the mounting flange of the bracket. This strategy was fine until new legislation required that all tow brackets fitted to non-commercial vehicles registered after 1 September 1998 had to be TUV approved. The requirement also meant that large bolt-on devices like this were deemed illegal, unless they had been included in the original TUV test of the bracket to which they are fitted.

A further problem with some 4x4 off-road vehicles concerns towball height. Even though the height is required to fall within certain limits, there are some instances where manufacturer-supplied towbars for all-terrain vehicles leave the ball too high, even when

a drop plate is fitted. Although its elevated position might be fine for towing agricultural trailers, it can cause a caravan to tow nose up and tail down, as the accompanying illustration shows.

Stability aids

It is important to emphasise that a well-balanced outfit with a good weight ratio should provide a pleasantly stable towing experience. However, there are often external forces like a strong gust of wind, a bad road surface, or the suction effect from a passing high-sided vehicle that can cause sudden sideways deflections. Normally a caravan soon comes back into line and it is most unlikely that the instability will get worse and develop into a condition referred to as 'snaking'.

As stated already, these moments of instability are caused by outside forces and their effect can be reduced to a large extent if a stabilising device is fitted. It's important to recognise that these devices should not be fitted in an attempt to cure an inherently unstable or badly matched outfit. Nor should they be used to provide a quick-fix cure for a major fault like a twisted chassis. However, they can help to suppress the effects of external forces that briefly upset a caravan's stability.

A recent Land Rover fitted with an approved tow bracket and drop plate did not allow this caravan to tow at a suitable level, or slightly nose-down angle.

Stabilising devices like this have been successfully used on caravans for over 30 years.

The Winterhoff coupling-head stabiliser fitted on many chassis from BPW dampens both lateral and vertical movements.

As long as a towball is kept clean and free of grease, this friction pad helps to dampen lateral movements.

Many stabilising products employ a friction component to suppress unwanted movements, and some of these are built into the coupling head.

Other types like the one being fitted on page 81 don't apply friction to a towball but have a damping turntable mounted at the end of long steel lever. Either way, many owners use a stabiliser and an increasing number of caravans are being fitted with a friction-type coupling head device as standard equipment.

A different approach to achieving stability has also been developed and monitoring devices have also been fitted recently in several types of vehicle. For example, electronic aids like EPS systems are being fitted in some cars and these products can also detect when a trailer has been coupled-up. If there's instability during a drive, a series of computer-generated responses are duly activated in order to reduce unfavourable movements.

Products have also been designed to perform similar functions in caravans. For instance, AL-KO Kober introduced the ATC Trailer Control in 2007 and this compact unit is mounted near the axle of a caravan. If its lateral acceleration sensors housed inside the unit detect instability, a caravan's brakes are promptly applied for a few seconds to re-establish a safe driving condition. A similar

Many of the caravans constructed on an AL-KO Kober chassis are sold with a stabilising coupling head as standard.

The ATC trailer control is either fitted from the outset by a caravan manufacturer or it can often be added retrospectively.

electronic control system called the Intelligent Drive Control (IDC) is also being fitted on some BPW caravan chassis.

Of course, there are thousands of caravans being towed behind well-matched cars that are not being helped by control systems like these; what's more, their owners seldom complain about instability. On the other hand it is pleasing that products are continually being developed in the quest to make caravanners' towing experiences both safer and more pleasant.

Towbars

When a vehicle is fitted with a towbar (sometimes referred to as a towing bracket), the assembly of steel members has been designed with a particular type of towball in mind. In fact four main types of towball are manufactured:

1 A 'swan neck' towball. (*Note: There are a number of different stem patterns*.)
2 A standard bolt-on tow ball. (*Note: The decorative paint sometimes applied to a new ball must be removed with emery cloth before it is put into use*.)
3 A bolt-on towball with extended neck. (*Note: This gives the essential clearance needed to accommodate an AL-KO or Winterhoff ball-acting stabiliser. AL-KO [UK] sells these through*

The Intelligent Drive Control (IDC) designed to fit BPW chassis is mounted close to a caravan's jockey wheel.

83

There are many patterns of swan neck towball, many of which provide unsuitable mounting points for accessories.

It is most important that the tightness of the bolts securing this type of towball is checked using a calibrated torque wrench.

Which towbar should be fitted to your car?

Cars registered before 1 August 1998

- A non-EC Type-approved towbar can be legally constructed and fitted. However, purchase a good quality product from a well-respected manufacturer.
- The bracket should comply with BS AU113 and BS AU114. Ball centre height must be between 350 and 420mm (13.8–16.6in) above the ground when the vehicle is fully laden; further information is given in the 'Technical Tip' box with regard to drop plates. The ball centre should lie a minimum of 65mm rearwards from the vehicle body.

Changes in the law

The implementation of European Directive 94/20 introduced new requirements, and the Directive attained legal standing in Britain following an amendment in the Road Vehicle (Construction & Use) Regulations 1986. However, the new requirements do not apply to cars registered *before* 1st August, 1998.

Cars registered after 1 August 1998 (S registration or later)

- Almost all cars registered on or after this date will have a VIN plate bearing an 'E' mark and number to denote EC approval.
- All cars bearing the 'E' mark must only be fitted with a towbar that complies with European Standard 94/20/EC and which similarly displays a plate or label to confirm compliance. This is often referred to as a 'Type-approved' towbar.
- Vehicles exempt from these requirements include specialist cars built in small numbers whose accreditation is achieved by passing the Single Vehicle Approval (SVA) scheme.
- Also exempt are vehicles imported directly from a non-European country, often referred to as 'grey imports'. These models do not bear a European VIN plate, and sometimes have different mounting points. This can cause problems when trying to fit a Type-approved towbar. The Mitsubishi Pajero ('grey import' Shogun) is one example, although Witter Towbars does produce a Pajero conversion kit. In addition, Watling Engineers builds bespoke towbars for the Pajero and other vehicles that do not have to comply with European Standard 94/20/EC.
- Light commercial vehicles (LCVs) have fallen outside this legislation, so motorcaravans built on a commercial base have been permitted to have non-TUV-approved towbars designed, built and fitted. However, this dispensation is planned to end in 2012.

 Technical Tip

Towball height and drop plates

Nowadays, towbars are manufactured to comply with the towing heights given in Directive 94/20/EC. Problems arise, however, with some older caravans that have an unusually low coupling head. The same effect occurs, too, if a car is only partially laden and is riding high. In these instances, it would help if a towball was slightly lower.

Unfortunately the height of a swan neck tow ball cannot be altered. However, drop plates are sold which allow you to lower the height of a bolt-on towball. In fact if your towing vehicle was registered before 1 August 1998, fitting a drop plate is permitted and this measure can immediately remedy the problem of a caravan that assumes a nose-up inclination. But this practice is not permitted on the more recent Type-approved towbars unless a drop plate or spacer was fitted when the bracket went through its Type-approval tests. Check this with the towbar manufacturer.

Note

1 Although a drop plate can be used in some instances to lower a towball, it should never be used to raise the height of a towball.
2 If there's a problem, take the matter up with your vehicle manufacturer. There are some modern vehicles whose approved towbars do *not* allow a caravan to assume its required stance.

This BMW removable towball is neatly designed; some products are less easy to operate when the ball needs to be detached.

its Website and provides a mail order delivery service.)
4 A removable towball. (*Note: There are several different retention systems currently being fitted.*)

Just as there are different types of towball, there are also two categories of towbar, namely EC Type-approved towbars, and non-EC Type-approved towbars. The accompanying panel explains what this means in practice.

When European Standard 94/20/EC was implemented in the UK, it raised issues concerning drop plates and other accessory products (including bicycle racks) hitherto mounted behind the flange plate of bolt-on towbars. Introducing these items retrospectively to a Type-approved towbar is not permitted unless special arrangements were made when a prototype bracket was submitted for testing. In response to this, Witter now tests all its European Standard towbars with a 25mm spacer in place so that bolt-on accessories can normally be added at a later date.

ELECTRICAL CONNECTIONS FOR TOWING

It seems strange today, but at one time tow cars were fitted with just a five-pin socket to run the modest array of road lights required on the rear of trailers and caravans. Then, as more road lights were being fitted on vehicles, a seven-pin plug/socket arrangement was introduced in the early 1960s to take its place.

The use of a single seven-pin plug and socket continued until October 1979, at which point two seven-pin sockets were fitted to vehicles intended for towing caravans. The 12N black seven-pin socket was used for road lights; the 12S grey (sometimes

A single 12N black plug for operating road lights was introduced in the 1960s and is still being used on boat trailers.

white) seven-pin socket was intended to run several of the caravan's 12V accessories using power drawn from the tow car. Meanwhile, boat and goods trailers continued using just a single 12N connection.

The idea of having a pair of sockets was generally approved by UK caravanners although the pin allocations did have minor changes in the mid-1990s. For the technically-minded person, these developments are described in considerable detail in *The Caravan Manual* (Fourth Edition, 2009) by John Wickersham, also published by Haynes. Wiring diagrams are provided too, which show the changes to pin allocations as ideas evolved.

However, in mainland Europe some caravanning countries didn't adopt twin plug/socket connections. In Germany, for example, a single 13-pin socket was developed instead. As a result, German cars imported by UK dealers in the 1990s and purchased for towing purposes were often fitted with an imported towbar complete with a 13-pin socket.

This was not always well-received and a costly adaptor lead was usually purchased to couple up to a UK caravan's twin-plug arrangement. But one thing was clear. The precise and positive coupling

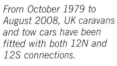

From October 1979 to August 2008, UK caravans and tow cars have been fitted with both 12N and 12S connections.

The ISO 11446 socket and its partner plug achieve a more sound engagement than was possible with seven-pin connectors.

system employed on these 13-pin sockets produced a better electrical connection than was achievable with 12N and 12S products. A few caravanners have even found that 12S sockets can get warm because of sparks jumping across poor connections.

Recognising that standardisation offers many benefits between European neighbours, it was decided after lengthy debates that UK caravans built from 1 September 2008 would be fitted with a 13-pin plug that complies with ISO 11446. Like any changeover exercise, the transition will take time to work through. Moreover, to make sure that UK caravanners are not faced with tiresome problems, a variety of adaptors are on sale. Let's have a look at the products now being used.

Towing adaptor connections

Thousands of cars and thousands of UK caravans are presently equipped with a 12N and 12S connection. If the pins on both the plugs and sockets are correctly wired and everything works as it should, there is no need to make any changes.

In a similar way, if you've purchased a new caravan fitted with a 13-pin plug and your tow car has been fitted with a matching socket, all should work well. Just one small warning, though. When a car is fitted with a 13-pin socket at a franchise garage, it's not unusual for only the pins serving the caravan's external road lights to be connected-up. Some garages are not familiar with the supplementary connections needed to run a caravan fridge during towing, or the principle of charging a caravan's battery from the tow car's alternator. In consequence a knowledgeable towbar fitter is needed to add the appropriate wiring. This can be an exacting task and it isn't a cheap undertaking.

Now let's look at the mismatch situations using photographs to show a suitable adaptor.

Situation 1

The tow car has a properly connected 13-pin socket

Solution to Situation 1

The blue-collared plug on the right fits the 13-pin socket on the car; the twin sockets on the left accept the caravan's 12N and 12S plugs. Secure the adaptor to the caravan's draw bar.

Solution to Situation 2

The black and white plugs at the top are connected to the twin sockets on the tow car; the socket at the bottom needs to be secured to the caravan's draw bar to accept its 13-pin plug.

Solution to Situation 3

These inexpensive adaptors sold in car accessory shops fit into a 13-pin plug on one side and the 12N black socket on the other. They enable the caravan's road lights to operate but none of the internal caravan functions – those depend on a supply from the car's 12S socket.

whereas the caravan is fitted with 12N and 12S plugs. This adaptor will make the right coupling.

Situation 2

The car has a pair of 12N/12S sockets connected up in compliance with the pin allocation that has been applicable since 1 September 1998. The caravan has a 13-pin plug.

Situation 3

Your car already has a pair of 12N/12S sockets that work well. However, you've ordered a 2009 model-year caravan that will be supplied with a standard 13-pin plug. You want to collect your new caravan but haven't managed to get hold of the adaptor shown in Situation 2. The alternative small adaptor shown here is an inexpensive way of bringing the new caravan home with all its road lights working correctly.

Solution to Situation 4
When post-2009 Bailey caravans are ordered, you can either have the standard 13-pin plug and single cable on the left or the 12N and 12S twin plug and cable system on the right.

Situation 4

Your car already has a pair of 12N/12S sockets that work well. However, you've ordered a post-2009 model-year Bailey caravan which will be ready to collect fairly soon. You don't like the idea of strapping an adaptor lead to the caravan's drawbar and don't want to change the 12N/12S sockets on the car either.

Bailey recognised that many existing caravanners weren't eager to change the sockets on their tow car but still wanted to purchase a new Bailey caravan. Although a 13-pin socket and lead is now the standard provision on all Bailey models, it is easily unplugged and the dealer can immediately replace it with a pair of 12N/12S plugs and cables at a reasonable cost.

In summarising the electrical connections that have to be fitted to tow cars, the complexity of wiring in modern cars has ended the efforts of DIY installers. The use of electronic aids in cars has brought safety benefits, improved fuel economy, provided better performance and so on. However, the downside of these changes is the fact that you can no longer couple cables to the rear lamp clusters on your car and take power feeds into the 12N socket for running the caravan lights. The advent of multiplex wiring in cars and the use of computer systems to send data signals to activate accessories has created a minefield of complexity. For this reason a car must be wired up for towing duties by an experienced and fully trained automotive fitter. Even the electricians in 'main dealer' garages have wired up sockets incorrectly in a few reported cases.

To keep pace with all the radical changes in car electrics, the National Trailer and Towing Association (NTTA) has created a national programme of training

It is more important than ever before to appoint a towbar installer who understands both the mechanical and electrical complexities of modern cars.

The NTTA runs training courses for towbar fitters and its Quality Secured Accreditation scheme enables caravanners to secure the services of highly experienced installers.

The NTTA Quality Secured Scheme

This scheme means that accredited centres:

- Have qualified fitters with the right knowledge, skill and training.
- Have adequate resources and the right equipment.
- Are subject to regular assessment and approval by independent assessors.
- Adhere to the National Trailing and Towing Association code of practice.
- Use the best-quality components and work to established standards.
- Charge a fair rate for each job.
- Offer good customer care.
- Give a guarantee of good workmanship and component quality.

The growing list of Quality Secured Accredited fitters can be checked on the NTTA website at www.ntta.co.uk. Information is also obtainable by telephoning 01926 335445.

Reversing this 4x4 vehicle using its side-mounted camera revealed that a final alignment can be hard to achieve.

courses for towbar installers. Equally, there's an ever-increasing chain of accredited towbar specialists. For example, the NTTA's establishment of its nationwide Quality Secured Accreditation scheme ensures that the installation of a towing bracket and its electrical connections is carried out correctly and to the highest standards.

OTHER VEHICLE ACCESSORIES

In the short time since the earlier edition of this book was published in 2002, many new automotive accessories have been introduced. For instance, many drivers now use satellite navigation systems; equally, a surprising number of vehicles are being fitted with reversing cameras.

This is not the place to review a large range of 'must-buy' products and there are always issues that retailers fail to mention. For example, some routes recommended by navigation systems are fine for cars but too tortuous for caravans. There's also a tiny reversing camera fitted to one well-known 4x4 vehicle just to the side of its rear number plate. When the author endeavoured to reverse this vehicle unaided towards an imaginary coupling hitch, the camera's location made final alignments quite hard.

This tiny camera retrospectively fitted by Alpine Electronics UK enables reversing up to a caravan to be done on your own.

This was not the case when an Alpine reversing system was fitted retrospectively, with its camera mounted centrally. This central location together with a controllable close-up viewing mode mean that reversing up to a caravan can sometimes be done on your own.

All in all, driving aids take time to refine; but once they work well they are often regarded as essential accessories.

FURTHER INFORMATION

Overall, the subject of towing is detailed and complex. If you want to find out more, get a copy of *The Caravan Towing Guide*, published in 2008. This 32-page booklet is available free from its publisher, The National Caravan Council (NCC), and was produced by the NCC in co-operation with The Camping and Caravanning Club and The Caravan Club. The author helped its compilers and supplied photographs to support the text. To obtain a copy, contact The National Caravan Council using the address given in the Appendix.

Another source of information is *The Essential Towing Handbook* by Philip Coyne, initiated by the Police Foundation at the suggestion of the National Trailer

Free copies of The Caravan Towing Guide are available from The National Caravan Council.

and Towing Association and Brink UK. The first edition was published in 2000 by the Stationery Office and has nearly 200 pages devoted to towing matters.

In addition, a chapter entitled 'Towcar Preparation' in *The Caravan Manual* (Fourth Edition) by John Wickersham and published by Haynes goes into technical issues in much greater depth.

Finally, literature available to members of The Camping and Caravanning Club and members of The Caravan Club is also extremely helpful.

TOWING SKILLS

Many drivers start towing a caravan without receiving any formal instruction. Whether this is a wise thing to do rather depends on your previous driving experiences. For example, if you have previously towed a small trailer, you will already appreciate that it is necessary to take a wider sweep than usual when negotiating tight corners. Ignore this in a town and your caravan might ride up on the kerb with potentially dreadful results.

Parking against a kerb is difficult too, because of the width of most caravans. And then there's that elusive skill of reversing.

There's no doubt that to acquire the relatively simple skills of towing, it is wise to join one of the caravan manoeuvring courses organised by the two major caravanning clubs.

Manoeuvring courses
Both The Camping and Caravanning Club and The Caravan Club run manoeuvring courses at private locations around the country. Typical venues are

Below right: Club manoeuvring courses include advice on choosing and using extension mirrors.

Below: The Camping and Caravanning Club provides you with a caravan with which to practise manoeuvres on the instructional courses.

Using guide poles, participants on towing courses are able to practise coupling up a caravan on their own.

Restricted vision means reversing into a nearside opening is harder than reversing into an opening on the offside.

former airfields and agricultural show grounds – so there's plenty of space that's empty of traffic.

Illustrated technical talks, supporting literature and instructional videos usefully support the practical sessions. There's only one warning – these courses are popular and you usually need to book a place a long time in advance.

The topics usually cover items like selecting and adjusting extension mirrors, coupling-up a caravan with and without a helper, checking noseweight, and general safety tips about items like tyres.

Participants at manoeuvring courses are taught useful signals to adopt when helping a driver reverse up to a coupling hitch.

This imported Airstream built to United States specification needs a heavy towcar and owners who passed their driving test after 1 January 1997 would need to take a supplementary test to tow a heavy outfit like this.

Practical tasks include straight-line reversing, reversing into an offside location and the harder task of reversing into a nearside opening. Plastic cones usually define the target zones and are flattened on a regular basis by wayward caravans. But practising manoeuvres with an experienced instructor is the way to learn these skills, even though many drivers regard reversing as a black art beyond their compass.

Other issues
Driving test
Remember that if you passed a driving test or obtained a full driving licence before 1 January 1997, this automatically permits you to tow a caravan. If you passed the test after this date, however, you will be required to pass a further test if the intention is to tow a very heavy outfit. Frankly, the obligatory test does not apply to the majority of UK outfits and the specification is as follows:

The need to take a special towing test applies where the combined weight of the tow car and caravan exceeds 3,500kg and the maximum weight of the caravan exceeds the unladen weight of the towing vehicle. If you're thinking of towing a colossal caravan with a very large vehicle and need to take a test, contact the Driving Standards Customer Services Unit, Tel: 0115 901 2515.

Motorway lane use
When towing a caravan you are not permitted to use the right-hand lane of a motorway which has three or more lanes – unless special notices indicate otherwise. Permission may be given when roadworks have caused lanes to be closed.

Parking
When parking a car and caravan, you are not permitted to use parking meter zones.

Passengers
It is illegal – and highly dangerous – to carry

passengers in a caravan when you are towing on public roads.

Deflection and snaking
When towing on fast roads, large overtaking vehicles will cause your caravan to deflect from side to side. This buffeting is quite normal but if you're not paying attention to your rear-view mirrors these unexpected movements can be rather frightening. Once the vehicle passes, a well-balanced outfit will realign itself quickly, and if you take your foot from the accelerator the dissipation of movement is usually hastened. But don't try to cure deflections by braking heavily. Stabilisers that help to reduce lateral deflection have already been discussed earlier in this chapter.

Note: These deflections are NOT what is meant by a 'snake'. A snake occurs when an ill-matched or damaged outfit gets out of control with the help of strong side-winds and thoughtless driving. In a snake, the caravan swings so far to one side and then the other that the articulation of car and caravan approaches an angle of 90°. In the unlikely event that you experience a snake, the advice is to immediately lift your foot from the accelerator, resist the temptation to apply your brakes, and hold the steering wheel steady rather than trying to steer with the movement.

Hopefully, anyone heeding the advice in this book will enjoy their caravanning without ever experiencing reptilian attacks.

Whether you are overtaking the lorry or the lorry is overtaking you on a motorway, there's usually a brief moment of buffeting which affects the caravan's stability.

CHAPTER SIX

ACCESSORIES

To describe all the accessories available for caravanners would take a whole book – and a very thick book at that. Many products have arrived with a flourish and then disappeared without ceremony. Others are 'must have' items that are not supplied when you buy a caravan from a dealer. Accessories like water containers, gas cylinders and a spare wheel are virtually essential. In addition, a good quality security device is a worthwhile purchase whatever the age of your caravan.

Portable dishes, satellite receivers and flat screen TV sets are popular purchases at present.

In recent times, caravan manufacturers have been required to supply a mains hook-up lead with their new products. In contrast, a wheel brace has been a standard accessory for much longer – though some have been disappointingly fragile. Looking to the future, components like a spare wheel might well become standard equipment as well. In fact, current regulations even require that a step of stipulated size is now supplied with all new tourers.

This is pleasing if you're intending to take delivery of a brand new model. However, most purchasers start caravanning with a pre-owned 'van – a strategy which always makes sense. Differences aside, this chapter draws attention to a wide range of accessories for both new and second-hand models.

Incidentally, towing items like extension mirrors are discussed in Chapter Eight so they're not mentioned here. Nor, for that matter, are awnings, which are described in Chapter Seven.

MATTERS OF WEIGHT

The previous chapter emphasised the point that all types of caravan have a maximum weight limit (MTPLM). Features like its empty weight were discussed too, and then related to the maximum weight it's allowed to attain. Subtracting the empty weight from its MTPLM produces a figure that covers its permitted 'payload'.

In consequence, you can only load up a limited amount of personal gear together with items like gas, water and toilet chemicals. However, if you subsequently decide to add an accessory item, the weight it imposes takes up part of your 'payload'. For example, if your caravan was already running at its maximum weight, installing an accessory will necessitate a corresponding reduction in the personal items being carried.

In practical terms, if your caravan's already running near its weight limit and you want to have an air conditioner fitted, that appliance equates with a veritable mountain of shoes, socks, shirts and frillies that would have to be left back at home.

Suffice it to say, reflect on your priorities and get a weight check of your caravan when it's packed for a typical holiday *before* spending money on heavy additional items (using a weighbridge was described in Chapter Five); and remember that products like motorised movers, portable generators, air conditioners and awnings are particularly heavy accessories.

ROAD ITEMS

It is most important to have a spare wheel and it's sometimes possible to stow this on an under-floor carrier.

Spare wheel

You can caravan for years without getting a puncture, but if it happens, the mishap can prove costly, especially if you don't carry a spare wheel with a sound tyre. Prior to the launch of 2002 models, most new single-axle caravans were built on 13-inch wheels, and when touring abroad, buying a tyre to fit a 13-inch rim is usually difficult.

So in 2001 a few manufacturers introduced 14-inch wheels on their single-axle caravans. The idea gathered momentum and in the 2002 model year, most (although not all) new caravans had 14-inch wheels. Again, this is no help to owners of older caravans, and it's one of many reasons why you should always carry a spare.

When you buy one, be absolutely sure it fits. It's surprising how often dealers supply a spare wheel where the fixings do not match those on the caravan, or where the tyre is incorrect. This often passes unnoticed until a puncture necessitates a roadside wheel change. That is neither the time nor the place to discover the error. As regards the tyre, it should be:

☐ The correct size (both in diameter and width).
☐ The correct type (see Tip overleaf).
☐ Of the appropriate speed rating.
☐ Of the appropriate load rating.

Note: *Throughout much of mainland Europe, motorists are required to wear high-visibility reflective jackets or waistcoats if they leave a vehicle to attend to a puncture or perform similar tasks. In some countries you have to carry such items whether you intend to change a wheel or not. Check the requirements for countries you visit.*

In many countries you are obliged to wear a high-visibility jacket when attending to roadside repairs.

A large range of tyre gauges are available by mail order from the International Tool Company.

Tyron Safety Bands

When a car or caravan tyre punctures badly, the collapsing casing often falls into the well of the wheel, whereupon its metal rim starts skidding along the road surface. This sudden loss of adhesion can cause all sorts of problems.

To cure this, Tyron Safety Bands comprise steel sections that are bolted into the well of a wheel, thereby preventing a deflated tyre from dropping into the recess. In consequence, the rubber of a punctured tyre continues to intervene between the rim and the road so that the vehicle doesn't slip all over the place. Even though the tyre is likely to get ruined, both car and caravan can be driven with reasonable control and steered to a safe point by the roadside.

Towing demonstrations held on redundant airfields in which a tyre is punctured by a detonation device are extraordinary to witness. The Tyron

Once a deflated tyre has been depressed with a clamp, the Tyron Safety Band is installed in the well of a wheel.

In spite of a high-speed blow-out, rubber from this tyre – rather than the rim of the wheel – kept in contact with the road.

A scissors jack is compact enough to be positioned under a caravan's axle even after a bad puncture.

Safety Band certainly achieves what its promoters claim and some caravan manufacturers have fitted them as standard. Alternatively, they can be fitted retrospectively by Tyron's recommended specialists.

Jacks

When lightweight chassis were introduced in the early 1980s, the positioning point for a jack became critical in order to avoid damage to the main longitudinal members. Many caravans are lifted using a portable jack although more recent models now incorporate a side jacking system. It's a good arrangement and these lifting assemblies can sometimes be fitted retrospectively. This depends on the age and the type of chassis; manufacturers like AL-KO Kober and BPW can give guidance.

Where lifting clamps can't be fitted to chassis side members, you need a jack that can be positioned at the outermost ends of the axle tube, even when your caravan has slumped close to the ground due to a puncture. A compact scissors jack usually meets this requirement, but these devices take considerable arm strength to lift a heavy caravan. It's certainly worth doing a 'practice run' at home or in a storage compound rather than carrying out your first wheel change by the roadside.

Chassis manufacturers often show their side jacking systems at caravan exhibitions.

Although this jack has been positioned correctly near the end of an axle tube, elevating a heavy caravan can be tough.

A telescopic wrench makes it notably easier to loosen over-tightened wheel fixings.

Telescopic wheel brace and torque wrench

These inexpensive tools are invaluable should you ever wish to remove a wheel yourself. The additional leverage offered by an extending telescopic bar means you don't need great strength to loosen an over-tightened wheel bolt. Telescopic wheel braces are obtainable from most car accessory shops and are sold with sockets to fit four different sizes of fixing.

That said, it's very important that the fixings (*ie* wheel bolts or wheel nuts) that secure a replaced wheel are tightened to the specified level. There are reports of caravan wheels becoming mysteriously detached, and it's normally the nearside one which is the first to loosen. That's why a caravanner who's prepared to change a wheel is advised to purchase a torque wrench. The 'torque setting' should be given in a caravan owner's manual and this figure has to be set on a scale adjacent to the torque wrench handgrip. When the fixing reaches the tightness required, a ratchet goes 'click', whereupon the wrench will tighten no further.

If you don't own a torque wrench and tighten-up using guesswork, a fixing that's insufficiently tight may come loose; equally disturbing, an over-tightened nut can deform its seating in the wheel, whereupon it then comes loose on account of the damage.

Once you know the required tightness of a wheel fixing, the specified amount is set on a scale near the handgrip of a torque wrench.

Wheel chocks are inexpensive items that can often perform an important job.

Chocks

These are obligatory in Germany, and if you have to change a wheel after a puncture chocks are most important accessories. Chocking the wheels when you're parked on a steeply sloping pitch is also strongly recommended. Frightening stories of caravans rolling down slopes are well documented.

Regrettably, however, some of the plastic chocks on sale have a habit of slipping when used on a smooth road surface. This can cause a serious problem if you've just removed a wheel. Sticking a layer of rubber matting on the underside of the chocks often helps, but you might prefer to get some larger wooden wedges constructed by a carpenter in which the curvature matches the shape of your caravan's wheels.

SITE ITEMS

Spirit level

There are several levelling aids on the market but a small spirit level takes some beating. Laying this on the floor directly above the axle is a logical place for both lateral and longitudinal checks. However, a few owners position a level on the A-frame at the front; others use the horizontal line of a front or rear window to check lateral levelling.

This type of spirit level sold at accessory shops is sometimes fixed permanently near the jockey wheel.

DIY caravanners often make their own ramps for lateral levelling.

Various types of ramp systems are sold in accessory shops.

On soft ground corner steadies need a base pad, and small pieces of wood are fine.

Ingenuity is often helpful too. Some caravanners carry a rectangular plastic jerrycan which they part-fill with water and then lay on its side over the axle.

Levelling boards and ramps

Getting a caravan level from side to side is harder than levelling from front to back – which a jockey wheel achieves with ease. The classic and inexpensive answer is to pull your caravan forwards on to some wooden boards prior to unhitching. Some DIY enthusiasts make their own simple system.

Alternatively there are several types of wedge-like ramp on sale at accessory suppliers. There are also wind-up devices that lift a wheel, but these are usually heavy and rather cumbersome to carry.

Corner steady pads

To prevent lowered corner steadies from sinking into soft ground, four small pads help to distribute the load. Small blocks of wood are perfectly adequate although a number of owners like to use purpose-made moulded plastic pads.

These are often attached to corner steadies with a steel pin although some versions have a habit of shaking around when you're towing. One type of pad used to be made with a channel that you had to fill up with water. This acted as an effective moat, thereby preventing colonies of ants from climbing up corner steadies to share the caravanning experience.

Steps

There are plenty of step designs on the market, some of which offer uncertain stability. A number of caravanners take DIY steps that double-up as tool boxes. Heavy tools hold them in place, but there's the risk that their contents could be stolen. Milk crates with a ply top are also popular – and provide bottle storage when you're towing. Anyway, whatever strategy is preferred, it's essential that steps are stable and safe.

SERVICE SUPPLY ITEMS

Hook-up mains lead, socket adaptors and socket tester are described in Chapter Twelve and the quality of cable needed to connect with the hook-up pillar is clearly explained. There have been instances where sub-standard cable has been sold at an attractive price – but whose specification does not comply with European Standards.

Leisure battery
Choosing, using and understanding the purpose of a leisure battery is discussed in Chapter Thirteen.

Fresh and waste water tanks
Trolley types, rolling barrels and simple jerrycans will all be seen on caravan sites. Some of these are described and illustrated in Chapter Ten.

Gas cylinders and regulator
Important tips on choosing the right type of gas and the subject of regulators are covered in Chapter Fourteen.

SECURITY DEVICES

There are two main concerns in respect of security. On the one hand there's the risk of a break-in while your caravan is unattended. On the other, there's the risk it might be towed away.

The latter has become increasingly worrying in the last few years and here are some points to bear in mind:

☐ It's claimed that 'buying time' is important. Most security devices can be beaten by an experienced

Many hitchlocks include a metal insert which takes the place of a towball.

This Bulldog hitchlock is robust and will even enclose the coupling head when your car is attached – that's useful when using a roadside restaurant.

This Bulldog hitch lock that fits a Winterhoff stabiliser achieved Silver Standard in the Sold Secure tests.

Some wheel clamps are heavy duty models for storage use; this portable version, however, is more compact to take on holiday.

This sturdy wheel clamp is more suitable for securing a caravan that's being stored.

thief, but more robust types take much too long to defeat. Anxious not to be 'caught in the act', most thieves move on to easier pickings.

☐ It often pays to fit more than one device. Hitch locks are useful, but a well-designed wheel clamp is usually harder to overcome. Fitting both is an extra deterrent.

☐ The locking mechanism is usually the easiest element to defeat. Devices employing an unsophisticated padlock are often easy to force open.

☐ Note the difference between heavy duty wheel clamps designed to protect caravans when stored for long spells and lighter 'portable' wheel clamps intended to be taken on holiday for caravan site use.

☐ Locking posts and barriers are often worth considering if your caravan sits outside your house on a drive. Some types are made to couple-up with a hitch lock as well.

☐ Electronic devices are reliant on a battery and some have a nasty habit of leaping into life due to a false alarm. Whereas some are mainly to register a break-in, others include a switch that incorporates a blob of mercury that starts rolling when a caravan is moved. This immediately triggers the alarm.

The Centinel locking post is one of several security barriers and posts used when a caravan or trailer is being stored by a house.

☐ Check the advice in the section overleaf regarding the Sold Secure testing scheme.

Taking these points into account, it is fair to state that some mechanically-based security products are tough to beat; others are less effective. In response to this, AL-KO Kober worked with the National Caravan Council to produce a wheel lock that operated in conjunction with an AL-KO Chassis. The AL-KO Secure Wheel Lock was then introduced in 2005 after a rigorous development programme. Today there's a wide range of installation kits that enable the product to be retrospectively fitted to caravans built on the Company's chassis from 2001 onwards.

The AL-KO Secure consists of two main elements. Firstly there's a highly visual locking bolt component. Secondly, there's the bolt receiver unit, which is fitted behind the brake drum.

These two components are secured with a nine-pin anti-pick radial lock, and this is the only caravan wheel-locking product to achieve Sold Secure Diamond Standard. Initially the product was introduced for use with alloy wheels of various patterns but a version is now available for securing steel wheels as well.

A wheel has to be in the right position to access the AL-KO Secure bolt receiver unit.

More recent AL-KO Secure wheel locks are made to fit steel wheels.

The attack tests conducted at the Sold Secure test house use an armoury of portable tools as well as sophisticated machines and lock picks.

Useful Tip

Owner vigilance

Since there are skilful thieves looking for caravans, an owner should be constantly vigilant. If your insurance policy allows you to store your caravan at home with a wheel removed, and provided the wheel is hidden elsewhere, this is a surprisingly effective deterrent.

During a long winter lay-up it is also wise to remove all the upholstery items and store them somewhere that's both warm and dry. Soft furnishings, seat backs and bases are remarkably costly to replace and thieves are seldom interested in stealing a caravan if all its upholstery items are missing.

A lock is usually the most vulnerable part of a security device – but some types are very resistant to sustained drilling.

In practice, it is fairly straightforward to lock an AL-KO Secure to a single-axle caravan; fitting the version made for twin-axle models is not quite so easy.

Sold Secure Test House

It is extremely hard for caravanners to evaluate which security devices are most likely to deter someone who wants to break into a caravan, or defeat a thief who wants to drive off with the whole lot in tow.

So the Sold Secure initiative is particularly noteworthy. Not only is this a way that manufacturers of security aids can gain recognition from an independent, non-profit-making agency; it's also a means whereby a caravanner can check which products have passed the very stringent attack tests conducted at the Sold Secure Test House.

Understandably, you won't be able to find out which products fail these tests, but at least the published Approved Products list gives you guidance on successful ones. Note, too, that products passing the test are rechecked on a regular basis, just to ensure that no shortcuts or quality faults subsequently creep into the manufacturing process.

The testing involves a five-minute sustained onslaught by locksmiths with all manner of picks, together with heavyweight attacks with wrenches, bolt cutters, drills, hammers and so on. There's also a saltwater bath to check rust degradation and a parallel test facility for checking the integrity of electronic systems.

Caravan accessories are the main interest in this book and products tested by Sold Secure include parking posts as well as wheel clamps, hitch locks and other devices. However, for caravanners who take bicycles on holiday, there are also Approved Product lists for cycle locks. Other Approved Product lists cover house alarms, car alarms, motorcycle alarms and so on.

With a new blade fitted for every test, hacksaws are used in an attempt to defeat a security device.

A long bar is used in an attempt to lever a clamp away from a caravan tyre.

Information and Approved Product lists are available free by telephoning 01327 264687. Alternatively, information is available on the Sold Secure website at www. soldsecure.com.

INTERIOR ACCESSORIES

Bedding

This is really a personal matter. Some caravanners take the sleeping bags they previously used for camping. They're notably easy to stow whereas duvets can take up a lot of space in a bed box. Other caravanners hate being 'bagged up' and prefer a traditional bed in spite of the effort involved in using sheets and blankets. There has also been a recent arrival of specialist manufacturers like Jonic which have developed caravan-specific bedding products. Both summer and winter grades are on offer.

Underlay

If a bed mattress rests on a sheet of plywood (as opposed to a slatted support), air cannot freely move around underneath. This leads to large damp

A fibrous non-slip underlay from The Natural Mat Company helps overcome the problem of damp patches forming under mattresses.

It's always wise to check the distribution of Fire Points when you visit a site.

For some fires, a fire blanket is extremely useful to have readily to hand.

In this demonstration, the moment half a cup of water on a long rod was emptied into a burning chip pan, a large explosion of flame erupted.

patches appearing on the underside of mattresses and these soon encourage mildew if a mattress isn't turned and aired periodically. The phenomenon seems to be more prevalent in winter.

Putting large towels under mattresses makes a small improvement, but it's not a cure. However, there are several products now available that help air to circulate – some of which are sold by boat specialists too. These include:

☐ The Natural Mat Company's 15mm fibrous rubberised, non-slip underlay.
☐ Ventair 15 underlay.
☐ Vent Air-Mat from Hawke House Marine.
☐ DRY Mat from Ship Shape Bedding.

Cutlery and crockery

This is another personal matter. To save weight, most owners buy plastic wine glasses, melamine dinner services or similar items from a caravan accessory shop. Only when you purchase a top tourer like a Carlight can you expect to find a bone china dinner service; this was standard equipment when a Carlight was originally sold new.

Fire precautions

Smoke alarms now have to be installed in all NCC-approved new caravans, but they're unlikely to be found in older caravans. Their inclusion makes good sense, although in the close confines of a caravan they have a habit of reacting extremely easily.

When visiting a caravan site, it's also wise to check the provision of fire fighting equipment and alarms. In addition you should strongly consider the merit of fitting a fire blanket (made to EN 1869). The problem of fat fires in caravans and the terrible mistake of trying to extinguish one with water is often demonstrated with devastating effect

at outdoor shows. This impressively reveals why a fire blanket is important, and once it has been put in place it should be left covering a pan for up to 30 minutes. This is because hot fat has an ability to reignite.

It's also wise to install a general-purpose fire extinguisher. A dry powder type is recommended as the best 'all-rounder' for typical caravan problems.

When fitting these items, remember to mount them within easy reach but not too close to a source of heat or enveloping flames.

Carbon monoxide alarm
These battery-operated devices are readily available and are often on sale in DIY superstores.

First Aid
It's obviously wise to take a First Aid outfit on holiday just as you'd have this provision at home. Some modern cars include one as standard but if that's not the case, get one to keep in your caravan too.

Toilets
Caravans have been fitted with cassette toilets for a number of years. If you've bought an old caravan, a fixed cassette toilet can sometimes be installed retrospectively provided the washroom cubicle is large enough. Don't worry if that's not the case. The smaller portable cassette toilets from Elsan and Thetford are almost as convenient. Turn to Chapter Ten to find out about treatment chemicals and related matters.

OTHER ACCESSORIES

TV systems
Since an earlier edition of this handbook, flat-screen TV sets have tumbled in price. Many caravanners now own one and several models are also fitted with a built-in DVD player as well. Also fitted inside recent TV sets are digital receivers, and that is important if you don't own a separate 'set-top' box (often called a 'digibox'), because at the time of writing analogue transmissions are progressively being terminated throughout the United Kingdom.

However, digital television programmes are only available when a signal is strong. If the reception permits, a good-quality picture is a pleasure to watch. Alternatively when reception is poor, analogue transmissions give disappointing pictures whereas

A dry powder fire extinguisher is often recommended for caravan use.

with digital systems you get nothing at all. This all-or-nothing feature applies to both digital TV captured using an aerial *and* digital TV captured using a satellite dish.

In consequence, you need either a good directional aerial (for terrestrial TV) or a good dish (for satellite TV). Both need to be pointed in their required directions and both will be affected by obstructions. In addition, your aerial or dish has to be reset every time you move to a new site; similarly, your TV set often needs retuning as well. Being able to watch TV in a caravan is undoubtedly more involved than watching programmes at home.

Given the options, some caravanners decide to use an aerial in order to watch terrestrial TV coming from land-based transmitters. With the Freeview service and a good reception you can enjoy over 40 TV stations and over 20 radio stations from caravanning venues in the UK.

Other caravanners decide to change to satellite TV using non-subscription programmes from either Freesat or Free to Air systems. With a suitable set-up you can also pick up many UK stations when you're on holiday elsewhere in mainland Europe.

However, things are changing at such pace that it would be inappropriate to go into any more detail here. One of the best overviews of television in leisure vehicles is published each year in RoadPro's free annual catalogue. Furthermore, most of the terrestrial and satellite products offered for sale are tested in Europe by members of the RoadPro staff.

Terrestrial TV equipment

For several years, caravans have often been supplied with a roof-mounted TV aerial as a standard item. The circular types are known as omnidirectional aerials because they don't need to be pointed towards the nearest transmitter. That's a useful feature, but an omnidirectional aerial is not able to pick up signals as efficiently as a 'directional' type. This weakness has become particularly evident now that digital transmissions have arrived.

It is true, of course, that many caravan aerials are fitted with a 12V booster amplifier. This helps to improve a signal in a weak reception area; in addition, these devices can also *reduce* signal strength when a caravan site is too close to a transmitter.

Notwithstanding the merits of amplification devices, the advent of digital systems has found that caravanners are better served by using a pole-mounted directional aerial. Two examples are the

Terrestrial TV products

An omnidirectional aerial will not obtain as good signals as a directional aerial like the one on the left.

Once permanently fitted, a Status 530-10 directional aerial can be completely controlled from indoors.

When a directional aerial is rotated, LED indicators on a signal finder confirm where the signal is strongest.

Get one of these coupling boxes fitted to an external wall if there's a cable to connect from an aerial outside.

Grade UK Status 530-5 (short pole) and the 530-10 (long pole), which are made for permanent installation in caravans. Once fitted, the user is able to push the pole upwards and to rotate it from indoors while watching the results on a screen. In addition, there's a control handle to tilt the mast-head aerial through 180° to suit those transmitting stations which need an aerial's elements to be in the vertical plane. In summary, a Status 530 aerial is a good product that can often be fitted in older caravans as long as its pole can be suitably hidden indoors.

A less expensive alternative is to purchase a sectional mast in order to mount a directional aerial on the top. Caravanners often route the connecting cable for linking-up to their TV set through a part-open window, but a better arrangement is to have a coupling point fitted as shown in the example on the previous page.

Otherwise a Freeview set-top box is needed, although modern flat-screen TVs have this product built in. *Note: Freeview is a terrestrial service that has nothing to do with satellite TV. Don't confuse it with Freesat.*

In summary, the success of a terrestrial system is strongly influenced by the location of a caravan site. That is equally true with satellite systems.

Satellite TV equipment

Some caravanners are choosing to purchase portable satellite systems in preference to improving their terrestrial TV reception. Several specialists are supplying the items required and guidance booklets are available from both Maxview and RoadPro.

Obviously a dish needs to be set up every time you arrive at a new site, and many caravanners use an inexpensive satellite finder to establish when the signal has reached its optimum strength. Although satellites are moving through space, their speed is set to match that of the earth; doubtless this is an over-simplified explanation but it illustrates why a dish has to be set in a fixed position when you arrive at your pitch.

Although there are automatic satellite-seeking domes for installing on roofs, portable dishes are far less expensive and are usually easy to tilt at the right angle and to point in the right direction.

Another necessary purchase is the receiver, and at the time of writing dozens of free programmes are available using either a Freesat or a Free-to-Air receiver. *Note: Don't confuse these with Freeview receivers that capture terrestrial TV systems via an aerial.*

More information on these seemingly complex products in the fast-moving world of modern TV are obtainable from specialist suppliers.

Satellite TV products

An increasing number of caravanners are purchasing portable satellite dishes complete with a tripod.

Once a dish has been mounted on a tripod, it has to be tilted to achieve the elevation angle needed by the chosen satellite.

A satellite finder enables a satellite to be found quickly using signal strength LEDs and an audible noise.

This 12V/230V receiver enables you to watch programmes in high definition that are broadcast free of charge.

In very hot conditions, a refrigerative air conditioner achieves impressive levels of cooling.

Air conditioning appliances

Caravans can get extremely hot inside when parked in direct sunlight. When temperatures rise, caravanners use both 12V and 230V fans to improve their comfort, and suitable products cost around £12 to £30.

That's a sensible strategy, but if you regularly take holidays in really hot places you might decide to have an air conditioning unit fitted as well. These fall into two broad categories: refrigerative air conditioners, and water evaporative coolers.

Refrigerative air conditioners

A refrigerative appliance employs a compressor-driven cooling unit just like the types fitted in fridges used at home. Without doubt one of these units will make a caravan very much cooler inside and some appliances are mounted in a bed locker; others are fitted on the roof and use an aperture like the ones used for roof-lights. Some models are made to produce mild background heat in winter as well.

Although their performance is remarkably good, these appliances are not often installed by UK owners for a number of reasons. For example:

- ☐ Roof-mounted models need a robust roof structure.
- ☐ They are heavy; an average unit weighs 32kg (70lb).
- ☐ They are costly; *eg* a Dometic B1500S costs over £1,000, plus fitting.
- ☐ On most products, the cooling unit requires a 230V supply.
- ☐ Some appliances are noisy and are irritating when left running at night.
- ☐ Summers in several European countries have few days of high temperatures.

Water evaporative cooling units

To understand the water evaporative principle, cover your mouth with a wet cloth on a hot day and inhale. The intake of air will be cool until the rag eventually becomes dry. The reason for this is simple: when water evaporates it absorbs heat, although the phenomenon is far less evident in humid conditions.

Several water evaporative products have been built employing this principle, including the Trav-L-Cool and the Webasto NiteCool appliances. These are roof-mounted products whose vents use a standard roof-light aperture. They are unlikely to create the level of cooling achieved by a refrigerative product but have several points of note. For example, the Trav-L-Cool model:

☐ Will fit on most caravan roofs without needing structural alterations.
☐ Weighs only 8kg (17.6lb) in a dry state.
☐ Runs on a 12V or 24V supply depending on the model.
☐ Has little to go wrong in its mechanism.
☐ Costs around £900 plus fitting.
☐ Is fairly quiet in operation and causes minimal disturbance at night.

Caravan motorised movers

When a caravan has to be manoeuvred into a difficult storage place, it can be an exacting job. In particular, elderly and disabled owners often find this difficult, especially if conducting the operation on sloping ground.

There are several answers to the problem and electrically driven tugging trolleys are one solution. Run by a 12V battery, these often have a dummy towball on top of the casing. A few couple-up with

To keep the interior of a caravan cool, a product like the NiteCool can be left running all night.

Caravan movers

The Move Control from Reich is fitted within a smart casing; another Reich model is made for twin-axle caravans.

A variety of friction products are used to drive a caravan's wheels; Powrwheel products have this abrasive coating.

Part of a wireless motorised mover is the central control box; its aerial receives signals from the handset.

A Powrwheel handset now includes a line drawing of a caravan so that it's easy to work out which button to press.

118

the jockey wheel clamp, although some specialists feel that this pulling point might cause minor chassis damage. Overall, these 'mini tractor' units don't add any weight to a caravan and are around 75% the cost of a permanently fitted mover. However, if you wanted to lift one into the back of your tow car they're quite heavy (around 23kg/50lb without the battery).

An alternative is to have an electric motorised mover fitted which drives your caravan's wheels. When the Carver Caravan Mover was first launched it certainly allowed thousands of elderly owners to continue caravanning, secure in the knowledge that they wouldn't have to push a caravan on to a pitch or into a confined parking place.

Carver ceased manufacturing caravan products around 1999 and several other manufacturers then started to produce 12V motorised movers as well. Whereas the first models had a coupling cable for the hand-held controller, wireless control pads appeared very soon after. Once you've practised with the simple controls, moving a caravan is much like operating a child's radio-controlled car.

Not that having a motorised mover is the sole preserve of elderly owners. On the contrary, there are caravanners of all ages who are not good at reversing a caravan with their tow car. Many struggle when siting a 'van on a pitch with spectating neighbours witnessing their every mistake. Other owners want to keep their caravan parked in a tight spot at the side of their house. In situations like these, a motorised mover provides a practical answer.

Unfortunately, though, these devices are heavy in weight and greedy on power. They're not cheap either. Recognising that a caravan's leisure battery is soon left in a badly discharged condition after a few manoeuvres, some owners buy a second leisure battery, which adds even more weight.

Fine though caravan movers might be, it's a dreadful mistake to have one fitted if you haven't first checked your available payload. Even without its own battery, the addition of an accessory that tops the scales at around 35kg (77lb) represents a very large chunk of a caravan's payload. That's sufficient to put some holiday-packed caravans well over their MTPLM, as explained in the previous chapter.

To be certain that your caravan is legal for use on the road, a weighbridge visit must precede the purchase of heavy products like a motorised mover.

The AL-KO Mammut
In 2010, the chassis manufacturer, AL-KO, is introducing its own motorised mover. To be known as the Mammut, the factory-fitted version of its two models will *not* reduce ground clearance under a caravan. This is achieved by mounting it adjacent to the main chassis members.

CHAPTER SEVEN

CHOOSING AND USING **AWNINGS**

If you park a caravan on a pitch for an extended period, an awning can be a great asset. Not only does it add to your personal space, it provides undercover storage for wet clothing and bikes. Some caravanners use an awning in summer for food preparation or as a venue for campsite banquets. Others fit a purpose-made sleeping compartment to provide an overflow bedroom. Even a small porch awning serves as a useful shelter when you're removing muddy wellies. It all depends on your needs...

121

This large Isabella awning doubles the amount of living space.

A Fiamma Caravanstor sunblind is not just effective, it's quick to set up.

A lightweight porch awning can be erected in minutes.

Though larger than a porch awning, a 'combi' or 'half-awning' normally fits several types of caravan.

Below: This awning is intentionally made as an accessory to fit on a Carousel folding caravan.

Below right: The zip-on bedroom extension shown here simply takes the place of a side-wall panel.

A good way to gain extra living space without buying a bigger caravan is to purchase an awning. However, these useful accessories come in a wide range of sizes, styles and materials. Types currently on sale include:

☐ Simple sunblinds consisting of just a roof and supporting poles.
☐ Sunroofs that permit the addition of a zip-in front panel and side walls to increase protection against mild winds and moderate rain showers.
☐ Small porch awnings that are especially useful in winter to keep draughts from your caravan door and to provide a place for wet wellies.
☐ 'Combi', 'universal' or 'half-awnings' which fall midway between a porch and a full awning. These are intended to fit a wide range of models – which is important if you're changing your caravan and don't want to spend money on a replacement awning.
☐ Traditional full-sized awnings whose size has to match your particular 'van. These usually have a rectangular floor plan and their side walls are stitched permanently to the roof panel. However, more expensive versions have 'zip-out' removable sides so that you can opt for either a roof-only sunshade or a full enclosure – depending on how long you're staying.
☐ Purpose-made awnings that are made for particular types of caravans, such as folding models.
☐ Awnings that offer a facility for adding an extra sleeping compartment to one of the sides.

☐ Massive multi-sided units whose overall internal dimensions are far greater than those of the caravan to which they're attached.

Though not the largest type of awning, this example would still weigh a lot when both its fabric and poles are packed.

Points to note:

1 Large awnings are especially heavy and it is often better if they can be carried in a tow car rather than a caravan. If you follow the advice in Chapter Five and take a holiday-loaded caravan to a weighbridge, it then becomes clear whether a heavy awning can be included without exceeding the 'van's Maximum Technically Permissible Laden Mass (MTPLM).

2 Universal and porch awnings are usually easy to transfer from one caravan to another. However, you need to check that there are no obstructions at the points where their sides rest against the caravan's wall. For instance if they cross the face of an acrylic window, this is likely to get scratched when the fabric gets blown in the wind. Similarly, the canvas should neither cross a refrigerator vent nor obstruct the fridge's flue outlet.

3 A resourceful owner is usually able to erect an awning unaided, although it isn't always an easy task. When it's dark and especially if it's breezy, it is wise to wait until later. Either way it is much easier if you have helpers. Bear this in mind before buying one of the mansion-like structures that look impressive in catalogue illustrations.

4 Instead of purchasing caravan-specific awnings, some owners prefer to use free-standing structures that can also be erected on the lawn back at home. Gazebos are particularly popular but they *must* be pegged down securely, especially when it's windy. However, these structures are less likely to suffer from wind-lift when zip-in side panels are added. Other types of free-standing enclosures are sometimes used for outdoor cooking or for housing a portable toilet. In addition, Ventura has included a small store that is useful for hiding away campsite furniture, bikes, toys and barbecue equipment.

A gazebo is more secure in winds if it has zip-in side panels; it can also be used on the lawn back at home.

Tents and awnings in the Khyam range are very quick to erect on account of the pole linking system.

MATERIALS

Many awnings are now manufactured using a synthetic fabric, and various forms of proofing are used. For example, ultra-light materials (often used for hike tents) are treated with a non-permeable coating on the inner face. These occupy little space when packed in a carrying valise, but the fabric isn't breathable so condensation quickly forms on the inside. That's one reason why natural cotton canvas is sometimes preferred, but it soon rots if packed away in a damp condition. In consequence, more expensive awnings are often made using breathable, treated synthetic products that feel similar to cotton.

Different types of poles employing various materials are also available, as the section below describes. Some pole structures use clip-together couplings which significantly speed-up the time it takes to set up an awning. Tents and awnings from Khyam, for example, have used couplings like this for several years.

Rigid and flexible poles

☐ **Coated steel rigid poles** – Strength is a point in their favour: weight is their disadvantage. An anodised finish is used on more expensive poles; cheaper products start to rust prematurely, especially when the coating gets damaged.

Steel poles are sturdy but heavy; when emptied from their bag they pose a daunting assembly problem at first sight.

Aluminium folding poles are used very successfully in roller-blind sunshades like the Fiamma Caravanstore.

☐ **Rigid aluminium poles** – At one time, manufacturers like Salou supplied alloy poles with their awnings. Alloy tubes are light and corrosion-resistant but usually lack the strength of a similar steel product. Today, awnings supported with rigid aluminium tubing are less common, although Fiamma uses this material to good effect on its Caravanstore sunblinds.

☐ **Glass-fibre tubing** – This product will neither corrode nor discolour. It is also very light, though it tends to be costly. It also lacks the rigidity of steel tubing and if there are large areas of unsupported fabric, a pole structure can flex and might even break. In winter, for example, an overnight fall of snow will place considerable weight on a roof. As the author found on a trip to the Alps, glass-fibre poles are less able to cope with inclement conditions.

☐ **Flexible hoops** – Influenced by the structures employed on many lightweight tents, more and more awning manufacturers supply flexible hoops instead of rigid poles. When fed through stitched sleeves in fabric panels, rods that are no thicker than your smallest finger assume a pronounced curve. Provided the sections only support light, nylon-proofed material, and guy ropes are used to resist deformation in strong gusts of wind, enclosures are often surprisingly rigid.

Fabrics

☐ **Cotton** – Depending on its grade, cotton is usually a light fabric and it has the advantage of 'breathability'. This means that it doesn't suffer from condensation problems associated with several types of synthetic materials. At the same time it's less tolerant to ill treatment. Pack it away damp for several days and the rotting process starts. What's more, the inevitable marks left by mould are almost impossible to remove. On the other hand, if you look after a cotton awning it can last for at least 15 years of seasonal use.

Many Isabella awnings are sold with the option of either good quality glass-fibre poles or coated steel products.

125

Flexible hoop assemblies, originally developed for backpacking tents, are now used on lightweight porch awnings too.

☐ **Synthetic** – Several types of synthetic materials are used by awning manufacturers; some are as soft as cotton but more resistant to wear. Good quality synthetic fabrics can be surprisingly expensive and the proofing process means that many types are not able to 'breathe'. Having ventilation in an enclosure is therefore essential to disperse condensation. The condensation problem becomes particularly acute if you use your awning as an alternative kitchen or a drying room. However, it's not as bad as it is inside non-breathable hike tents because there's a greater airflow in a large awning.

Features of synthetic products
Acrylic is light in weight, hard-wearing, virtually rot-proof, resistant to fading and it doesn't shrink.
Polyester fabrics can offer a small measure of 'breathabilty' depending on the coating used. The product is lighter than acrylic but not as hardwearing. To improve performance it is often coated with proofing treatments like polyurethane (PU) or polyvinyl chloride (PVC).

Note: In many awnings, more than one material is used. For instance, there are awnings where the roof is weather-resistant coated polyester whereas the sides are cotton. You may also note that there are often PVC-coated panels at the foot of the walls. This provision is particularly beneficial because it copes with splash-up damage in downpours and spray damage from canine leg-lifters.

The dark blue PVC-coated panels at the lower edges of this Ventura product offer useful practical benefits.

ATTACHMENT TO THE CARAVAN

Manufacturers use different ways to secure awnings and poles to the sides of caravans. Older models, for example, sometimes have large rubber suction pads fitted to the ends of the roof poles. However, these fail to achieve satisfactory suction on an aluminium surface that has a textured finish.

Other systems require eyelets to be mounted on a caravan's walls, and that necessitates drilling the external cladding. When mounting these eyelets you are seldom lucky enough to find a wood strut behind the aluminium or GRP skin to provide a firm fixing. In consequence you have to rely on tight-fitting self-tapping screws. Inevitably this addition produces potential leaking points, so it's important to use stainless steel screws and to bed the attachment plates on a flexible sealant.

Since the act of drilling a new caravan might invalidate its water ingress warranty, some awning manufacturers have designed pads complete with a pole 'docking' arrangement which are slid into the awning rail as separate items. An alternative strategy is to slide roof support poles through sleeves that form part of the awning fabric itself. In some instances, you'll also find fabric pockets that are fitted with zips to retain the poles.

When comparing various attachment methods, it is undoubtedly better to have a roof pole support system that eliminates the need to drill a caravan's side wall.

MEASURING-UP

It is important that an awning fits well. If the fabric starts to flap in a wind, it not only keeps residents awake at night; it can also damage a caravan's painted side panels and the surface of acrylic windows.

At one time, awning poles were nearly always hooked into plastic eyelets that had to be mounted on a caravan's walls.

In this model, roof poles are zipped into a sleeve that runs along the top of the awning's side panels.

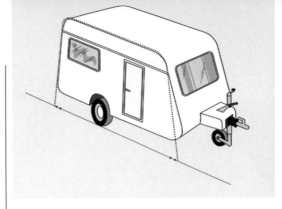

The red dotted lines indicate the required measurement around the awning channel including projections down to the ground at either side.

A good quality awning has taped edges and impeccable stitching on all the seams.

When comparing awnings, look carefully at the quality of the zips.

With a conventional full awning, as opposed to a porch or combi design, it's most important that the measurement from the ground and all along the trackway is going to match the dimension of the awning you plan to purchase. In a good Owner's Handbook, the caravan manufacturer will advise what size awning is needed for your particular model of caravan. If this information has been overlooked you sometimes find that awning manufacturers and retailers hold records of measurements relating to the more popular recent caravans. Failing that, check the panel below.

BUYING TIPS

☐ When comparing products, check the quality of construction, especially the stitching. Look closely, too, at the zips; replacements can be costly to have fitted.

☐ Check the 'optional extras'. Some manufacturers can supply a useful pocket panel for storing holiday items; others offer items like coat-hanger bars. Inner tents are also available if you want to use an awning as an overspill dormitory.

☐ Look for storm guy fixing points. Some models

ⓘ Useful Tip

Measuring-up tips

To establish the size of awning required you will need to carry out the following procedure:

1 Park your caravan on level ground and lower the corner steadies.

2 Working from the diagram above, hold a tape measure around the awning channel that normally runs round the perimeter of the side walls and the roof. Include in your measurement the bottom projection from each end of the trackway down to the ground.

3 Even better is to run a length of non-stretch cord around the trackway itself – just as you would the attachment cord of an awning. Carry both ends down to the ground, then remove it and measure it carefully.

4 Since the angle on the sides of an awning usually splays outwards, you need to take this into account when establishing the point where the bottom of the awning will touch the ground.

All sorts of 'extras' are available – including a rack of coat hooks.

Fancy curtains and Georgian-style glazing bars on the windows are popular at present.

are better suited to exposed, windy locations than others. There may also be storm straps listed in the catalogue. Failing that, several independent component specialists can supply these items.

☐ Ask if there's an after-sales service in case of an accident. It's not unusual for a pole to fall over when an awning is being erected and sharp spikes on the top can easily puncture the fabric.

☐ Enquire if you can purchase spares like rubber expansion loops for the pegging points. Find out how easy it is to purchase a replacement pole. In a strong wind it's possible for a pole to become so badly bent that it cannot be straightened.

☐ Check the colours of awnings as well. Some manufacturers have moved to light pastel shades which look very pretty. However, colours that look good on their own might not match the colour of the caravan.

Left: Note the storm guy fixing points, but use guys rather than 'bungee' rubbers.

Above: Storm straps are often sold at outdoor shows; these types have tightening clamps.

These connecting loops on an Isabella awning are easy to fit.

Ground sheets left down for a long time can ruin a pitch; breathable floor coverings are much to be preferred.

A specially-formulated 'carpet cleanser' will effectively remove most stains without damaging a Bolon covering.

The woven-vinyl breathable floor covering from Bolon can be cut from the roll.

Edging clips can be purchased which are made with pegging holes.

GROUND-COVER MATERIAL

Think carefully about the type of ground-cover that you want to use. Traditional groundsheets kill the grass, so there are special carpeting materials with 'breathable' characteristics. Some examples can be bought from the roll and priced according to size.

Perhaps the longest established product is Bolon woven-vinyl breathable floor coverings, which are manufactured in Sweden. The version of Bolon carpet sold for caravanning is marketed by Isabella Awnings and this 'extra breathable' material is fireproof, stain-resistant and kind to grass. To secure it without puncturing the material, Bolon also manufactures special pegging clips.

SPARES AND EXTRAS

☐ If you need spares for an awning, it's unlikely that you'll be able to purchase these at an indoor exhibition. Smaller companies who specialise in awning components are more likely to attend the

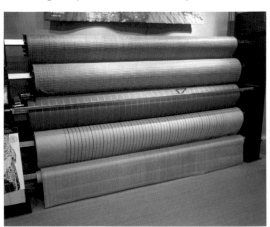

outdoor shows and rallies that are held in the warmer months of the year.

☐ With the increasing use of hard standings on campsites, there's often a need to have a selection of heavy duty items called 'rock pegs'. As their name suggests, these are also useful on rough ground, and several campsite operators sell rock pegs in the reception office.

☐ If you have the misfortune of colliding with a tree or wall and compress the awning channel, W4 accessories has the answer – a tiny dumbbell with bullet-shaped ends designed to be tapped through the channelling with a hammer, thus re-establishing the shape of the aperture as it passes through. Don't prize open an awning channel with a screwdriver or pliers because you'll damage it.

Spare poles are often on sale at major outdoor shows like The Camping and Caravan Club's Feast of Lanterns event.

Independent specialists sell awning spares – and you'll see them at outdoor rallies.

On rough ground like this, the plastic pegs supplied with many awnings are of little use.

Rock pegs are useful additions and many caravanners also carry a hammer in their peg bag.

Spray with silicone then tap the appropriate end of this re-forming tool through a damaged awning rail.

Granger's Fabsil contains silicone and can be used on both cotton and synthetic fabrics.

132

CLEANERS AND REPROOFING PRODUCTS

Marks and stains are a fact of life, hence there are several specialist fabric cleaners available from caravan accessory and camping suppliers. For instance, Camco Awning cleaner has been especially popular in the last few years. The Camco range from America is stocked and available by mail order from ABP Accessories in Leicestershire.

Bear in mind that stains like bird lime should be removed at the earliest opportunity, whereas mud is best left until it's completely dry. Other stains include car exhaust marks. Apart from proprietary awning cleaners you can often shift marks using warm, soapy water – but never use detergent. Of course, there's sometimes a tendency for a tidemark to appear around the treated area, so you then have to extend your effort and clean the entire panel. However, this isn't always a problem because some marks are confined to a small panel with stitching boundaries.

The trouble with determined and regular cleaning is that this can hasten the need for reproofing. However, specialists like Grangers and Nikwax market a number of reproofing products and their application is straightforward provided the weather is on your side.

As a rule, it's best to erect an awning before tackling the reproofing work. It also needs to be clean. Ideally you want warm, dry weather – but not hot, direct sun. On the other hand, Nikwax Aqueous Technik for PU-coated materials is better when used on a damp fabric. Similarly, Nikwax Spray-on TX Direct and Nikwax TX 10 Cottonproofer can be applied to wet or dry fabrics. So before getting to work, check carefully the instruction leaflet supplied with the product that you intend to use.

Many treatments like Granger's Fabsil would normally be applied with a brush, although some owners use a pressurised garden atomiser spray, which is rather more convenient. Using a long lance attachment, for example, allows you to reach the roof panels much more easily.

Needless to say, a full reproofing operation will take an hour or more. However, if you merely want to reproof a small area – perhaps where you've carried out a spot-cleaning operation – you can purchase reproofers in aerosol cans for localised application.

Avoid bad locations
If you ever make the mistake of erecting an awning under a lime or similar tree that exudes a sticky sap, you'll never do it a second time. These substances soon coat the entire roof fabric and need washing-off at the earliest opportunity. Even then, you might find you remove the water-resistance of the fabric and need to reproof it.

PACKING AN AWNING AWAY

If circumstances force you to pack away a wet awning when leaving a caravan site, you need to open it up and dry the fabric as soon as possible. In a very short time, mould marks appear whatever the type of fabric. Hence on long trips back to the UK from abroad, many caravanners realise the importance of taking an overnight break to re-erect their damp awning to start the drying process.

At the end of a season, the need to ensure that its fabric is completely dry is again important. With some awnings costing a four-figure sum, these are expensive products needing care and attention. Although it's usually fine to store an awning in a caravan when the weather's warm, it can get too damp in a 'van during winter. So if you've got room, transfer it into your home.

REPAIR WORK

Damage can occur in a number of ways, although a falling awning pole complete with a spike is one of the mishaps that tears a lot of awnings. Whilst a few owners subsequently use their domestic skills to carry out repairs, most seek the help of a professional equipped with industrial sewing machines.

Some awning manufacturers such as Isabella (UK) carry out repairs for customers. In fact this company can even make small alterations to an existing Isabella product so that it can be fitted to a larger or smaller caravan. That's a useful service for owners who want to purchase a different-sized caravan without getting rid of their current awning.

There are also independent awning repairers whose services are often listed in the classified advertisements of both caravan and camping magazines. In addition, both major caravanning clubs offer advice. For example, The Caravan Club records 19 specialists nationwide in its latest awning repair list.

Repairers will also replace damaged zips, and some caravan breakers cut out zips from scrapped awnings and sell them in their accessory shop. It's not unusual to see a bundle of second-hand zips on display in various lengths and colours.

Tip

New awnings that leak
On some brand new awnings, the sewing needles used to stitch the seams leave large puncture holes – especially in coated synthetic fabrics. When it rains, you then find that your new awning starts to leak; but don't get too dismayed. Provided the dampened thread and fabric swells, the tiny puncture holes diminish in size and the problem solves itself. Some manufacturers even advise purchasers to erect a brand new awning before leaving for a holiday in order to spray it with a hose. It's a one-off job that seldom needs repeating, but if the leaks persist you might then have to apply a proofing compound along the stitched seams.

133

Specialists at the Isabella UK headquarters will repair or alter awnings the company has supplied.

ERECTING AN AWNING

Some awnings are sold with very poor erection instructions. In fact if you don't set up your awning on a regular basis, it's a good idea to colour-code the ends of each pole using PVC tape.

If the awning is being erected for the first time, you might also find that the feed points on your caravan's trackway need widening slightly. Do this very carefully and try to use a blunt tool – the sharp corners on a slotted screwdriver can all too easily damage the surface of an aluminium extrusion. Alternatively you can prise open the feed slot using a small wedge of wood; this avoids a metal-to-metal contact.

Once this preliminary preparation is complete, the awning should go up fairly easily. The accompanying

Check the poles and the way they assemble. If you need a step to reach the roof, have it to hand.

Find the openings in the awning track where the cord on the roof panel can be inserted.

134

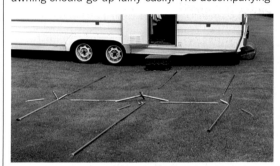

Left: Carefully pull the roof section around the awning rail. On this Combi awning it has to leave the groove at a specially enlarged outlet.

Above: Once the roof panel is centralised, the frame is assembled and coupled to the caravan – but its vertical legs are kept partly folded.

photographs show a Combi awning being erected, and my caravan's free-standing step proves especially useful when reaching up to the awning rail. Drawing the roof panel through the channelling can be quite a stretch!

Incidentally, different people put up awnings in their own favourite ways. This is my preference, in which the sides are zipped out and reinstated later. It means the roof section, which goes up first, is lighter to handle.

Lengths of foam are coupled to one part of the vertical wall using white sleeves. This is where a Combi awning touches the mid point of the 'van's wall.

The size of Combi awning was chosen so the caravan window wouldn't be obscured; foam pads attached to the awning protect the caravan's paintwork.

With the roof still untensioned, the legs are now lifted. Now the side panels can be zipped-in, the canvas tensioned and the pegs driven into the ground.

To prevent the walls flapping in a breeze, tie tapes allow the canvas to be secured to the poles.

It is important to zip-up all the doors of an awning before pegging-out the wall panels.

For 'fine tuning', there's usually a facility to adjust the position of poles and telescopic couplings which allows the tension of the fabric to be altered.

CHAPTER EIGHT

HITCH-UP
AND GO

When getting ready for a trip away, there are several jobs to carry out before leaving. Packing a caravan correctly, checking its noseweight, and fitting the extension mirrors on your car are some of the points discussed in this chapter. Then you have to couple the car and caravan together. Nothing's particularly difficult, but several key tasks should be noted.

Let's imagine the situation. Your caravan has been serviced for the season, it bears the same number plate as your tow car, you've turned all the gas cylinders off, the tyre pressures are correct and you're now loading your personal gear. When your possessions have been duly stowed, that's when the caravan's noseweight needs checking.

An assistant using prearranged signals is a great help when you're reversing a car towards a caravan's coupling hitch.

Coupling components referred to in this chapter

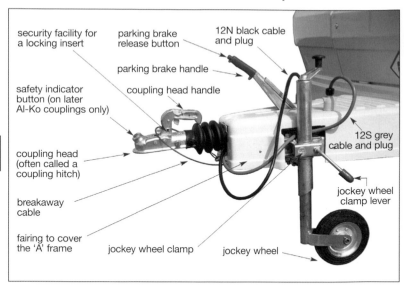

security facility for
a locking insert

parking brake
release button

12N black cable
and plug

parking brake handle

safety indicator
button (on later
Al-Ko couplings only)

coupling head handle

12S grey
cable and plug

coupling head
(often called a
coupling hitch)

breakaway
cable

jockey wheel
clamp lever

fairing to cover
the 'A' frame

jockey wheel clamp

jockey wheel

NOSEWEIGHT

The weight that bears down on the rear of a tow car is determined by the distribution of possessions inside. Their placement determines the load on the towball; this is referred to as 'noseweight'.

If the entire weight of a caravan is distributed so that everything balances over its axle (or axles), no weight at all will be bearing down on the car's towing ball. That might sound a wise strategy, but it's a recipe for disaster. You'll find that the balanced load above the caravan axle will see-saw up and down as soon as you start towing. The towing vehicle then receives relentless lifting and lowering movements and the outfit becomes alarmingly unstable.

For safe towing, noseweight is a crucial commodity. What's more, it's an easy thing to adjust. Repositioning heavy items of equipment inside the 'van such as an awning or a toolbox immediately alters the load on the towball.

To achieve the most stable arrangement, it is generally advised to create a noseweight that is around 7% of the total weight of your fully laden caravan. To calculate this in a precise way necessitates having your loaded caravan checked on a weighbridge as described in Chapter Five. The total weight of the 'van is

To measure noseweight, the coupling head is lowered on to a noseweight gauge.

Some caravanners purchase a purpose-made gauge to check the noseweight.

then divided by 100 and multiplied by seven to establish the ideal noseweight. That said, there are limits on the load that a towball can manage.

Both towbar and vehicle manufacturers prescribe the weight limits for their respective products. For example, the maximum carrying capacity of recent towbars is marked on a plate as shown on page 70. So whereas towing stability might be at its best when the noseweight's 7% cent of a caravan's laden weight, there are instances when the calculated figure can't be used because it *exceeds* the car and the towbar limits. Check the accompanying panel for further advice.

Others check noseweight using a short pole, a pad and some bathroom scales.

 Technical Tip

Noseweight limits

As a general rule, stated maximum noseweights typically fall between 50 and 75kg (around 110–165lb). Moreover, it was mentioned in Chapter Five that nearly all towbars (sometimes called 'towing brackets') fitted to post-1 August 1998 vehicles have to bear a Type Approval plate declaring maximum loading capacities. One of the listed figures gives a towbar's noseweight limit, which is sometimes called the 'S' value.

It's true that a few cars have remarkably high limits. Examples include 4x4 all-terrain models and vehicles with self-levelling suspension like some Citroën saloons. But that doesn't help if the permitted carrying capacity of the towbar you later have fitted is designed to handle much lower noseweights. So remember:

- Generally it's helpful to have as heavy a noseweight as possible, but this depends on a number of constraints.
- For example, you need to find out: (1) the towbar's noseweight limit, and (2) weight limits applicable to the towing vehicle. You must then ensure that you don't exceed these figures.
- Once these constraints have been noted, you can then ascertain how close you can get to the 7% noseweight, which is believed to achieve the best level of stability when you're towing.
- Unfortunately, if you own a particularly heavy caravan you might not be able to achieve this ideal figure. That's because the calculated 7% figure turns out to be higher than the limits applicable to your car or its towbar. That doesn't necessarily mean that you mustn't tow the caravan. To comply with these limits you can usually reduce noseweight to a lower percentage of the caravan's weight provided you recognise that the outfit is unlikely to be quite so stable.

Some owners use a purpose-made device like the ones shown on pages 138 and 139.

Useful Tip

An alternative way to measure noseweight
If you don't own a gauge, a popular way to measure noseweight is to use a cut-down length of broomstick handle or a similar length of timber. When no one's looking, you then 'borrow' the family bathroom scales. Thereafter the procedure is much the same as it would be when using a purpose-made gauge. For example, one end of the wooden stick is inserted into the coupling head; the other is positioned on the central part of the weighing platform – preferably on a small piece of wooden board to prevent damaging the plate. Once you've lowered the 'van using the jockey wheel, take the reading from the scales.

Procedure for checking noseweight

Some owners use a purpose-made device like the ones shown on pages 138 and 139. These products are used as follows:

1 Park the caravan on flat ground. If there's the slightest chance of movement, chock the wheels.
2 Make sure the jockey wheel is in contact with the ground and that the caravan brake has been engaged.
3 Raise all the corner steadies; then lift the coupling head using the jockey wheel handle.
4 Insert the top of the noseweight gauge into the coupling head and hold the device vertically. If you can't do this because the coupling head's too low, turn the jockey wheel handle to gain extra height.
5 Once the device is in place, lower the front of the caravan until all the noseweight is being borne by the piston on the gauge.
6 Take the noseweight reading.

Altering noseweight

Increasing or reducing noseweight is achieved by moving your stowed items either towards the front or the rear end of the caravan. But there's a warning. If there's excessive noseweight you might decide to eliminate this in one easy move by putting a heavy item at the extreme back of the 'van to compensate. **That, however, is bad practice**.

Loading heavy items at opposite extremities creates what is called the 'dumb-bell effect'. This means that if your caravan starts to sway from side to side when it's being towed, the inertia in these heavy items tends to perpetuate a pendulum action. Even with a stabiliser fitted, the unwanted lateral movements take longer than usual to correct.

In consequence, if you need to *reduce* noseweight it's better to move items hitherto stored near the front of the 'van to a location much closer to the

Technical Tip

'Dumb-bell effect'
Carrying a spare wheel on a caravan's rear wall is a highly questionable strategy. A spare wheel, complete with a tyre, is surprisingly heavy so it should be stowed low down and as near the axle as possible. Similarly, it's very unwise to fit a cycle rack on the rear wall of a towed caravan. A physicist would point out that lateral instability is much harder to bring under control when heavy items are stowed at the extreme ends of a caravan. In spite of this potentially dangerous phenomenon, you'll often see caravanners who are oblivious to the implications of a 'dumb-bell effect'.

It is not good practice to carry bicycles on the rear wall of a caravan.

axle. In fact, as many heavy items as possible should be loaded low down over the axle. You certainly don't want a large amount of weight at the extremities. This is why you mustn't be tempted to use up all that inviting space in some of the latest gas cylinder lockers at the front. In fact on some caravans, a correct noseweight can only be achieved by carrying no more than two small gas cylinders in this locker – even though there's space to accommodate much larger products.

A rear-mounted spare wheel might seem convenient but positioning heavy items at the extreme ends of a caravan can make the reduction of lateral instability difficult.

The space might look inviting, but it's all-too-easy to exceed the noseweight limit if you pack too much into a front-end gas locker.

When loading up a caravan, the distribution of personal effects should follow this pattern.

Key

☐ - Heavy items   ☐ - Medium-weight items   ☐ - Light items

Note
The Type Approval regulations have an exclusion clause regarding towball height for off-road vehicles. In consequence the ball height for these vehicles may be too high to allow a caravan to adopt a level stance when hitched up. If you experience this problem, seek advice from the manufacturer's customer relations department.

LOADING A CARAVAN

Not only does wise loading of your personal possessions help to achieve the ideal noseweight, it has other implications for stability when towing.

For example, when negotiating a sharp bend, a caravan travelling at brisk speed is likely to develop 'body roll'. This is why heavy items should never be stowed in roof lockers. Caravans are fitted with rather a lot of lockers these days, but that doesn't mean you have to fill them all up.

There are several basic principles that you should follow when loading a caravan and the accompanying diagram gives helpful advice.

Inclination

When you're towing at normal speeds, both the car and caravan should assume a level stance. This inclination should be checked on level ground when the outfit is stationary. However, it's worth noting that a slight nose-down inclination is often regarded as acceptable when a caravan is parked. That's because there's usually a small lifting effect brought about through turbulence which helps the 'van assume a level stance once you're on the move.

☐ If you've achieved the correct noseweight but find that the rear end of the towing vehicle sags when the caravan's coupled, your car might need

To achieve a level car and caravan, it is sometimes helpful if a drop plate is fitted to the bracket so that the tow ball height is lowered.

replacement rear springs or an approved spring-reinforcing device. These products were mentioned in Chapter Five.

☐ If it's the caravan's tail which sags, then you might resolve the problem by fitting a drop plate, but check the comments in the accompanying panel.

Loading food

The practice of loading up a caravan's cupboards with as much food as possible is fortunately losing its appeal. Even if a caravan site doesn't have a shop of its own, supermarkets are seldom far away – whether you're at home or abroad. So why give the tow car a tough assignment by transferring half your kitchen to the caravan?

To repeat the point made above, don't carry heavy items in roof lockers. Even if a roof locker might seem a logical place to store the marmalade jar on-site, it's not the place to keep heavy items when you take to the road. (Should we ever meet on a future occasion, ask me to relate the story of the jar of red cabbage in vinegar and my first, brand-new caravan that was fitted with a primrose yellow carpet.)

As regards refrigerator products, try to pre-cool the fridge before taking to the road. Also ensure that you load it following the recommendations given in Chapter Eleven.

MIRRORS

The so-called 'through vision' created via a car's internal mirror is not likely to be very helpful when you're towing. Even if your caravan has large windows front and back, a few drops of rain will turn a rearward image into a fuzzy blur. Even in good weather, modern plastic windows rarely provide accurate information about road conditions behind you. Moreover, it is a legal requirement that a vehicle is equipped with at least two mirrors

A nose-up caravan is unstable because the caravan will be susceptible to a wind lift effect which develops under the forward end of the floor panel.

Drop plates
Nowadays, tow brackets are manufactured to produce a standard towing height. Directive 94/20/EC specifies that the centre of a towball should be between 350mm and 420mm (13.8–16.6in) from the ground when a vehicle is laden to maximum weight.

However, problems arise with some older caravans which have an unusually low coupling head. The same effect occurs, too, if a car is only partially laden and is riding high. In these instances, it would help if the towball was slightly lower.

The subject of drop plates was discussed in Chapter Five, where the key issues are explained in the panel entitled *Towball height and drop plates*.

144 *The extension towing mirrors from Smat Nord Spa have been used in the UK for many years and recent models bear the mandatory E-markings.*

Once you've taken to the road, it's not unusual to have to pull into a lay-by fairly promptly to make fine adjustments to the towing mirrors.

and when a caravan is coupled-up, that effectively means external mirrors are needed on both the nearside and offside.

Since most caravans are considerably wider than their towing vehicle, extension mirrors are normally essential. Many types have been marketed in the last 30 years and frankly the ones that clip to door-mounted mirrors are usually better than old-style 'wing mirrors'. However, some extension products don't fit snugly and paintwork on a tow car's mirror housing can get scratched by road dirt trapped under the clamping straps. So the application of protective tape may be worth considering. Similarly, PVC electrical insulation tape is often useful for remedying a vibrating or ill-fitting unit.

Many people opt for convex rather than flat glass in an extension mirror because it provides a wide-angle image. Unfortunately its greater capture of rearward vision is spoilt by the fact that any following vehicles are actually much closer than the reflected image suggests. For that reason, it is often recommended that an offside extension mirror is better fitted with flat glass instead.

Once both external mirrors are mounted on your towing vehicle, carry out some checks to confirm their adjustment. A bit later, after you've left home, it's often necessary to pull into a lay-by to make further 'fine adjustments'. This is also a good opportunity to double-check that the electrical coupling cable between your car and caravan hasn't started to sag more than you anticipated.

External mirrors

- People who tow with a wide, commercial vehicle might not need extension mirrors added to the towing vehicle. But that's only a minority of caravanners.
- A driver is required to have a good view down both sides of a caravan together with a sideways vision extending to 4m (157.5in) at a distance of 20m (787.5in) rearwards of the caravan. For most vehicles, this requirement clearly necessitates the addition of extension mirrors.
- When your caravan has been unhitched, extension mirrors must be detached before you drive on the road.
- The extension mirrors fitted to old towing vehicles should not project more than 200mm (8in) beyond the widest part of your caravan. On more recent vehicles the maximum permitted projection is 250mm (10in).
- Extension mirrors now being sold have to be 'E-marked'; if you are using an older, unmarked product make sure that it is fitted with safety glass.

COUPLING-UP

Preliminary manoeuvres before coupling-up

Your car now has mirrors, the 'van is loaded and its noseweight is satisfactory. It's time to couple them together.

Reversing a car up to a caravan coupling head is undoubtedly easier if you've got a helper. Although a garden cane in soft ground can act as a useful marker when you're on your own, you'll still need to hop in and out of the car to check finer details. So what makes a good assistant?

Organising clear signals and agreeing on key words is important. For instance, the word 'good' is too vague. To a reversing driver it might mean, 'good … keep coming slowly' or 'good … you've got there'. Imprecise verbal communication might lead to a dent in the back of your car or a pointless dispute with your partner.

I wouldn't dream of giving adult readers a prescriptive list of commands. Develop your own but make sure they're not ambiguous – especially if you use different assistants to help you. For instance, it's not unusual to find that well-meaning neighbours on a caravan site employ a completely different sign language.

However, there are some common practices. For instance, many assistants start by raising a hand vertically above the caravan's coupling head. This conveys a visual clue to the driver concerning the alignment of the coupling components.

Then, as the car reverses, agreed hand-signals will reveal progress, including a measure of the closing distance and deviations from the intended course. Note that a caravan's coupling head should be slightly higher than the top of the towball. If that's not the case, wind down the jockey wheel to lift the coupling head.

In the final stages of reversing a tow car, some instructors discourage an assistant from standing directly between a caravan and a reversing car. It's certainly true that when grass is damp, a wet shoe might slip off a clutch pedal. An alternative approach is shown in the accompanying photograph.

Some caravanners like to reverse the car until the

Running out of jockey wheel elevation

Sometimes the threaded spindle inside your jockey wheel tube reaches the end of its travel. That's annoying if you still need to raise the coupling head even further to clear an approaching towball. Here's the remedy:

1 Temporarily lower the front corner steadies to support the 'van.

2 Wind up the jockey wheel with its handle so that the wheel pulls well away from the ground.

3 Unclamp the jockey wheel and lower it further in its clamp assembly than it was before. Make sure the wheel now touches the ground.

4 Tighten the clamp firmly once more.

5 Prepare to elevate the caravan using the jockey wheel handle. It will now have a lot more threads available on its spindle

6 Since the front corner steadies have now completed their brief supportive function, raise them up once again.

In the final stages of coupling preparation, experts recommend you give the driver progressional guidance from a side position.

coupling head is directly over the towball. Others are content if the coupling head is slightly to one side, because the flexibility of tyres allows minor alignments using a judicious nudge of a leg against a caravan's draw bar. On a light caravan, that can work without releasing a caravan's brake or removing the chocks; however, it's not so easy with a twin-axle 'van.

Step-by-step coupling procedure

Now let's reinforce the recommendations above with a visual step-by-step coupling operation. The sequence presumes that your caravan is loaded up in your preferred way, the noseweight has been confirmed, and the gas has been turned off at the cylinders.

Using the hand lever, fully apply your caravan's brake.

Use chocks on its wheels, especially if the ground is sloping.

Lower the jockey wheel tube; clamp it when the wheel touches the ground.

Lift all corner steadies; retrieve their pads; raise hitch with jockey wheel.

Working with your prearranged signals, slowly reverse the tow car.

Be precise in the final stages so that the coupling head causes no damage.

Apply the handbrake on your car; release the brake on the caravan, recognising that the wheels have been chocked.

If fitted, lift the stabiliser lever; check alignment with the towball.

Lower on jockey wheel with one hand as you also lift the coupling lever.

Above: When the coupling head embraces the ball, this indicator shows green.

Right: If there's a coupling head stabiliser, push this down to add ball friction.

Right: With the car now supporting the coupling, fully raise the jockey wheel.

Below: Check that the breakaway cable feeds straight through the guide eyelet.

Right: On this ball the cable's passed round its neck and clipped back on itself.

Below: The two plugs are connected to the car's 12N and 12S sockets.

Right: Retrieve chocks and carry out a rear road-light check before leaving.

- It's always very important to check that a caravan's coupling head (sometimes called the coupling hitch) has clasped itself fully around the ball and isn't merely resting on the top. If your caravan doesn't have the red/green safety button shown in the accompanying sequence, a simple way to confirm a successful union is to raise the locked-on coupling head a small amount using the jockey wheel. If the coupling-up has been correctly achieved you'll see the rear of the towing vehicle starting to rise on its springs.

- Once a caravan has been coupled correctly, completely raise the jockey wheel by turning its handle. Then release its clamp to pull the jockey wheel tube to its high-level towing position. Re-clamp the raised jockey wheel tube, ensuring that it's tight. Alternatively, some owners like to achieve better ground clearance by removing the entire jockey wheel assembly. This is then stowed in the back of the tow car. There are 'fors' and 'againsts' in both strategies and on some caravans a jockey wheel isn't readily detached.

- Always remember to turn off your gas supply at the cylinder(s) before driving an outfit away from its pitch. (To ensure the fridge keeps its contents cool when you're towing, switch its control to the 12V operating mode.)

Breakaway cables

One of the most frequently misunderstood components is the 'breakaway cable'. Many owners connect these up incorrectly and there have been instances where this error has caused a caravan's brakes to fully engage and then burn out amidst billowing smoke. But why is this cable important?

Sacrificial operation

If, for some reason, a caravan becomes detached from a towball, a correctly fitted breakaway cable will tighten, apply the caravan's brakes, and then

When a breakaway cable was too tight for the job, this caravan's brakes were totally ruined.

This coupling eyelet is too far to one side of the towball.

promptly snap on account of the load. This provision is intended to leave the 'van unattached, albeit with its brakes safely engaged. It is believed that parting company like this is better than having an unhitched caravan being dragged behind a tow car on the end of a sturdy safety chain. To achieve this preferred disconnection, a sacrificial clip or crimped fitting on a breakaway cable is intentionally designed to snap as soon as it has fully engaged the caravan's brakes.

Operational success

The effective operation of a breakaway cable is dependent on a number of factors. To begin with, it needs to follow a straight line from its fixed attachment point at the lowest point of a caravan's handbrake lever right through to its clipping point on the tow car. Within this path, it should be fed through a collar on the caravan itself as shown in the earlier coupling-up sequence, and not tidily bunched-up with the electrical cables. Moreover, if coupled to a tow car eyelet that's situated further than 100mm (4in) from the centre point of a towball, it's unlikely to engage a handbrake as needed. Being able to pull in a straight line is really important.

Burnt-out brakes

If a breakaway cable is inappropriately short, or if it has been wrongly wrapped twice around a towball stem, it will prematurely pull on a caravan's brakes. Similarly, if you are negotiating a very sharp corner this manoeuvre can also tighten an over-short cable and pull on the brakes. Unwanted brake activation also occurs on some off-road vehicles whose clipping point is too far forward of the towball itself. This equally leaves too little slack in the cable.

Each of these situations applies a caravan's brakes far too often, and that's when they start getting warm. However, the real problem occurs on caravan handbrakes that are fitted with a gas-strut spring. These well-intentioned products help owners to *fully* engage a brake without exerting a lot of

A breakaway cable of the correct length should never be wrapped twice round the stem of a towball.

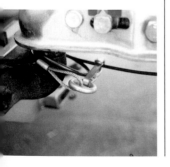

Just a small tug on this handbrake that has gas-strut assistance will fully engage a caravan's brakes.

151

muscular effort. In other words, the slightest tug on a brake lever that's supported by a gas-strut assister causes the brake to fly on to its limit. That reaction is also triggered *if a breakaway cable goes taut prematurely*.

With most tow cars, you'd immediately notice that your fully braked 'van is very much harder to pull – so you'd stop to see what's wrong. However, some 4x4 vehicles are so powerful that their drivers haven't detected any problems and have kept on driving until they've seen smoke. A surprising number of brake systems have thus been totally ruined and that's one reason why breakaway cables must be coupled correctly. Careful coupling's particularly important on 'vans with gas-strut assisted handbrake levers.

Clips and clipping
Although recent tow brackets have an eyelet to accommodate a breakaway clip, many offer nothing at all. Some owners buy a bolt-on 'pigtail' from an accessory shop which then affords a means of attachment. Others wind the cable once round the neck of the towball. This isn't the preferred method of attachment, because in an emergency breakaway situation the cable might flip over the top of the towball. It then couldn't pull on the brake. On the other hand, if there aren't any eyelets, this is sometimes the only way to fasten a cable.

As regards the clips themselves, the most common type which has been used for many years is *not* designed to attach directly to an eyelet. If you do this, a clip can chatter around during towing, settle in an upright position and then stand the risk of unacceptable distortion when it's needed to apply an unhitched caravan's brake. To ensure that the cable *does* function correctly, this type of clip should be passed right through the eyelet then clipped to its own cable to form a noose.

That's fine, but you also find that many of the eyelets are too small for the clip to pass through. In

The new type of clip on the left can be directly clipped to an eyelet, but the older version shown on the right can't.

This bolt-on plate offering an attachment point for a breakaway cable is too small for a clip to pass through.

consequence a new type of spring clip has recently been introduced that costs only a few pounds to have fitted instead. Based on the mechanism used in rock-climbing safety couplings, this revised product *can* be clipped directly to an eyelet. In fact, all caravans really ought to have one installed.

Plug connection

If your caravan is fitted with 12N and 12S plugs, these will need to be eased into their respective sockets, noting that a small notch in the plug in its 'six o'clock' position, engages with a lug in the socket. That ensures the plug is correctly orientated and inserted the right way up. There's a similar lug in the latest 13-pin plugs, but the moulding also incorporates a twisting collar that helps to achieve a locking effect.

Make sure there's enough 'cable slack' for the

ⓘ Technical Tip

Breakaway cable replacements

It's extremely important that the brake assembly on a caravan is fitted with a breakaway cable of the correct length. Caravans built on an AL-KO Kober chassis use a cable with a *red* sleeve: BPW chassis should have cable with a *blue* sleeve.

This red-sleeved cable is designed to fit AL-KO Kober brakes; note that this one is fitted with an old-style clip.

This new-style clip is fitted on a blue-sleeved cable whose length is made to suit a BPW braking system.

Their respective lengths are not the same. Other chassis are often fitted with thin steel cable that lacks a coloured sleeve, and very old caravans were fitted with a small chain. Any replacement must be of the appropriate length.

Caravan road-lamp failure

1 If a lamp fails to light on your caravan, give the towbar plug a gentle shake in its socket. This sometimes improves a connection and signifies that some of its pins are probably dirty.

2 In rear light clusters, the holders securing the bulbs are sometimes starting to rust; an inoperative bulb may start to work when these sockets are given a clean.

3 There may be a faulty bulb – and you are always wise to keep spares in your caravan.

4 If there's a detached wire somewhere in the system, you may need to call a mobile towbar fitter.

5 Further advice is contained in *The Caravan Manual*, published by Haynes; this book is specifically concerned with caravan repairs.

caravan to articulate at sharp angles without trying to wrench the plugs from their sockets. At the same time, make sure there's not so much slack that the cable drags on the road. Some owners tidy up slack cable on the caravan drawbar using an elasticated strap. That's fine, but don't include the breakaway cable.

With the plugs in place, now carry out a road-light test to confirm the connections are sound. This doesn't take long although it helps if you've got assistance from a partner. My preference is to follow a particular sequence and I always operate the lights as follows: right flasher, left flasher, brake lights, side and number plate lights, and fog lamp where fitted. The checker at the rear has to call out these words, to confirm the lights are working correctly. Incidentally, on recent caravans there's often a reversing light for checking as well.

OTHER ISSUES

Finally, you may have a stabiliser to fit, or need to check the self-test results of an AL-KO ATC Trailer Control system. Stabilising products were discussed in Chapter Five.

Other routine tasks include checking that everything's secure inside the caravan, including items like roof vents, windows, cupboards, doors and so on. These procedures are also discussed in Chapter Nine, where Site Arrival and Site Departure checklists are provided. Have a look at these, because they're equally applicable when you're about to leave home.

CHOOSING AND USING A SITE

Selecting a site, choosing a pitch and adopting a leisurely routine are some of the pleasures of caravanning. Here's advice on how to select the kind of site you like best and what to do when you get there. Sometimes the pitches are grass-covered, some are hard-surfaced, some are sloping and some have trees to avoid. Don't worry! The hints and tips here will help you find places that provide what you need.

155

This site round a lake at Horsley in Surrey is a Camping and Caravanning Club gem.

Over 30 lakes and pools surround The Camping and Caravanning Park site at Kingsbury Water Park in the West Midlands.

Where can you go? And what must be done on arrival? These key questions are addressed in this chapter, so we'll take them in order and start with a warning. Newcomers to caravanning are initially confused by the diverse array of places to stay. Here are several examples:

Club sites

This category comprises venues that are owned and managed by (a) The Camping and Caravanning Club and (b) The Caravan Club. These are the two large clubs that look after the interests of Britain's caravanners. Many of their 300+ sites are purpose-built and are noted for their high standard of facilities. Only 36 or so sites require visitors to use their caravan's own toilet; the majority provide first-class heated toilet/shower/washrooms, many of which have cubicle washbasins and provide appliances like hairdryers. The clubs' sites are kept notably clean and are run by experienced staff.

The Caravan Club also has some 'Management Agreement Sites', most of which are owned and maintained by Local Authorities or racecourse companies. The Club appoints wardens and

The New Forest Caravan Club Centenary Site was built from scratch on an old Second World War airfield.

undertakes the day-to-day running of these facilities. Not surprisingly, racecourse sites are only used for caravanning *between* meetings, and although they might not have the same level of provision as Club-owned sites they are fascinating places to visit.

Similar co-operative ventures have been organised by The Camping and Caravanning Club. For instance, the establishment of 'Forest Holidays' involves a partnership between The Camping and Caravanning Club and the Forestry Commission.

Some of the sites run by both clubs are exclusively for members whereas others welcome non-members, albeit with a surcharge. You can often join the club on arrival as well.

Holiday parks

Owners of caravanning facilities sometimes give their venues the title of 'park' rather than 'site'; places which adopt this practice often have a distinctly 'holiday' focus. For example, the provision of facilities at a 'holiday park' is usually aimed at families and you often find attractions like children's amusements, a swimming complex, climbing frames, club houses, restaurants, discos and on-site supermarkets.

The old converted railway station at Presthope near Much Wenlock, Shropshire, is one of the few sites that doesn't have a washroom block.

Many holiday parks are equipped with several swimming pools to suit the needs of their visitors.

Sites in the UK are often equipped with climbing apparatus, but some sites abroad have climbing walls too.

One large holiday park in North-East England is especially diverse in the range of activities on offer; it even includes a fishing lake, an on-site theatre, a betting shop and donkey rides.

Naturist sites

Whilst it is presumed that most naturist visitors will decide to leave their clothing in their caravan, some of these sites accept clothed caravanners too. For obvious reasons, naturist sites are usually found in warm areas and there are a number of well-known examples in parts of mainland Europe. For instance, 24 high-quality naturist sites are listed in the current Alan Rogers Sites Guide for France. Moreover, in Croatia a very large proportion of caravanning sites include naturist facilities.

In addition to drawing a nature-loving clientele, these types of site often attract clients who are especially sensitive to environmental issues. As a result, the venues are amongst the tidiest and cleanest you'll find in your travels. Naturism might not be everyone's cup of tea, but caravanners who have used these sites often report that they are notably smart.

Average-size commercial sites

Commercial sites vary in the facilities they offer in accordance with their owners' objectives. Fundamental provisions normally include a

Riverside Camp Site in Snowdonia is a typical mid-sized commercial venue with a restaurant for clients and mountains nearby.

Banned! A growing number of sites are exclusively for adults, and children are not accepted.

washroom, showers, toilet block, fresh water taps and toilet emptying points. Most sites also offer several pitches served by a 230V hook-up point, although in many parts of Europe, this extra feature incurs an additional charge. For a lot of caravanners that's all they need, whereas others look for commercial sites that offer facilities such as a children's playground, laundry facilities, a small shop, a dog exercise area, Internet coupling facilities and so on. Overnight charges will reflect what's on offer.

Restricted sites

Recently there has been an steady increase in the number of 'Adults Only' sites – a title that might imply they run sleazy nightclubs. In fact, they are usually quiet, football-free places, and one such restricted site accepts no one under 30 years of age. Another UK Adults Only site offers a curious concession: children are accepted at certain times, but the management requires them to reside in a special compound – a strategy which doesn't sound welcoming for future generations of caravanners. In fact quite a number of elderly visitors enjoy taking their young grandchildren on occasional caravanning treats and have been deeply hurt when refused entry to this type of site.

This matter is very contentious and letters published in caravanning magazines reveal two extreme viewpoints. Some people are acutely opposed to any form of prejudice which affects caravanners' freedom: others are strongly in favour of sites which impose some form of segregation or which exercise exclusion clauses in one form or another. 'No large, all-male groups' is one such restriction at a well-known Lake District site; bad experiences by the management have led to this ruling.

In addition to these discretionary measures, there are also sites where dogs are disallowed, especially on farm sites during lambing seasons. In contrast, other sites welcome dogs and have special 'dog walk' routes that provide for an animal's 'exercise' rituals.

A growing number of sites now have special dog walks where owners can exercise their pets.

Sites like this one in the New Forest run by The Camping and Caravanning Club in conjunction with The Forestry Commission attract many country-loving caravanners.

Some site owners also disallow travelling trades people; others refuse to accept caravans that are towed by commercial vans or lorries. In view of these restrictions, it's important to recognise that not all sites are open to everyone.

Forestry Enterprise sites
(Formerly known as Forestry Commission sites)
These wooded locations can be found all around the UK; some have fairly extensive facilities whereas others are more limited. If you like woodland and wildlife, these are delightful places. They're usually peaceful, too, and don't suit caravanners who want an on-site restaurant, a bar or bingo.

Forest Holidays
In 2007 a new partnership was formed between The Forestry Commission and The Camping and Caravanning Club. Forest Holidays are now organised at some 20 sites in England, Scotland and Wales, a few of which have cabin accommodation for visitors who don't own a caravan. Further information is obtainable from the Club, on the Internet at www.forestholidays.co.uk or by telephoning 0845 130 8224.

You'll often see these signs when driving around rural areas.

Small informal sites
Some caravanners seek out simple sites that offer no formally marked pitches, where grass in the field may rise above the ankles and access roads are muddy tracks. Facilities are abundantly simple and overnight fees are a fraction of those charged at well-equipped sites. Be prepared to accept that other visitors may only be butterflies, birds and grasshoppers.

Certificated Sites and Certificated Locations
Some small venues are run by owners who are permitted to accept no more than five caravans or motorhomes at any one time. In addition there's a

maximum 'stay limit' of 28 successive days, and these five-unit sites are only available for members of the national club that has issued the appropriate certificate. The Camping and Caravanning Club calls the venues in their listing 'Certificated Sites' (CS), whereas The Caravan Club listing refers to their recognised venues as 'Certificated Locations' (CL).

Typically a CS or CL is located in a rural area, and since a large number provide no more than a tap and a toilet-emptying point your caravan needs to be well-equipped. The modest fee is hugely different from the overnight charges at well-equipped sites and The Camping and Caravanning Club and The Caravan Club record several thousand examples in their Members' Site Guide Books. Although some caravanners don't want the peaceful solitude offered at these rural hideaways, some caravanners joining the Clubs have clearly stated that one of the main reasons for seeking membership was to gain access to the national chains of Certificated Sites and Locations.

Year-round sites

This descriptive term usually implies there'll be some hard-standing areas – a provision that assumes special importance when winter weather renders grassy pitches unusable. Although not normally open

161

The legal position relating to Five-Van caravan/ motorhome sites.

The Camping and Caravanning Club explains the position as follows:

'Under the Town and Country Planning General Development Order 1977, sites of no more than five caravans can be granted a certificate of exemption which exempts them from the provisions of the Public Health Act 1936 and the Caravan Sites and Control of Development Act 1960.' (Press Release, 9 August 2005.)

Arising from this exemption, both The Camping and Caravanning Club and The Caravan Club are empowered to issue landowners and occupiers a Certificate which permits the operation of a caravanning site for recreational use without the need for planning permission. The site must not accommodate more than five 'units' at any one time, and a 'unit' is either a touring caravan, a motor caravan or a tent. The facility is only available to the respective club members for up to 28 consecutive days. These certificated venues may be open all year round if the owner wishes.

Specially drained and gravel-topped pitches are a feature of sites that are open in winter.

Above: At some year-round sites, The Camping and Caravanning Club has developed hard pitches that use a robust plastic mesh.

Above right: Well-placed for the National Exhibition Centre, Chapel Lane at Wythall is a Caravan Club site that's open all year; it accepts non-members.

for a full 365 days, a few site owners erect a large, heated marquee and organise Christmas Caravanning Packages complete with meals and seasonal cheer. However, these celebratory occasions are popular and have to be booked in advance.

CHOOSING SITES

Recognising that there are many different types of site, you need to make your choice carefully when consulting guidebooks. Using the benefits of modern technology, the publishers of some guidebooks work with a large computer data base of addresses. This means that an impressive list can be assembled, but experience shows that information sometimes gets out-of-date quickly.

There are also special marketing groups whose site owner-members pay for inclusion in a free promotional booklet. In this country, the Best of British chain is an example and the caravan sites of member-owners have to fulfil certain criteria before acceptance into the scheme. Typically these are all high-quality 'five star' holiday parks.

In France, Les Castels (formerly called Camping

Highfield Farm Touring Park near Cambridge is one of the prestigious, five-star sites in The Best of British chain.

& Castel Group) is a similar marketing initiative for high-quality sites that have a chateau or historic building within the grounds. There's also the French Sites de Paysage chain, which offers well-equipped sites in country settings. In most cases, site guide booklets published by these marketing groups are distributed free of charge at major indoor caravan exhibitions.

Then there are independent guides which only contain sites that have been inspected by specialist assessors. The *Alan Rogers' Site Guides*, for example, are published by a committed team of caravanning site assessors who travel all around Europe. The close scrutiny of each listed site takes a considerable time to complete and the owner is visited unannounced and at least every two years. In fact if standards slip a venue is immediately taken out of these annually published guidebooks.

On a different note, there's also an increasing number of site-searching facilities on the Internet. Caravanning clubs, magazines and other organisations also hold databases with site information.

In addition there are national competitions

As a member of Les Castels chain, Le Petit Trianon de Saint Ustre, five miles from Chatellerault, occupies the grounds of a French Chateau.

Below left: The Pencelli Castle site is a national award-winning location near Brecon.

The awards displayed at the Reception of Pencelli Castle and Camping Site near Brecon speak for themselves.

Below: Tick and star schemes often give a clue about the quality of a site and its facilities.

organised to find the best sites of the year in England, Scotland and Wales.

There are various categories of site in these award schemes and the competitions are contested eagerly by owners. Not surprisingly, winning sites are always very impressive and well worth visiting. On a similar note, both of the caravan clubs conduct a contest to find the best Certificated Location/Certificated Site of the year.

Lastly, there are 'tick' and 'star' schemes run by tourist boards and the motoring organisations which add further measures of quality.

When it comes to booking a site, procedures vary from place to place. Normally the process starts with a telephone call and sometimes a deposit might later be required. However, like other commercial ventures today, caravan sites can often be booked on the Internet and this booking procedure is becoming increasingly popular.

ARRIVAL PROTOCOL

Prior to your arrival, it's important to establish when the site reception office is open, especially if you

Like a growing number of sites, Ferry Meadows near Peterborough has a robust security system.

expect to arrive late in the evening. For security, more and more large sites are now protected by a barrier, and you need a code number or a swipe card to lift the bar.

If you can arrive on time, there may be an opportunity to make your own choice of a pitch. Whether a view over the sea is more important than a pitch close to a toilet block or the clubhouse is a matter for you to decide. However, try to avoid pitches under trees that shed sap; as Chapter Seven on awnings points out, this can cause you a lot of work later. That said, on some sites a member of the reception staff will lead you to a recommended pitch – often with the help of a bike.

If you decide to use a mains hook-up, ask how many amps the coupling supplies. The term amps is a measure of quantity and the amount you can draw at any one time varies from site to site. If you use too many appliances at once, the site's trip switch will automatically terminate your supply. So the matter of amps is important, and guidance in Chapter Twelve explains which electrical appliances you'll be able to use.

As regards late arrival procedures, some sites have a small compound near the entrance where you can stay overnight, pending the reopening of reception next morning. Most caravanners are unsympathetic with anyone who sets up on a pitch in the middle of the night. Even the most experienced owner is unable to position a caravan without making a noise.

For that reason, enquire before arrival when the gates are closed or when barriers come down for the night. Ask when reception closes too. If you arrive after the office is shut – and as long as there's no access barrier – a warden sometimes puts your name and allotted pitch number on a 'Late Arrivals' noticeboard. This system enables you to proceed to the allocated pitch, thereby leaving the completion of forms and payment of fees until the reception office is open next morning.

At this Camping and Caravanning Club Site, the manager often uses his bike to lead visitors to an allocated pitch.

To prevent noise in the late evening, many sites have a 'Late Arrivals Area'.

Many of the club sites are equipped with vegetable preparation and washing-up sinks with hot and cold water.

If you've ever seen the damage that can be done by a caravan fire, you'll appreciate the wisdom of checking the location of a site's fire points.

FINDING THE FACILITIES

On arrival, nature often dictates that you'll seek out the toilet block first. Washrooms and showers will be checked, too, along with fresh water taps, waste disposal points, chemical toilet emptying points, ironing rooms, washing/drying rooms, and so on. Some sites even have dedicated washing-up sinks and vegetable preparation areas.

It is also wise to establish where the fire points are situated. A few club caravanners place a fire bucket alongside their caravan, although it's a practice seldom pursued now. More and more caravans are equipped with a fire extinguisher and a safety fire blanket.

If there's a swimming facility, check to see what safety precautions are in place. You won't always find a lifeguard on duty and some pools don't even advise which is the deep end. Several locations abroad are especially lax in these matters.

And the rest depends on you. Parents may want to find the children's playground whereas owners of dogs might head for a dog walk.

There are many magnificent swimming pools on summer sites abroad, but safety measures vary in standard.

PITCH SPACING

With good sense and with safety in mind, the requirement on club pitches is that each resident's caravan should be sited no closer than a specified distance from a neighbour. Although this is mainly a precautionary fire measure, the stipulation also makes sense where noise is concerned. To give an example of a typical ruling, The Caravan Club makes the following statement:

'Where numbered pitch markers are provided on site, please check with the Site Warden as to the position of the outfit in relation to the marker peg. Normally and at the discretion of the Warden outfits may be positioned on the pitch in any way, provided that there is not less than 6 metres (20 feet) spacing between facing walls of adjacent caravans, motor caravans or trailer tents and that there shall be left a minimum clear space of 3 metres (10 feet) between adjoining outfits in any direction, in order to restrict the spread of fire.' The Caravan Club, Club Site Rules, 7 The Pitch (a), Sites Directory & Handbook 2009/2010.

No one likes too many rules and regulations, but the prescription above makes good sense. The wisdom of this becomes even more apparent when you see some commercial sites on a public holiday weekend where the tight packing of caravans is neither safe nor satisfactory.

SETTING-UP PROCEDURE

When arriving at your pitch, the following tasks need to be carried out:
☐ Unless there are site regulations prescribing outfit orientation, decide where you want to position the 'van, the car and perhaps an awning.

At a National Holiday weekend, the units here were sited far too closely together.

Above: Purpose-made spirit levels are sold at caravan accessory shops.

Above right: Caravanners who use a jerrycan for collecting water often mark the container with tape to act as a levelling device.

Wood blocks or purpose-made ramps allow you to level up from side-to-side.

Blocks are needed under corner steadies, especially when the ground is soft.

☐ Either reverse your caravan or drive it forward on to the pitch.

☐ In readiness for lateral checking, place a small spirit level or a part-filled translucent plastic water container on the floor.

☐ Try not to step inside since this puts considerable strain on the unsupported chassis members and may upset the reading.

☐ A side-to-side slope needs a remedy now. A few caravanners carry a special wheel-jacking accessory, but driving on to blocks is often easier. Angled plastic blocks are available from accessory shops. Leave the level-checker in place for later.

☐ Apply the handbrake on your caravan, and if the pitch is sloping chock the wheels. Chocks are important accessories to carry in a 'van.

☐ Unclip the breakaway cable, disconnect the 12V plug(s) from the tow car, lower the jockey wheel to the ground, tighten the clamp on the jockey wheel. Incidentally, if the ground's soft, put a small board under the jockey wheel.

☐ Lift the coupling head lever and hold it in the ball-release position while you operate the jockey-wheel handle. When the rising coupling head clears the towball, it's time to drive the car away.

☐ If it's greasy, fit the towball cover before you get marks all over your trousers. Also remember to remove the extension mirrors before driving your car solo on public roads.

☐ Again refer to the spirit level or part-filled water container to check the caravan's front-to-back line of inclination. Lifting or lowering the jockey wheel by winding its handle soon gets this right.

☐ Once you've got your caravan level, lower the corner steadies. If they're not fitted with feet pads, use small blocks underneath each 'leg' to prevent it sinking into the ground. Some owners speed this process up by using a purpose-made socket that fits into a cordless drill.

On steeply sloping pitches, you may need a pile of blocks under the corner steadies.

☐ Position the step by the door and go inside. On the 12V fused distribution control panel, set the selection switch to 'caravan' as described in Chapter Thirteen.

☐ If you intend to use a mains hook-up, follow the strict coupling procedures given in Chapter Twelve and leave spare cable loosely unravelled underneath the caravan.

☐ Turn on the supply gas cylinder and then get the refrigerator into operation as discussed in Chapter Eleven. If coupled to the mains, you have a choice whether to run the fridge on gas or 230V.

☐ Set up the waste water container and couple the drain hoses as discussed in Chapter Ten.

☐ Top-up the fresh water container and couple to the caravan. Connecting-up advice is given on page 177 and guidance on pumps is also included in Chapter 10.

☐ If the toilet hasn't been prepared for use, add one litre of water to the waste tank followed by a chemical additive. Top up the flushing water and consider using a rinse-clean additive to keep the bowl shiny and clean.

☐ If you're a TV enthusiast who uses a directional

Couplings are available for fitting into a rechargeable electric drill so that corner steadies can be operated quickly.

Notes

1 When setting up on a steep slope, the jockey wheel sometimes reaches the end of its travel before a level position is attained. The procedure for overcoming this situation is given on page 145.

2 Where do you place a spirit level to check the 'van is level? This leads to opinionated debate among caravanners and here are some options to consider:

• On the A-frame section of the chassis not far behind the coupling head.

• On the lower edge of the forward-facing central window.

• On the bottom of a sink to ensure waste water runs down the outlet and doesn't collect at one edge.

• As far as a fridge is concerned, the shelf in its freezer section used to be seen as the point of reference, but now there are models without a freezer shelf.

• Probably the best place of reference for the caravan as a whole is on the floor directly above its axle. This presumes the floor hasn't sustained damage and that a fitted carpet or floor covering material hasn't puckered. On a twin-axle caravan you can take readings over both axles and then make a decision.

Most caravanners fit a lightweight coupling lock or wheel clamp when stopping at a site.

Below: Most caravan sites have safe places for children to cycle; repeated cycling around toilet blocks can be a nuisance to users.

Below right: Children often like playing with a hose and squirting water, but waste water disposal points are not appropriate places to play.

aerial, you'll need to get this pointing in the right direction to achieve the best possible signal.

☐ Most caravanners fit a portable security device while staying at a site; thefts have become increasingly prevalent in recent years.

SITE ETIQUETTE

No one likes sites with an abundance of 'Don't Do This…' signs. At the same time, you'll come across instances where thoughtless behaviour spoils the pleasures of other caravanners. A common complaint is the fact that young children have a persistent habit of cycling around toilet blocks, which could obviously lead to an accident. But are youngsters to blame, or should parents be more aware of their unattended children elsewhere on the site?

On that note, here are some problems to ponder:

Note: *Thanks to the parents who gave permission for their children to appear in these 'staged' photographs cycling, kicking stones and playing with water.*

Many caravanning sites permit visitors to bring a dog, but as shown here, it should always be kept on a lead or a tether.

It's easy to trip on badly laid cables when it's dark. Neither these TV nor mains cables had been thoughtfully uncoiled, and a rabbit agrees.

Stones on areas of grass can damage a mower, so playing with stones on a hard standing is something to be discouraged.

Safety barrier cards should be returned at the end of a stay. In spite of collection points like this, they still get taken home accidentally.

DEPARTURE PROCEDURES

Once you've prepared the car with its towing mirrors, prepare the caravan for departure. The list that follows looks at both indoor and outdoor jobs to attend to, but they are not presented in a particular order. For example, dealing with a mains supply appears in both lists.

Inside

Get into a routine here and consider creating a checklist. This might vary from model to model but is likely to include these reminders:

☐ Close roof light(s)
☐ Close windows
☐ Secure cupboards
☐ Clear the open shelves
☐ Secure the fridge door
☐ Select the 12V operation on the fridge's fascia controls
☐ Turn off the fridge's gas operation controls
☐ Turn the 12V panel switch to 'car' setting if your owner's handbook says this is necessary
☐ Turn off the mains isolating switch on your caravan's 230V consumer unit as described on page 227
☐ If it can't be loaded into your towcar, stow a packed awning over the caravan's axle.
☐ Secure a water container that has been part-filled with just enough water for picnic drinks and check 'setting off' on page 176
☐ Stow the emptied waste container, the step, levelling ramps and other items
☐ Make sure the toilet waste tank is emptied

Note: *Thetford's instructions have sometimes recommended that a flushing water tank is emptied, although most caravanners leave a little water in the system.*

Several different types of door catch are used on refrigerators. Be absolutely sure it has engaged correctly before towing a caravan.

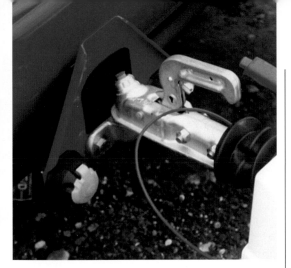

To protect the rear of the car when coupling a caravan, this towing bracket has an over-run bump plate.

Outside
TURN OFF THE GAS SUPPLY AT THE CYLINDER
- ☐ Disconnect the mains supply cable as described in Chapter Twelve
- ☐ Retrieve, coil and stow the mains hook-up cable
- ☐ Remove water containers and coupling hoses
- ☐ Retrieve any blocks of wood left under the corner steadies and wheel ramps

HITCHING UP

Refer back to the illustrated step-by-step sequence in Chapter Eight that goes through tasks involved in a hitching-up operation. Note, too, that when leaving an uneven pitch, a caravan sometimes lurches when releasing its brake. So chock the wheels where necessary. If it rolls forward a little, the coupling head can sometimes make unexpected contact with the back of the tow car; dents in the rear body panel of a caravanner's car are not unusual. Some owners reduce this risk by having an over-run bump plate fitted behind the towball.

LEAVING THE SITE

Road safety advisers sometimes assert that road accidents often occur in the first few moments of a journey. Without doubt, if the exit gate of a site takes you into a country lane that doesn't have road markings, extra vigilance is needed – especially in countries which don't drive on the left. A surprising number of sleepy British drivers leaving a foreign camping site have a momentary lapse of concentration and take up their position on the wrong side of the highway.

WATER AND SANITATION **SYSTEMS**

In the 1950s, fresh water was often brought to a caravan in a white enamel jug that stood alongside the sink. Piped systems became popular in the 1960s with either foot- or hand-operated pumps delivering water to the sink from a container left outside. Water heaters appeared in the 1970s and electrically-operated pumps arrived around the same time. Shower rooms were then added and toilets were built-in as well.

Anyone who takes up caravanning after holidays spent in tents is often surprised by the sophistication of the sanitation systems. The provision of hot and cold water, a shower and a cleverly designed 'cassette toilet' means that you are pretty well self-contained. In fact, if you pull into a lay-by during a journey you can step from your car into a well-equipped home.

This also means that you can stop at simple farm sites whose facilities are little more than a cold-water tap and a toilet emptying point. Self-contained independence undoubtedly has its advantages.

Some sites clearly mark the taps that are installed solely to provide your drinking water.

In spite of this, some caravanners still miss the simple arrangements of the past. Certainly, if you purchase an old 1970s 'van solely for summer touring and your intentions are to stop at well-equipped caravan sites, its lack of facilities is hardly a problem. Many modern sites have good showers, hairdryers, and designated washing-up sinks with hot and cold water.

Today, however, modern caravans are sold with every conceivable facility – whether you want them or not. It is probably true that most people purchasing new caravans expect to find shower rooms in the layout, even though many caravanners normally use sites' showers instead.

Notwithstanding anomalies like that, caravans have changed radically in the last few years. In view of the many improvements, this chapter adopts a broad overview of water and sanitation systems for these reasons:

☐ Many people start caravanning by purchasing an older caravan. Accordingly the operation of earlier components is explained.
☐ Others purchase new caravans, so many of the latest systems are discussed as well.

Within this review of products, the text and illustrations show how things are put into operation. However, the information doesn't include repair guidance, nor does this chapter provide ideas for updating elderly installations. Practical projects of this nature are included in a companion book, *The Caravan Manual*, also published by Haynes.

SETTING OFF

You'll probably want to travel with a small amount of water on board for roadside picnics. In addition, a supply of water may prove useful if the tow car's radiator or windscreen washers need topping-up. However, don't completely fill a caravan's fresh water container because water adds considerable weight to the outfit. As a guide, a gallon of water weighs around 10lb; a litre of water weighs 1kg.

Also be aware of a further problem: surging water in a part-filled container can affect stability and braking. To avoid this, some caravanners carry their 'picnic' water in plastic bottles that they store in the fridge. Whichever strategy is preferred, always make sure that a water-filled container is well secured. If a large water container like an Aquaroll gets thrown around inside, it is likely to create serious instability when you're towing.

Position the fresh water container near the caravan's inlet; if it has a submersible pump lower this into the container.

CONNECTING-UP ON ARRIVAL

Once your caravan has been levelled on its pitch, you'll need to set-up the fresh and waste water systems as follows:

☐ The full fresh water container should be positioned near your caravan's fresh water inlet.
☐ Remove the screw cap from the waste water container; store this somewhere safe, and put the container near the waste outlet.
☐ Connect the fresh water coupling hose to the caravan's inlet – this might be fitted with a submersible pump on one end – as explained later.
☐ Alternatively, some 'vans just need a short length of hose or plastic pipe because there's a separate pump fitted indoors.
☐ Couple the waste pipe from the caravan's outlet (or outlets) to the waste water container.
☐ Modern caravans have an electric pump so switch on the 12V system at the main control panel inside.
☐ Check that water is delivered to the sink and let the tap run for several seconds to clear any stale water that may have been left in the pipes.
☐ Put on the kettle for coffee or tea ... at least, that's what most people do.

If a caravan has a fixed inboard pump, coupling-up just needs a short length of hose or purpose-made plastic pipe.

Couple the waste pipe to your waste water container; on some caravans there are two outlets.

Some sites now provide fresh water coupling points to serve individual pitches.

The Whale Aqua Source includes a pressure reducer so you can connect mains tap water directly into your caravan's supply system.

Above right: This Truma Waterline is coupled-up to a caravan and then connected to a tap reserved for the pitch.

This caravanner used some waste pipe and blocks to create a gradient – thereby creating his own draining facility.

This site in France even offers permanent outlet points for pitch occupiers using direct drainage hose.

ⓘ Technical Tip

Direct coupling

There are a few sites in Britain where you can connect up directly because every pitch is equipped with its own tap. However, to enjoy this facility you need a special coupling hose that incorporates a pressure-reducing valve to protect the joints in your caravan's pipework. Direct coupling kits include:

1 The Truma Waterline, designed to couple with Truma Ultraflow inlets.
2 The Whale Aqua Source, which couples to the Whale Water-master socket or (with an adaptor) to a Carver Compact inlet.

Some pitches also have a pitch-specific waste water disposal point too. To take advantage of this you merely need to purchase a length of waste water hose, which will be fitted to your caravan's outlet nozzle.

WATER CONTAINERS

The connecting-up procedures described above presume that you've already purchased fresh and waste water containers. These are seldom supplied with a new or second-hand caravan, and anyway, many people like a clean start.

It's a matter of choice whether you purchase an inexpensive plastic jerrycan, a rolling water barrel like the Aquaroll, or a trolley-type water container such as the Wastemaster. As a point of interest, many caravanners in mainland Europe don't like fresh water containers being left outdoors, so facilities are built to store them inside. Some UK manufacturers, eg Avondale and Bailey, have noted this preference and a few models in their ranges have been built with an indoor tank compartment as well.

As regards waste water containers, buy one which is flat enough to stay close to the ground. That's because caravan waste water outlets are often fitted near the chassis and don't provide much scope for creating a downward gradient on the coupling pipe.

If you don't mind carrying a five-gallon jerrycan back from a tap, this is the least expensive fresh water container.

Several purpose-made water barrels are available but models in the Aquaroll range are especially popular.

Fiamma markets a wheeled container and some caravans have an indoor compartment where this can be coupled.

The shallow height of a Wastemaster container just permits a gradient on this caravan's waste pipes.

(i) Technical Tip

1 If you drape a waste water hose so that it rests on the bottom of its receiving container, as soon as the container starts to fill the discharge of water from sinks and washbasins will slow down significantly. You'll find that water runs much more quickly out of a caravan's pipes if the end of the connecting hose is positioned near the entry point to the waste container rather than on the bottom.

2 Ensure that a fresh water container's inlet is covered to keep out slugs, snails and other inquisitive creatures. If your connection hose arrangement doesn't include a plastic cap or shield, fabric shrouds are available from Gardner of Wakefield.

Winter caravanners often bring water containers indoors at night; some carry a back-up container too.

For short-term protection, it's useful to put a water container inside an insulated bag when it's cold.

This supply system fitted in a Bailey Senator uses an inboard tank with three-way options.

WINTER STRATEGIES

More owners are starting to use their caravans in cold weather, and when it's frosty it's wise to transfer the water containers indoors at night. Some intentionally carry back-up containers as well. There are also outdoor activity bag manufacturers that sell insulated fabric bags to prevent water containers freezing-up too easily.

INBOARD TANKS

A few caravans, including models from Avondale, Bailey, Bessacarr and Vanroyce, have been fitted with an inboard water tank. You shouldn't travel with this full, of course, because it would cause instability – and water takes up your valuable payload. So take a couple of plastic bottles of water for a roadside brew by all means, but make sure the tank's left empty until you arrive at a site.

The trouble with an inboard tank is the fact that if you occupy a pitch for several days, you would have to tow your caravan to a site tap now and again to replenish the tank. That's a nuisance, so many people carry a long hose or even take an additional plastic container and a funnel to top-up the tank.

To overcome this, Whale introduced a dual-function installation which embraced the best of both systems. By using two switching controls you could activate one of three options, namely:

1 Setting the controls so that an internally-fitted pump would draw water just from the inboard tank.
2 Setting the controls so that the pump would draw water solely from an external water container for immediate use in the 'van.
3 Setting the controls to divert water drawn from the external container to top-up the inboard tank.

Avondale fitted a system like this in late Landranger models. Bailey fitted the Whale system in some of the more recent Senator models.

FRESH WATER AND WASTE PIPES

When checking the water systems inside caravans, plumbing components differ in several ways. At one time, *all* caravans used to be fitted with plastic hose that was coupled using fittings such as Jubilee clips. The trouble with flexible hose is the fact that unreinforced plastic tubing can develop kinks over a period of time. This seriously restricts the flow of water, but in spite of that several well-known manufacturers continue installing fresh water supply systems using flexible hose and clips.

A disadvantage of plastic hose is the fact that kinks often form on sharp bends.

181

Better installations employ semi-rigid plastic pipe with push-fit couplings, which have been used domestically since the 1960s. But old habits die hard.

In the 1960s and '70s clear plastic hose continued being fitted in caravans, and since this allows the light to penetrate, algae and other deposits develop inside. This was one reason why opaque red and blue plastic pipes were later used for hot and cold supplies respectively.

If you purchase an older caravan, clear plastic pipes are certain to look dirty inside. It's not a reassuring sight, especially when you consider that this is the supply route taken by your drinking water. The subject of sterilising water systems is described in the following section and some caravanners also decide to purchase 'bottled water' for drinking purposes.

Then there's the waste water plumbing. Sadly, in many caravans this is the most primitive example of plumbing you're ever likely to find. Far too many manufacturers fit a convoluted plastic hose that features reinforcing ridges. These ridges might add strength, but on the inside they capture food remnants like rice, peas, meat and so on. Added to this is the fact that on some runs of waste pipe, a 'fall', or gradient, is scarcely discernible – which is one reason why caravan sinks empty so slowly. Sections of pipe might even travel uphill for short distances.

Look under the floor and you may find that a lack of support clips causes the waste pipe to hang like a Christmas garland. In consequence, food remnants and greasy washing-up water accumulate in the dangling loops.

This criticism might sound harsh but in many caravans the waste water system hardly exemplifies state-of-the-art plumbing. Oddly enough, it's very easy to replace convoluted hose with rigid PVCu pipe. This is fitted in our homes and is sold at builders' merchants. In fact, the upgrade work is

Ridges on convoluted waste water pipe, together with poor gradients, trap food and reduce flow rates.

Some practically-minded owners upgrade poorly performing waste water systems.

described in more detail in *The Caravan Manual*, published by Haynes.

It is also pleasing to report that some caravan manufacturers are starting to respond to my persistent criticisms. Recent models are sometimes being fitted with straight runs of 25mm (1in) PVCu waste pipe. This type of rigid pipe is readily obtainable because it is used domestically as overflow pipe on household toilet cisterns. Moreover, when Vanroyce caravans were being manufactured, these had wide-bore PVCu pipes and water traps fitted under the sink outlets too.

KEEPING THINGS CLEAN

☐ **Fresh water system** – At the start of every season (at the very least) flush this through thoroughly with plenty of water and then sterilise the pipes and your fresh water container using a product like Milton. This is the treatment used to sterilise babies' dummies, drinking bottles and so on.

Several sterilising products are sold for cleaning water supply system components in caravans.

Practical Tip

If you purchase an older caravan and have doubts about the cleanliness of the supply and waste pipes, it may be wise to have them replaced. In some instances the original system can be improved as well – some DIY projects can be found in Chapter Nine of *The Caravan Manual*, also published by Haynes.

□ **Waste water system** – A product called Wastemaster Superclean has recently been launched by F.L. Hitchman, manufacturer of the Aquaroll and Wastemaster. This is designed solely to clean waste water containers and tanks and must not be used on any of the fresh water components.

In addition, the waste system needs flushing out periodically and especially before a caravan is left in storage. One reason why a caravan interior smells unpleasant after a long winter break is the fact that odours from residual water trapped in the waste pipe creep up through the sink, basin and shower tray outlets.

183

Waste water containers can now be cleaned inside using purpose-made products like 'Superclean'.

FILTERS

Some caravans have filters fitted, but note that there are essentially three different types, these are:

1 **Grit filters** – one of these is needed if a caravan has a diaphragm pump as described later. A grit filter needs checking and cleaning periodically.
2 **Taste filters** – these can be easily fitted and are a great asset if you visit venues where tap water tastes ghastly. However, remember that a taste filter improves palatability but does not purify water.
3 **Purifying filters** – in this system, a filter achieves levels of purification and taste improvement that allow you to drink water coming from all kinds of uncertain sources. For instance, products like the Nature Pure Ultrafine from General Ecology are so effective they even enable narrowboat owners to drink the water drawn from canals.

Needless to say, taste and purifying filters need changing periodically. Ignore this and the filter might even start to collect waterborne germs.

Filters and purifiers

Right: Keeping the grit filter clean on a diaphragm pump is important.

Right: Some submersible pumps have a removable grit intercepting cap.

Below: Truma introduced this new taste filter product in 2007.

Right: These taste filter screw-in cartridges were introduced in the 1990s.

Above: Some cartridge taste filters are mounted in the supply hose itself.

Below: If a diaphragm pump is fitted, this submersible filter is sometimes used.

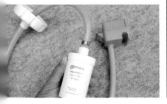

Right: If it's hard to remove a screw-in cartridge, this tool can be made to help.

Below: For water purification, the Nature Pure Ultrafine is a remarkable product.

PUMPS AND TAPS

The final part of this section looks at water pumps and taps. By intention it takes account of older, non-electric systems as well as the very latest components.

NON-ELECTRIC SYSTEM
Caravans built before the mid-1970s were often fitted with just a hand- or foot-operated pump. These were only built to deliver *cold* water: in those days, water heaters and hot water systems were seldom installed in touring caravans.

Advantages
☐ Simplicity: there's only one set of pipes for cold water.
☐ Pump: these are relatively inexpensive items and spares are still available for a surprising number of models – some of which have been around for 30 years or more.
☐ Battery: no need for a 12V battery supply, which is a requirement when an electric pump is installed.
☐ Switching: no need for a switching arrangement, which is essential when electric systems are fitted.

Disadvantages
☐ Improvements: it's not possible to take a shower while you are simultaneously using a foot- or hand-pump! Hot water heaters cannot be added – they're designed to run in conjunction with an electric pump.
☐ Frost damage: some types are quite difficult to drain down prior to the onset of winter weather and it's often necessary to disconnect a pipe coupling to empty residual water out of a caravan's internal hoses.

Operating procedures
To run a non-electric cold water system you merely connect a length of fresh water hose to the caravan's inlet and hang this in the water container. Once you've pumped water up through the internal pipes to the sink you should find that the water won't drain back into the water vessel when you stop operating the pump. A loss of water every time the pump ceases to operate would be a distinct nuisance.

This retention of water in the pipes is sometimes helped by the pump itself but it's principally achieved because there's a non-return valve in the

Technical Tip

If your caravan has a foot-operated pump, the outlet at the sink is merely a shaped length of metal tubing, typically finished in chrome. If you check component specialists' catalogues, this is called a faucet rather than a tap. In this country, the term tap normally refers to an outlet that has a closure system like a screw-top or a lift-up lever to control the flow of water.

A few caravans built in the 1980s combined an inboard electric pump with a foot-pump as well.

system. Normally this small component is fitted in the supply line close to the external coupling point.

Unfortunately, non-return valves sometimes fail, although a replacement isn't expensive. Incidentally, it's this component which causes water to remain in all your pipe runs after every caravan trip. Moreover, stale water held in the pipes during a winter lay-up isn't pleasant and it needs flushing through before your first trip away the following season.

This is why many owners will disconnect one of the low-level hose couplings situated 'upstream' of the non-return valve so as to drain off all the remnants of water. There ought to be a proper drain-down tap, but although these products are available few caravan manufacturers fit them. This provision ensures there's no residual water left to freeze in the pipes. In reality, flexible plastic hose can cope surprisingly well with the expansion caused when ice starts to form, but pump casings can crack, as I learnt when I started caravanning many years ago.

COMBINED MANUAL AND ELECTRIC SYSTEMS

In the early 1980s several caravan manufacturers installed water systems that used both a manual pump *and* an electric one. These worked as a 'twosome'.

To couple-up one of these hybrid systems you first have to connect a plastic feed hose from the water supply container to the caravan's water inlet. Then, to activate the supply of water you have to operate the foot-pump. Its purpose is to draw water into the caravan in order to fill the chambers of the electric pump. The operation is called 'pump priming', and once that has been done the electric pump is able to take over the work.

When these types of pump are primed, they continue to do their job until air gets sucked into the system. That often happens when the water container is nearly empty. It also occurs when you disconnect the coupling pipe in order to tow your 'van to the next site. Nevertheless, the pump-priming task is hardly a chore.

Advantages
☐ Manual back-up: perhaps the main advantage of the dual system is the fact that you have a foot-pump (eg a Whale GP51) to fall back on if the battery becomes discharged or the electric pump develops a fault. The type of electric pump installed – usually a Whale GP74 – permits water to be driven through its mechanism when it's not operating on its own account. This is not possible with a number of other electric pumps.

Disadvantages
☐ Priming: some caravanners don't want the bother of priming the system, and when inexpensive submersible pumps appeared in the 1980s these became instantly popular. Strictly speaking, this type of pump does need priming, but the prime is achieved merely by immersing it in water.

ELECTRIC SUBMERSIBLE PUMP SYSTEMS

Most caravans are now supplied with a submersible pump which is a relatively cheap and reasonably efficient component.

On several models built around 1990, the pump and its supply pipe remained permanently coupled-up to the 'van. When leaving a pitch, the supply hose is folded flat, rolled up and stowed in a small

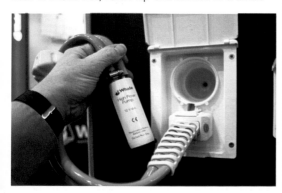

Whale Watermaster submersible pumps are available with couplings to suit both Whale and Truma Crystal/Compact inlet sockets.

Above: This Carver submersible pump fitted in late 1980s caravans is attached to roll-flat hose that is permanently connected to the inlet point.

Above right: This coupling includes both a water inlet and brass 12V connections for pump operation.

external compartment. This was an early Carver Crystal water system and some of these installations are still working well today.

More recently, however, the pump, connecting pipe and its electric feed cable are detachable assemblies. So when arriving on site, you have to plug the assembled system into the caravan's wall inlet. This usually requires a firm and sustained push, because there's an 'O' ring in place so that a watertight seal is achieved, together with electrical contacts which have to mate tightly.

Once you've made the coupling, the pump is dropped into a full fresh water container to activate the supply. However, check the Technical Tip alongside if water doesn't start to flow.

A submersible pump provision has both strengths and weaknesses. It's certainly wise to keep a replacement pump on board because these units can't usually be repaired. Equally, you're unlikely to find compatible units if you encounter a problem when touring abroad.

Advantages
☐ Cost: submersible pumps are far less expensive than the diaphragm pumps described next.

The 'O' ring on the water inlet nozzle ensures the coupling is water-tight but inserting the unit needs a sustained pressure.

On this Carver system, when the connector is pushed fully home, two retaining lugs help to hold it in place.

- Self-priming: whilst this type of pump has to be primed before it starts working, it achieves this automatically as soon as it's dropped into water.
- Damage: the mechanism is merely a paddle wheel (or impeller) that's driven by a small motor. If grit or other waterborne debris gets into the mechanism, it is more likely to survive the intrusion than a diaphragm pump, which is far less tolerant of grit.

Disadvantages
- Repairs: these are throwaway items and if the casing splits and water gets into the motor mechanism, it is irreparable.
- Battery dependence: like all electric pumps, submersible models rely on having a 12V supply.

ELECTRIC DIAPHRAGM PUMP SYSTEMS

Instead of having a submersible pump, some higher specified caravans have what is called a diaphragm pump. These are installed somewhere inside the living area, and on arrival at a site you merely need to connect a short length of hose from the external coupling inlet to your water supply vessel. Then it's 'all systems go'. Diaphragm pumps are well-engineered but are more costly than the submersible types.

Advantages
- Output: these self-priming pumps usually achieve a notable flow rate.
- Repairs: most manufacturers and importers of these pumps offer a repair service.

Diaphragm pumps like this Whale Smartflo are noted for their high flow rates, reliability and robust construction.

Recent submersible pumps have an air release hole to ensure that air bubbles don't get trapped in the casing.

189

Technical Tip

For several years, submersible pumps didn't have an air release hole on their casings. If you own one of these earlier models, air bubbles sometimes get trapped inside – even when it is lowered into a water supply container. When this happens, its motor will still spring into life when a tap is turned on, but water doesn't arrive at the sink.

If you have this problem, the answer is to swing the unit around in the water container by holding its connecting hose and ensuring that it remains below the surface. Making the pump bump against the side of the water container while it's below the surface then helps dislodge the trapped air bubbles. Sometimes it helps to uncouple the feed hose at the caravan connection point before swinging the pump about; this provides a further escape route for trapped air. Having followed this routine, water should then flow from the taps.

Disadvantages

☐ Noise: diaphragm pumps can be noisy, although this is often through poor installation.
☐ Damage: grit soon damages the tiny pistons that create water flow and a special filter has to be checked and cleaned periodically.
☐ Cost: these items are considerably more expensive than submersible pumps, although a diaphragm pump is likely to last much longer.
☐ Battery dependence: like all electric pumps, a diaphragm pump relies on having a 12V supply.

Exploded drawings of the mechanisms, guidance on grit filter cleaning and installation checks are given in Chapter Nine of *The Caravan Manual*, also published by Haynes.

PUMP SWITCHING

Like all electric motors, the ones fitted in caravans' water pumps need something to switch them into action. In most cases, a pump motor is controlled by miniature switches that have been mounted in the taps and the shower controls. As you turn the hand-wheel on a tap or lift its lever, two things happen – firstly the water channel is opened up and secondly the micro switch is triggered.

This control arrangement is fine, apart from the fact that these diminutive switches cease working if damp gets into their housing. On some taps, you then have to throw the whole unit away and purchase a replacement. That might be costly and it is fortunate that most tap assemblies are designed so that a faulty microswitch can be replaced. Only the matter of access makes this a difficult operation, especially under a kitchen sink. It certainly helps if

Handy Tip

It's always wise to carry a spare microswitch. Even if you have no intention of carrying out your own repair jobs, the spare can be given to a service specialist to fit. This is particularly appropriate if you're travelling abroad, because the water systems and associated products are often different.

The micro switch on this Whale Elegance mixer tap is fairly easy to change.

you're a contortionist, slight of build, and able to see in the dark.

Whereas microswitched systems are quite common, some caravans are fitted with a different switching system altogether. This involves a pressure-sensitive switch that detects when a tap is opened and then responds by setting the pump into action. In fact, a diaphragm pump usually has a pressure-sensitive switch housed inside its casing. Alternatively, it is possible to have a stand-alone pressure switch coupled-up within the supply pipe that serves the taps.

The only trouble with pressure-sensitive devices is the fact that they have a nasty habit of switching on a pump motor whenever a tiny failure in a pipe joint is sufficient to cause a slight air leak. That's why there's a pump isolating switch on many electrical control panels. In fact it's always wise to switch off a pressure-controlled system last thing at night so that you don't get woken up by a pump making a brief pulsing action.

Pressure-sensitive switching systems can also be affected when a supply battery gets low. In anticipation of this possibility, both diaphragm pumps and stand-alone pressure switches usually have a screw control for making 'fine-tuning' adjustments. However, this is sometimes hidden so that owners don't tamper with the adjuster and upset its calibration.

To summarise, neither microswitch nor pressure-sensitive systems are perfect performers. Whereas some components work for years and years without a problem, others have less impressive reliability.

WHICH PUMPING SYSTEM?

In light of the points made above, anyone buying a new or pre-owned caravan would therefore be wise to ask:

☐ What type of pump is fitted? And, in the case of a diaphragm type, where is it located?
☐ Does pump switching rely on a microswitch or a pressure-sensitive device?
☐ Are replacement microswitches readily available?
☐ How is the sensitivity of a pressure-sensitive device (if fitted) adjusted?
☐ Is it easy to purchase a replacement submersible pump of the appropriate type and with a connection to suit the caravan's water inlet?

Handy Tips

Many caravans have a double tap system for the hot and cold water supply. If a microswitch fails on one of the supplies – let's say it's the hot supply that cannot be switched into operation – you can sometimes solve this temporarily by 'cheating the system'. This is how you do it:

1 Open the hot tap a generous amount. Nothing will come out because we've established the microswitch has failed.

2 Now very, very gently turn the neighbouring cold tap (or any other tap in the caravan for that matter), listening for a tiny 'click' to indicate its switch is activated.

3 Don't open this tap any further – it just needs to be open enough to trigger the microswitch.

4 Hey presto! The pump will be set in motion but the water will come from the hot tap that was opened a generous amount.

Bench-type cassette toilets from Thetford have been fitted in caravans for many years.

TOILETS

It's a long time since the 'bucket and chuck it' toilet was used in caravans. Few modern caravanners would tolerate an open receptacle surmounted by a precarious seat. If using these toilets was primitive, caravanners' stories involving stumbling on the caravan's steps en route to the chemical emptying point with a full bucket were legendary, as you might imagine.

The portable flushing toilet with a connected holding tank was undoubtedly a great step forward in lavatorial luxury. Furthermore, these units could be transferred from caravan to caravan when you bought a newer model.

However, most toilets are now built-in and this alternative style of 'cassette loo' has been installed in most British caravans for more than 20 years. The first type to appear is referred to as the 'bench-type'; a later version is called the 'swivel-bowl' toilet. Either way, the care, use and end-of-season servicing are much the same for permanently-installed models as for portable flushers.

Swivel-bowl cassette toilets often fit better in small cubicles, which has made them increasingly popular.

When comparing all modern versions of these cassette toilets, several things remain much the same. They all need flush water, all use similar chemical treatments and all have a cassette that needs emptying – especially when its gauge reveals that it's full.

Not surprisingly, innovations appear now and again, and, to bring this overview right up to date, Thetford has now introduced a cassette that has wheels.

193

Since 2008, many caravans have been equipped with a Thetford C250 toilet whose cassette is fitted with wheels and a retractable handle.

Flush water
The procedure for adding a toilet's flushing water depends on the model. As the photos below show, a bench-type toilet has a fold-out reservoir whereas a swivel-bowl model has a purpose-made hatch.

Chemical treatments
The cassette, sometimes called the 'holding tank', needs a chemical to break up solids, and there are plenty of products on the market. They appear in several forms, too, including liquids, granular crystals

On a bench-style Thetford toilet, there's a fold-out reservoir for flush water and additive in the cassette compartment.

Swivel-bowl toilets fitted on caravans usually have a separate hatch and filler point for the flush water and additive.

Chemical treatment fluid needs measuring out carefully and this cassette cap includes markings to make the task easier.

Several manufacturers sell granular treatments; these are sometimes supplied in a plastic bottle with a widened neck which acts as a measuring dispenser.

Elsan Blue Bag sachets are another convenient product used to treat the contents of a toilet waste tank.

Introduced in 2009, water-based Blue Bio is a cassette treatment which is also designed to be a flush additive.

and dissolvable sachets. Pay careful attention to the mixing levels of the liquid products and always remember to put about a litre of water into the cassette first of all.

When purchasing chemicals, you'll find that some products are based on formaldehyde. This certainly breaks down solid matter, but there's growing

Handy Tips

- When adding a chemical, avoid spilling it on your caravan carpet at all costs. The marks of many treatment chemicals are virtually impossible to remove. Water-based Blue BIO is one of the exceptions.
- It is best to introduce liquid chemical directly into a cassette rather than via the toilet bowl. If neat chemical gets on to the rubber seal that keeps the open/close blade watertight, it can hasten its demise.
- Flushing water additive really does keep a toilet bowl shiny; it's not merely 'sales talk'. Similarly, purpose-made plastic cleaners can be very effective when cleaning washbasins, shower trays and toilet bowls.
- Toilet manufacturers have introduced many products, including fast-dissolving toilet paper, cleaning additives for the cassette tank and a cleaner for the flush water system. Over time, flush water reservoirs sometimes get coated with a black deposit that subsequently enters the toilet pan.

concern that it is detrimental to the environment. In consequence, several 'environmentally friendly' chemicals have been appearing as alternatives.

Taking such concerns further, most treatments are formulated to bring a halt to biological activity in a toilet cassette tank. Unfortunately, constituents like formaldehyde and glutaraldehyde have also been claimed to pose problems at sewage treatment plants.

In response to environmental concerns, new products are certain to appear, like Blue BIO which contains non-pathogenic enzymes. Their function is to break down the 'nasties', kill the odours and then continue to carry out these functions at the sewage treatment plant. This principle of operation is entirely different from more traditional approaches, and yet Blue BIO only has to be diluted at the parsimonious rate of one part product to 100 parts water. When used as a flush water additive, the prescribed dilution is then one part product to 500 parts water. Without doubt, this is a remarkably economic treatment.

Potty training

Explaining to adult readers how to use a fixed cassette toilet or a PortaPotti might seem demeaning and vulgar. But, if the job isn't explained here, how will you learn an all-important fact of caravanning life? It certainly never gets mentioned in other caravan handbooks. So here goes.

Many caravanners have 'house rules' that dictate that their toilet is only used for liquid waste. On most sites that's fine, but not when you stop at modestly-equipped farm sites where you have to be fully self-contained. The rule also ignores the fact of the 'human emergency'.

The time-honoured trick is to precede a 'performance' by flushing a small amount of water into the pan. Then a few pieces of toilet paper are carefully placed to float on the water like flower petals, making sure they make brief surface contact around the pan as well. This origami exercise may sound bizarre but it brings its rewards.

Once the 'performance' is complete, you find that as soon as the toilet emptying blade is swung open, the solids drop unhindered into the holding tank below and the paper encloses them completely with gift-wrapping panache. This means that no stains are left on the pan, or – more importantly – on the blade and its sealing rubber ring. Don't forget that you see this rubber sealing ring every time the cassette is taken for emptying, so you don't want soil marks. If this all sounds unseemly, believe me – it works!

Depressing the air release button while tipping a holding tank calls for dexterity, which comes with practice.

196 There's always a plastic catch to hold a cassette holding tank in place.

Immediately put a removed cap in a safe place. This shows how **not** to proceed – the cap can easily get knocked into the caravan site's emptying chamber.

Prior to laying-up a caravan, it's sensible to start by removing the toilet cassette first of all.

Emptying advice

There's definitely a knack to emptying a cassette, and using a brim-full container doesn't help you learn. Some points to bear in mind:

☐ When removing the screw cap, place it well away from the emptying bowl. Site owners are not happy if they have to try to fish out lost screw caps for butter-fingered caravanners.

☐ As you point the cassette's outlet spout to the receiving pan, immediately press the air release button. This can sometimes be difficult to reach, depending on the way you hold the cassette. However, if you ignore pressing the button, the contents tend to glug into the pan and you are much more likely to get splashed.

☐ Add some fresh water to swill the last remnants of paper out, but don't replace the screw cap and swirl the water around too vigorously. This has been known to damage the internal float mechanism that warns when a cassette is ready for emptying. Do it *gently*.

☐ Finally, it's always a good idea to precede your first-ever emptying operation by performing a 'dummy run' using a cassette full of fresh water

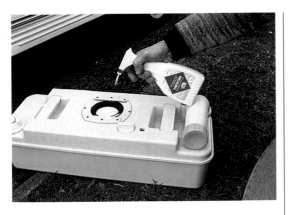

Thetford bathroom cleaner is used to remove deposits from the toilet seal.

rather than effluent. The operation might not be quite as straightforward as you had first imagined.

Lay-up procedure

Obviously it's catastrophic to leave a toilet un-emptied all winter, even though a cassette is built with a pressure-relief valve. But you won't make that mistake if you always remember to leave the blade in its open position prior to a lay-up period. Apart from acting as an emptying reminder, this prevents the blade sticking to the rubberised seal valve – which sometimes happens over a long storage period.

  You are also strongly advised to lubricate the seal prior to an extended lay-up period. Do this as follows:

1 Clean the rubber seal using Thetford Bathroom Cleaner or a lukewarm diluted solution of washing-up liquid; never use a household cleaner, which can damage the seal.
2 Dry thoroughly then spray with Thetford's Toilet Seal lubricant. Alternatively you can use olive oil, but never use Vaseline or any form of grease.
3 Leave the blade wide open throughout the period of storage.

An alternative to olive oil is Thetford's maintenance spray for toilet seals.

The seal is treated with olive oil, after which, the blade should be left open.

CHAPTER ELEVEN

USING A
REFRIGERATOR

A refrigerator is one of the most useful appliances in a modern caravan. However, it is different from the fridges we've got at home, and to get the best from one it helps to have a rough idea of how it works. For example, unlike household refrigerators, the appliances fitted in modern caravans operate on one of three sources of power. First, they can work on gas, secondly, they can operate on 12V electricity while a caravan is being towed, and thirdly, they can work using a 230V mains supply.

A modern refrigerator is one of the most useful appliances in a caravan.

This WAECO compressor fridge runs solely on a 12V supply, but it's more commonly fitted in small motor caravans rather than touring caravans.

Technical Tip

In almost all caravan cooling appliances the refrigerants are circulated by heat. This is called the 'absorption' process. However, in your refrigerator at home the chemicals are circulated by a compressor pump, and you can often hear the hum of its motor when a thermostat brings it into operation.

The noise from a compressor fridge is seldom a problem in a large kitchen but the intermittent hum can be a nuisance in a caravan – especially at night. Nevertheless, compressor fridges are sometimes fitted in small 'camper vans' and this alternative approach to refrigeration might gain ground in the future. Time will tell.

The idea of equipping caravans with refrigerators gathered momentum in the 1970s. One of the popular types at the time was manufactured by Morphy Richards, and its gas burner was accessed by removing a hatch fitted to an outside wall. It then had to be lit with a match, which was always a challenge in breezy weather. This was one of the early appliances designed specifically for caravans. Other products appeared soon afterwards.

For example, the Electrolux range became popular too, which included portable refrigerators for use on picnics. In time, Electrolux leisure models occupied a special division within the parent company, which was well-known for a diverse range of domestic appliances. Then the leisure division became part of the Swedish Dometic Group, and although Electrolux products didn't wear the new badge for several more seasons they remained a prominent force in the caravan industry.

Around the start of the new millennium, Norcold refrigerators, which had been prominent in the USA, were introduced to European markets. In the United Kingdom these appliances are now part of the Thetford Group, whose toilet systems have enjoyed a long-established presence in the leisure-vehicle market.

The refrigerants in products from Morphy Richards, Electrolux, Dometic and Thetford are circulated by the application of heat as described later. In contrast, there are cooling appliances made by WAECO whose refrigerants are circulated by a compressor pump rather than heat. These are often installed in small motor caravans but are not normally fitted in UK touring caravans. However, these products are mentioned because, in 2007, Dometic merged with WAECO International to form a large group manufacturing equipment for refrigeration, climate control and sanitation.

With this knowledge, purchasers of older caravans equipped with an Electrolux refrigerator will understand where caravan dealers obtain

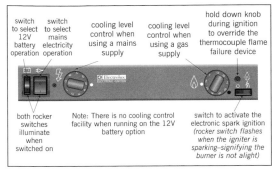

switch to select 12V battery operation

switch to select mains electricity operation

cooling level control when using a mains supply

cooling level control when using a gas supply

hold down knob during ignition to override the thermocouple flame failure device

both rocker switches illuminate when switched on

Note: There is no cooling control facility when running on the 12V battery option

switch to activate the electronic spark ignition *(rocker switch flashes when the igniter is sparking–signifying the burner is not alight)*

201

If you purchase an older caravan, here's an example of controls and their functions on later 1980s and early 1990s electronic ignition fridges.

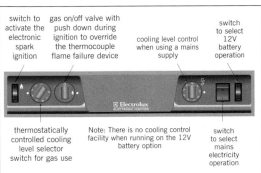

switch to activate the electronic spark ignition

gas on/off valve with push down during ignition to override the thermocouple flame failure device

cooling level control when using a mains supply

switch to select 12V battery operation

thermostatically controlled cooling level selector switch for gas use

Note: There is no cooling control facility when running on the 12V battery option

switch to select mains electricity operation

Example of controls and their functions on a mid and late 1990s electronic ignition fridge.

spare parts, acquire service training skills and gain general customer back-up. Also be aware that this chapter uses many photographs and descriptions of Electrolux products, since these are found in the majority of UK touring caravans. That said, contact addresses for both Thetford and Dometic appear in the Appendix address list. However, Morphy Richards' contact details are not included; although the company's leisure refrigerators were sometimes fitted in early 1970s caravans, they were seldom seen after that period.

STARTING A CARAVAN REFRIGERATOR

When you want to start a caravan's refrigerator, you have to decide whether to run it on gas or electricity. Provided the appropriate supply is available, it's then a matter of selecting your preferred operating mode on its fascia panel. Of course, if you choose to run it on gas, the burner will also have to be lit using the fridge's ignition control.

Unfortunately, a variety of fascia panels have been fitted over the years and if you've purchased a

When this fridge is running on gas, you adjust the level of cooling by using its gas control knob.

Older fridges were criticised for having complicated controls: this 2009 model is delightfully simple to operate.

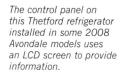

The control panel on this Thetford refrigerator installed in some 2008 Avondale models uses an LCD screen to provide information.

second-hand caravan and the handbook is missing, this may pose a problem. So the accompanying drawings show two of the more popular designs. Guidance about the function of the switches and selectors is shown on the drawings. You will also notice that you can set the level of cooling required.

However, with three supply sources on offer, which one should you use – and why?

THREE-WAY OPERATION

Refrigerator manufacturers talk about three-way operation in recognition of the fact that three power sources can be used to run these appliances. Each has its merits and there's good reason for giving caravanners three alternatives.

Whichever option you choose, the supply is used to heat the refrigerant chemicals stored in the cooling unit at the back of the casing. Once heat has been applied, the refrigerant starts circulating around a complex assembly of pipes. During its circulation, the refrigerant chemicals change to a gas and then back to a liquid — a process which is instrumental in drawing heat out of the food compartment. That's all you need to know about chemistry and cooling, although the Technical Tip panel on page 200 explains how caravan appliances differ from the ones in our homes.

Operation on gas

Applying heat from a small burner is particularly effective. Although this heat source is located low down at the back of the casing, a gas selector knob on the front panel of many older appliances controls the level of cooling. As shown in the accompanying photograph, this control raises or lowers the height of the flame. Incidentally a caravan fridge is made to run on either butane or propane gas without any need for alteration.

To ignite the gas burner, several different systems have been fitted. When caravan fridges first became popular around 40 years ago, you had to light the burner with a match. That was inconvenient, so spark ignition was developed next using a Piezo crystal. Plenty of fridges still in active service continue to use this system and a red push-button on the fascia is a familiar sight.

Even more convenient is the electronic system which was first introduced in the mid-1980s. Provided an appliance is switched on at the fascia, the electronic circuits will generate a spark automatically whenever the burner isn't alight.

Operation on 12V

It is very unwise to run a fridge on gas when your caravan is being towed; in addition it is illegal and potentially very dangerous to enter a filling station forecourt with an exposed gas flame. To avoid this, fridge manufacturers fit a heating element that runs on 12 volts as an alternative heat source. This means you can keep your fridge working while you're towing without using the gas system.

However, a refrigerator takes a lot of current to heat its refrigerants (around 8 amps) and the demand would discharge a 12V battery very quickly. So it is entirely impracticable to run this appliance from a caravan leisure battery when you are stopping at the site. Accordingly the caravan's wiring seldom includes a supply that links the fridge with its inboard battery.

Nevertheless, as long as your car's wiring has been correctly modified for caravanning use, a refrigerator is able to operate when you're towing and the engine is running. Current for the 12V heating element is drawn from the vehicle by taking advantage of its alternator charging system. In other words the alternator keeps the car battery charged even though there's a power-hungry appliance taking some of its current.

Operation on 230V

If you select the mains option, a different heating element comes into use for circulating the

203

Note
Ignition systems only work if a spark gap is correctly set at the burner. Furthermore, soot is created when a fridge runs on gas and an excessive coating around a burner assembly similarly upsets an igniter's efficiency. That's partly why it's important to have a caravan fridge serviced periodically, as explained later. One of the tasks involves cleaning the system and realigning the electrode where the spark should appear.

Note
When you've set a refrigerator's selector switch to the 12V operating position, you will not be able to control the cooling level of the appliance as you can when it's running on either a gas or a 230V supply. On a 12V setting, the refrigerator runs at a steady level, and altering the fascia cooling controls makes no difference at all. However, don't be misled into thinking that 12V operation is any less efficient than it is when running on gas or mains electricity. That is not the case.

On crowded sites in the summer, particularly in some European countries, the current draw on a mains system is considerable. This becomes especially acute in hot weather when fridges and air conditioning units are running flat-out. In some instances, heavy usage affects a caravan site's supply capabilities, and checks have revealed that some mains systems even drop below 195V. If this occurs, your fridge operation can be badly affected. Specialists at Dometic recommend that if you cannot get satisfactory cooling when running on mains, switch over to gas operation. This is likely to improve the performance, especially when you're using busy sites in hot locations.

204

chemicals. Equally, on older appliances there's another control knob with setting numbers for altering the level of cooling.

This operating mode is not only useful on a caravan site. It can also be put into use when your caravan is parked at home and you're packing it for a holiday. For example, it enables you to pre-cool the fridge before setting off without having to use your gas supply.

To carry out this operation, run the fridge using your caravan's hook-up lead, thereby ensuring that the RCD safety unit in the 'van is providing protection inside. This safety component is described in Chapter Twelve. Of course, you'll need a plug adaptor if you want to connect a hook-up lead to one of the domestic 13-amp sockets in your house. Moreover, it is strongly recommended to use a portable RCD unit in your selected 13-amp socket just in case anyone damages the external coupling cable running out to your caravan.

As regards fridge operation when stopping at caravan sites equipped with hook-ups, if you've paid to couple-up to a mains supply pillar, you'll obviously select the 230V mode rather than running your appliance on gas.

To run a fridge from a 13A mains socket at home, your hook-up lead will need an adaptor together with a portable RCD safety unit.

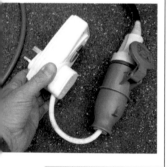

Handy Tip

If you accidentally run your caravan fridge on more than one supply at once, it can damage the cooling system. On pre-1992 models, this can occur by accident when you've been running the appliance on gas and then select the 12V option before driving away. Many caravanners wrongly presume that by turning the gas temperature control knob to its lowest setting, you'll duly extinguish the flame.

Unfortunately that is not the case. On earlier models the gas burner remains alight, albeit at just a glimmer. That's because the gas control knob on older refrigerators only selects the level of cooling. To extinguish the flame completely you have to turn off the gas at the supply cylinder.

In truth, you are *always* advised to turn off cylinders before taking to the road – but the job can get overlooked. In recognition of this, manufacturers of post-1992 Electrolux and Dometic refrigerators changed the fascia components so that a gas control knob *does* incorporate a shut-off valve.

If a refrigerator's gas burner doesn't ignite, check that the tap on the supply pipe is in the 'Open' position.

POSSIBLE PROBLEMS AND SOLUTIONS

As a rule, a refrigerator that's serviced regularly and installed correctly will be notably trouble-free. However, the following tips may be useful, especially if you're experiencing problems when trying to get it started:

If you find the refrigerator doesn't work on gas, check these points:
a Its supply cylinder still contains plenty of gas.
b The gas valve serving the refrigerator is open.
c If you can't ignite the burner after repeated attempts, arrange to have the appliance serviced.
d If the flame doesn't stay alight when releasing the gas control knob, the flame-failure device needs attention.

If you find the refrigerator doesn't work on 12V, check:
a The caravan's 12S or 13-pin plug is connected to the tow car's socket.
b The fuse serving the refrigerator on the 12V supply panel is intact.
c The 12V selector switch is in the correct position on the refrigerator fascia.
d The tow car's engine is running – the 12V option is for use when towing only and is not available when the engine is switched off.

If you find the refrigerator doesn't work on 230V, check:
a The 230V fascia switch is turned on.
b If the fridge is coupled to a caravan's mains circuit using a 13A plug that normally stays in a socket, check that the fuse in the plug is intact.
c Check that the miniature circuit breaker that controls the fridge supply hasn't tripped out on the 230V consumer unit.

A fridge can hold a lot of food, but don't pack it too tightly or the contents cannot cool effectively.

FOOD STORAGE ADVICE

To get the best from a caravan refrigerator there are also a number of tips relating to food storage:

Pre-cooling
Refrigerator manufacturers recommend that the fridge will perform best if it has been in operation for three to four hours before the caravanner sets off. During this period, some non-perishable items should be placed in the food compartment, *eg* bottles of water or some cans of drink.

Adding foodstuffs
When packing for a holiday, try to delay putting perishable foods in your refrigerator until its cabinet temperature has dropped considerably. If you are able to transfer items that are already cool from your kitchen fridge, so much the better.

Cooling efficiency is greatly reduced if a pack of drinks is placed directly over the heat extractor fins.

Loading-up

Avoid packing food tightly in the fridge and try to position items so that air can circulate around the cabinet. This is important because cooling is achieved by taking heat *out* of the food storage compartment.

Cooling fins

Heat withdrawal is carried out via a bank of silver fins at the rear of the food compartment and it's important not to cover these. Quite often poor cooling occurs when a caravanner stows a shrink-wrapped pack of drink cans hard against the cooling fins.

Covering food

Remember to pack strong-smelling commodities like pungent cheese or onions in a sealed plastic bag. Similarly pack any damp vegetables in a bag – especially freshly washed lettuce. Failure to do this leads to the formation of water droplets or frost on the silver cooling fins and this impairs performance.

Door catches

Get into a fixed routine of checking that the door security catch is engaged before taking to the road. Many caravanners have the dreadful experience of finding the refrigerator's contents strewn across the floor on arrival at their destination. But you only make this mistake once!

PRACTICAL OPERATING ADVICE

Freezer compartment

If your refrigerator has a small freezer compartment, decide what types of food might be usefully stored inside. There is usually a tray for making ice cubes, too, but don't fill this with water just before hitching-

Heat from the food compartment is drawn out via silver heat extractor fins.

207

Wet lettuce must be wrapped in a sealed bag before storing it in a fridge.

This 2009 Bailey Pageant has been equipped with a refrigerator whose freezer compartment can be removed if it isn't needed.

up and leaving. As a point of interest, some 2009 caravans are fitted with a Dometic fridge whose freezer compartment can be dismantled if it isn't needed. This frees-up space in the main part of the food storage compartment.

Igniting the gas burner

If your caravan has not been used for some time, it may take several attempts to get the gas burner to light. This usually means there's air in the gas supply pipe and it may take repeated attempts before all the air is purged. However, if ignition difficulties persist, this often indicates that the spark is weak, the electrodes are dirty or the spark gap needs realignment. Problems like that typically show that it's time for an appliance to be serviced.

Checking the flame

On older Electrolux models, there's often a small inspection port in the bottom left-hand side of the food compartment. This will have a clear plastic cover and it may be necessary to move some of the contents to see the glow of the flame. On a refrigerator with electronic ignition, you will hear the unit clicking when it detects that the flame has been extinguished. These clicking sounds also indicate that the igniter is generating sparks automatically in an attempt to relight it. You will also note a flashing red switch on the fascia which again confirms the burner is *not* alight and that ignition attempts are not achieving results.

Flame-failure devices (FFDs)

Like most gas appliances, a refrigerator has a flame-failure device (FFD). This means that if the flame blows out in a wind, the gas supply to the burner will be shut off automatically. The FFD uses a probe (called a thermocouple) that is angled into the gas flame; when it gets hot it creates a small electric current, which in turn keeps a gas valve open in the supply line. However, when you start the fridge from cold you have to hold down the main control for several seconds to manually open the gas valve while the probe is getting warmed up. If you find the flame goes out as soon as you release the control knob, the FFD probably needs attention – and that's one of the jobs included in an annual service. Don't be tempted to jam the control knob open, since you will override the all-important flame-failure facility.

Note: *Further information about flame-failure devices is given in the Technical Tip panel on page 288.*

Many of the older Electrolux refrigerators have an inspection port in the bottom of the food compartment through which you can check the gas flame.

208

For refrigerant chemicals to circulate correctly, it's important that your caravan is set up in a level plane. Indeed if your caravan was built before 1986 this is critical, and a refrigerator fitted at the time is unlikely to achieve cooling if it is 2–3° from level.

Since that date, Dometic, Electrolux and Thetford refrigerators are described as being 'tilt tolerant'. In practice this means:
- Models like the Electrolux RM122 and RM4206 will operate correctly as long as the degree of tilt doesn't exceed 3°. So do the Thetford N-series products.
- Models like the Electrolux RM4217, RM4237 and RM4271 will operate at angles up to 6° from a level plane.

Note: *When you're on the road, the pitch and toss of towing isn't a problem for fridge operation. As long as the refrigerator passes through a level plane every now and again, the cooling unit will remain in operation.*

Efficiency
As long as a refrigerator has been correctly installed by the caravan manufacturer, and provided the user-recommendations are followed, both Electrolux and Dometic refrigerators are able to operate efficiently in air temperatures as high as 38°C (100°F). Unfortunately, some caravan manufacturers have taken short cuts in the installation and these often prevent an appliance from achieving its full potential.

Ventilation
On an absorption refrigerator (as opposed to a compressor type), external vents are important contributors to the cooling process. For that reason, you should make sure that they don't get covered up. Occasionally sections of an awning can obscure a wall ventilator, and if this happens the fabric should be modified so that a clear airway is created. On some models a caravan's door opens directly across the vents, and this doesn't help either. Make sure a gap of at least 50mm (2in) is maintained when the door is held back, especially during warm weather.

Note: *If you buy a pre-owned caravan and find there's a small electric fan fitted on the inside face of the upper fridge ventilator, this is a modification to improve the flow of air across the cooling unit. This may improve cooling, although some manufacturers maintain that a fan is not normally necessary if an appliance*

209

On absorption fridges, efficient cooling is dependent on having external ventilators that allow air to flow across the cooling unit mounted on the rear of the casing.

Fans are sometimes installed at the rear of the large fridge-freezers that are now being fitted in a few of the more expensive touring caravans.

In very hot conditions try to open your fridge door as briefly as possible.

has been installed correctly. However, small fans are sometimes fitted on the large fridge-freezers installed in a few 'top-of-the-range' caravans.

Door

In very hot weather, try to open the door of a fridge as little as possible. The wisdom of this is self-evident but young children may not appreciate that cooled air quickly drops out of the food compartments of upright fridges. Anyone who opens a door when wearing shorts is soon made aware of this feature; disciplined use of the door makes good sense.

COLD-WEATHER CARAVANNING

Most caravanners take their holidays in summer and poor cooling is often a matter of concern. On the other hand if you use your 'van when outside temperatures are low, you can experience the opposite problem: over-cooling. It partly depends on the model fitted in your caravan.

Models prone to over-cooling

This problem is only likely on Electrolux models fitted with a gas valve, such as the RM212, RM4206, RM4230 and RM4200. It doesn't normally happen on models fitted with a gas thermostat like the RM2260, RM4237, RM4271 or more recent appliances.

Winter covers

Aware of the over-cooling problem, Electrolux introduced an accessory referred to as 'winter covers'. If your caravan has recent Dometic or Electrolux ventilators, you can purchase compatible winter covers from your dealer. These covers are designed to restrict the flow of air across the rear of the appliance and you're recommended to clip them

on to the ventilators whenever outside temperatures fall below 10°C (50°F).

Unfortunately, some of the cheaper ventilators fitted on caravans are of a different pattern and you can't buy covers that fit. As a rough and ready alternative some owners attach a piece of silver cooking foil over a small part of the upper ventilator. However, don't cover the lower ventilator, because on some refrigerator installations this also acts as a gas escape point in the event of a leak in the supply pipe.

Draughts

If a refrigerator has been installed in accordance with its manufacturer's instructions, the section at the rear of the appliance will be completely sealed-off from the caravan living quarters. In other words if a strong wind blows towards the external ventilators, it is prevented from reaching the occupants inside.

It is a matter of considerable regret that a number of caravan manufacturers fail to seal off the rear section as required. Not only does this impair a refrigerator's cooling performance in summer: it also leads to draughtiness in cold, windy weather. Some owners wrongly presume that winter covers are intended to overcome this. In practice they might ease the problem, but winter covers were *not* designed to act as draught excluders.

CHECKING AN INSTALLATION

If you're buying a caravan – whether brand new or second-hand – it is often possible to establish if the cooling unit at the rear has been sealed off properly from the living area indoors. For instance, if you look through the external ventilators you should not be able to see into the kitchen. In fact on the latest ventilators you can remove the grill by using a coin to undo the retention catches, which then reveals if there's a likelihood of a draught problem.

This winter cover from Dometic reduces the flow of air and is fitted when temperatures fall below 10°C (50°F). It is not designed to be a draught excluder.

On the latest Electrolux ventilators, the grill section can be removed independently from its frame below.

This is a good installation; when peering through a ventilator aperture it was impossible to see through to the kitchen.

Removing a drawer sometimes reveals why draughts reach a kitchen; it's usually the result of a poorly fitted fridge.

If a draining board gets hot when a fridge is running, the installation is unlikely to have followed the Electrolux guidelines.

Alternatively if you remove drawers in the kitchen near a fridge and peer towards the wall vents, you shouldn't be able to see any light from outside. Indeed, you shouldn't even be able to see either the upper or lower ventilators from inside.

At least one manufacturer, who should have known better (and now does), tried sealing off the top part of its installed refrigerators by jamming a length of sponge across the top of their casing. This was not approved by the fridge manufacturer, because sponge compresses and then gets dislodged.

There's a further test that you can carry out to confirm if your refrigerator is suitably shielded-off at the rear. This check should be made when a fridge is running on gas. If there's a worktop or draining board directly over the top of the appliance, put your hand on it. If it's warm, it's almost certain that the installation is not as good as it should be. Heat being produced around the cooling unit is not being confined at the rear as the refrigerator manufacturer prescribes.

If you carry out checks and find that an installation is disappointing, this is unlikely to constitute a risk to the occupants. Although the ventilation pathway at the rear should be sealed to create optimum cooling and a draught-free kitchen, don't get this confused with the flue system above the burner. Gases from combustion at the burner *do* have to be efficiently discharged outside via a flue, but that's a separate assembly – except in the case of Norcold appliances and large fridge-freezers.

Until recently, a surprising number of refrigerators were fitted unsatisfactorily. Poor-performing appliances often get blamed for mediocre cooling whereas it's usually a slipshod installation that provokes the problems. Furthermore, if you fail to get a refrigerator serviced regularly that can also affect performance. And without doubt, there are many caravan owners who stoically endure draughts in their kitchen whenever it's windy outside.

CLEANING AND LAYING-UP

On a 'housekeeping' matter, a refrigerator needs to be kept clean inside and free of mould.

☐ To keep the interior clean, Dometic recommends using a teaspoonful of bicarbonate of soda added to a litre of warm water. On Norcold refrigerators, Thetford (UK) is currently recommending the use of Thetford Bathroom Cleaner.

☐ Do not use other cleaners; some brands slowly react with the plastic lining material of refrigerators and the resulting damage isn't always apparent until several months later.

☐ To remove a food stain (like egg yolk discolouration) on the plastic lining of the cabinet, Electrolux has recommended that a very fine wire wool pad can be used, provided it's liberally lubricated with water to reduce its abrasiveness.

☐ Leave the door ajar using its security catch in the storage position. If the catch is broken or the 'van has a false wooden door to hide the fridge, rig up a system which will ensure the refrigerator door is held slightly open without being able to swing free if the caravan is moved during storage. The system must also prevent the normal magnetic closure device from pulling the door tightly shut.

To clean the inside of a Dometic fridge, the manufacturer recommends a solution of a teaspoonful of bicarbonate of soda mixed in a litre of warm water.

Thetford now recommends that Norcold refrigerators are cleaned inside using the Company's 'Bathroom Cleaner'.

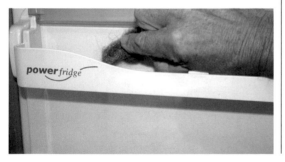

Electrolux recommends that food stains can be removed using very fine wire wool provided that it's copiously lubricated with water.

When this fridge door was completely closed before spilt milk was removed, mildew developed quite quickly.

Unfortunately this caravan manufacturer had fitted a false door front over the front of the fridge and omitted to fit a catch that would hold the door slightly ajar.

Most refrigerators have a catch that allows the door to be locked slightly ajar during periods of storage.

This more recent Dometic refrigerator has a central door catch offering two closing positions. It works well unless the door starts to drop on its hinges.

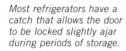

At first sight this strut fitted to a Norcold fridge might seem rather fragile. However, when it's secured at either end it effectively holds the door in a part-open position.

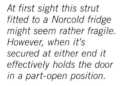

REFRIGERATOR SERVICING

Check your caravan's owner's manual for advice on refrigerator servicing intervals. For example, to ensure that their caravan refrigerators give good service, Electrolux, Dometic and Thetford recommend that their appliances are serviced every 12–18 months depending on the frequency of use. However, don't be misled into thinking that a fridge need not be serviced if a caravan remains stored for a couple of years. Rust will form in the flue and this can easily dislodge and fall on to the burner. Moths and spiders can also upset the fine operation of an electronic ignition system, or the gas supply itself.

One of the anomalies, however, is the fact that if you book-in your caravan for its 'standard' annual service, very little work is done on the refrigerator itself. Cooling is usually checked, and the appearance of the gas flame might be inspected by a gas engineer, but little else.

This is regrettable, and a full fridge service is usually regarded by caravan servicing specialists as a further task that is 'optional'. It is not an expensive operation, although one of the more time-consuming jobs is removing an appliance from a caravan to

One of the most demanding parts of a refrigerator service can often be the business of withdrawing the appliance in the first place.

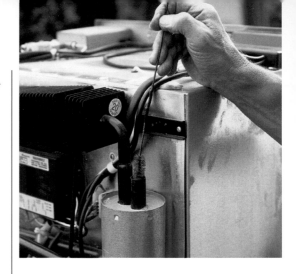

One of the tasks carried out by a service engineer is cleaning the flue and burner assembly.

obtain better access. Several service jobs are virtually impossible to complete if appliances are left in situ.

Service jobs include:
☐ Fitting a new jet, except on Thetford models.
☐ Cleaning the burner, flue, FFD probe and ignition assembly.
☐ Checking and realigning the ignition spark gap.
☐ Checking the operation of the flame-failure system.

Once a fridge has been moved to a bench, a servicing operation normally takes about an hour to complete. In a few cases the work can be done with an appliance left in situ, but that's unusual. Either way, the task should be entrusted to a qualified servicing specialist, and it is not a DIY job. Courses are run by refrigerator manufacturers so that caravan workshop staff know how to

Training courses in servicing operations and repairs are organised by refrigerator manufacturers for caravan workshop staff.

conduct service operations, diagnose faults and carry out repairs.

More detailed practical information on servicing, refrigerator operation and installation requirements is given in Chapter 11 of *The Caravan Manual*, also published by Haynes.

PORTABLE REFRIGERATORS

If you buy a very old caravan that hasn't been fitted with a fridge, it might be possible to have one installed. However, this can be a costly option, and alterations to your caravan's kitchen will probably be needed as well. A better alternative might be to purchase a portable refrigerator.

Don't get these mixed up with insulated 'cool boxes', which have a similar look but lack a cooling unit. Portable refrigerators are manufactured by several specialists, and many caravanners buy them to provide an additional cooling facility to use in an awning or to put into use back at home.

These appliances normally offer three-way operation and it is important to read the instructions most carefully when putting one into commission. Operation from gas, for example, must follow all the usual safety procedures.

Otherwise the points mentioned already about food packing and pre-cooling are applicable to portable fridges as well. In addition, if you decide to change your caravan you can transfer a portable refrigerator to its replacement.

Portable refrigerators can be especially useful appliances – both at home and on holiday.

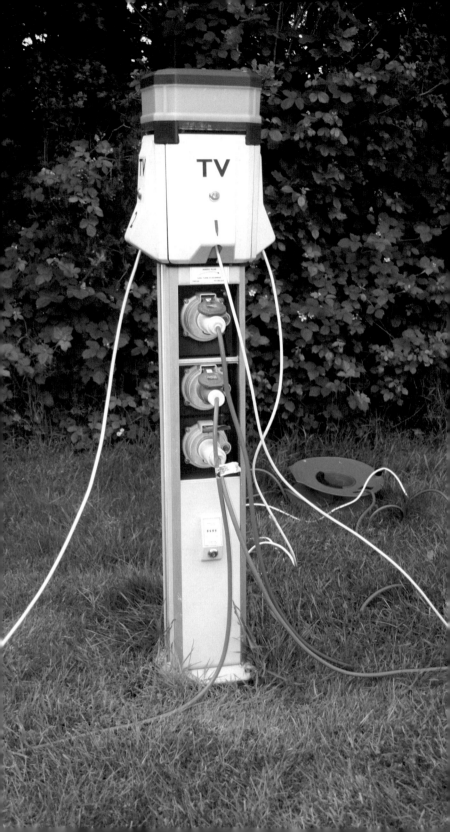

CHAPTER TWELVE

USING MAINS **ELECTRICITY**

Being able to use mains lights and 230V appliances in your caravan is especially helpful. Indeed, in the last 25 years more and more sites have been offering mains connection points, called 'hook-ups'. However, two matters must be recognised. Firstly, it's essential to observe the important safety procedures; mains electricity can cause fatalities. Secondly, you won't be able to operate some of the power-hungry appliances often used at home.

These hook-up pillars are often seen in Britain. This one also houses TV sockets linked to a large site aerial.

If you purchase a second-hand caravan and find that its handbook is missing, you need to find out how to use the 230V mains 'hook-ups' which are provided on many caravanning sites. Even with a new caravan, some owner's manuals do not go into much detail about site supplies, hook-up pillars and issues encountered abroad. To help new caravanners, this chapter covers the following areas of interest:

☐ An overview of components that are fitted in caravans to permit the safe use of 230V appliances.
☐ A summary of the coupling items needed for connecting a site supply to your caravan.
☐ Different types of hook-up pillars that you'll find in the UK and abroad – together with the use of adaptors.
☐ Establishing what appliances you can and can't run in your caravan. This varies from site to site and you need to ensure that you don't overload a site's supply system.
☐ The procedures, presented in step-by-step stages, for connecting up to a site supply.
☐ The issue of 'reverse polarity'. This term refers to a situation where there are 'crossed wires' in a site's supply system.

 **Technical Tip**

Amps, volts and watts

Expressed simply, the word 'voltage' refers to electrical 'pressure', and in Britain, a mains supply used to be rated at 240 volts (V). Other countries in mainland Europe often used lower voltages. However, as a result of European standardisation, supplies in EU states are now 230V AC – albeit with a permitted variation between plus 10% and minus 10%.

'Volts', therefore, relates to electrical *pressure* and isn't a measure of *quantity.* However, the matter of quantity is important, because some electrical appliances are certainly more greedy than others. Accordingly the *amount* of power consumed is measured in amperes (amps or A), which is also referred to as the 'current'.

It is helpful for a caravanner to understand these definitions because the *amount* of electricity available from site hook-up pillars is also expressed in amps. What's more, the amount of current available varies from site to site, and that affects what types of appliances you'll be able to use. That's why you ask at a reception office how many amps are available from a site's hook-ups. With that information, you then need to know how many amps are used by your various mains appliances. You might think that will be easy to find out, but then discover that appliance labels refer to watts (W).

The watts information on a label refers to an appliance's *rate* of electrical consumption, and watts embrace a combination of both amps and volts. In fact watts = amps x volts. Of course, it is widely understood that a traditional mains light bulb rated at 100W is brighter than a 60W bulb; it is also more costly to run. In fact, most electrical appliances are also rated in watts – which doesn't help the caravanner who really wants to know how many amps they consume.

But that's not a problem. You find this out by dividing the wattage of an appliance by the voltage of your electrical supply. So a domestic 2,000W (2kW) fan heater being run from a 230V mains supply consumes nearly nine amps (2,000 divided by 230 = 8.78). Help! That exceeds the current supplied by many hook-up pillars – and that IS important to know. Trying to run an appliance like that on some sites will cause the hook-up supply to terminate automatically. Issues like this are explained later in this chapter.

☐ The provision of a safe but independent 230V
supply in an awning.
☐ The use of portable generators and inverters.

On a technical note, it is worth adding that you don't
have to understand terms like amps, volts and watts
before switching on your lights at home. Nor, for that
matter, is it necessary to have this knowledge before
using electricity in a caravan. On the other hand,
the matter of coupling-up to a caravan site supply is
helped if you *do* have a rudimentary understanding of
words like 'amps'. For this reason the accompanying
Technical Tip panel is presented for readers who want
to know why this is helpful.

*This kit from Powerpart
provides all the items
needed to use a mains
supply.*

THE MAINS SUPPLY

New owners are often surprised to find that there are
two separate electrical systems installed in modern
caravans. These are: (1) a 230V mains system,
and (2) a 12V system that draws its supply from a
battery. This chapter, and the one which follows, look
closely at the two installations.

Virtually all caravans currently manufactured in
Britain are fitted with a mains electricity system as
standard. In addition, many older models which
were not originally equipped to run 230V appliances
often have a mains facility installed retrospectively.
This upgrading work can be carried out at a caravan
workshop or by a qualified electrician who has
a knowledge of the wiring products and special
components needed in caravans.

In addition, DIY installation kits are sold, and these
are ideal for owners who have the skill and knowledge
to carry out conversion work themselves. An approved
kit is strongly recommended, because the way that a
caravan has to be wired-up is quite different from the
way our homes are wired. Moreover, you may find
some kits – like the one from Powerpart – in which the
mains consumer unit is already pre-wired. This means
it is supplied with lengths of pre-connected cables
which you see extending from its casing. So most of the
fitting operation involves basic carpentry and general
practical skill rather than dealing with electrical issues.

With a supply system in place, all you then need to
connect up your caravan to a supply pillar or 'hook-
up' is a length of approved hook-up cable. Under no
circumstances should you use any other type of flex,
cable or coupling wire.

However, before describing the sequence of operations
needed to make the connection, let's identify all the
parts and find out their respective functions.

*The consumer unit in a
Powerpart kit is already
pre-wired.*

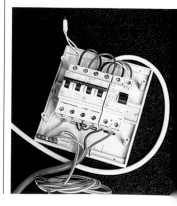

On this Belgian site, the hook-ups offer 220 volts.

In Britain, a mains supply was traditionally rated at 240V AC. The accompanying photograph taken a few years ago on a Belgian caravan site indicates that the supply in that country was then 220V.

As part of European standardisation, reference is now made to 230V AC, and the initial agreement included a permitted variation of +10% or –6%. However, from 2003 the permitted tolerance became +10% or –10%.

Throughout this book, reference is made to a '230V supply' in recognition of the latest European standards. In practice, however, it is often reported that the *actual* voltages supplied on caravan sites sometimes drops below the permitted tolerance of –10% (207V). It has been alleged by electrical specialists, for example, that on busy caravan sites, particularly abroad, a high demand for mains electricity sometimes means that hook-up pillars might only achieve 190V. That would explain why caravan refrigerators sometimes run less efficiently on their mains setting.

PARTS NEEDED IN AN INSTALLATION

Irrespective of the age of your caravan, look for the following items:

FIXED COMPONENTS
These include:
- ☐ An input socket.
- ☐ The consumer unit.
- ☐ A safety earth cable with bonding clamps.
- ☐ Earth labels.
- ☐ Internal cables and 13-amp sockets.

The input socket
In order to draw electricity from a site's supply point, a hook-up cable (described later) will have to be connected to a mains input socket mounted on your caravan. This socket has to be an industrial type that is suitably robust. At one time sockets were often fitted on the underside of caravans' floors, but in this location grit and rainwater can get into the connection when the 'van is being towed. It's possible, of course, to fit a protecting cap, but on balance it is better if the socket is mounted inside an external locker. Accordingly, it is sometimes fitted inside the box that also holds the leisure battery. On other caravans there are flush-fitting enclosures that are made just large enough to accommodate a socket on its own.

This 1990 Compass Rallye has an external locker which houses an input socket, a mains consumer unit at the top and a battery charger below.

Above left: On this 2007 Avondale Dart, the mains coupling socket is mounted inside the battery locker.

Consumer unit

Another essential component in a caravan's mains supply system is referred to as the 'consumer unit'. This not only enables a user to activate or isolate separate circuits; it is also an important safety device. Consumer units are situated in various places. Some, for example, are fitted in a caravan's wardrobe or a cupboard; others might be mounted in an external locker that provides storage for a hook-up cable and socket adaptors. There are also electrical component manufacturers who fit a mains consumer unit within an enclosure that's used to house 12V fuses and switches as well. Examples are shown on page 227.

The all-important function of a consumer unit and a description of its controls are discussed in the later section entitled 'Switches on a consumer unit' (page 226).

Some mains sockets are housed inside small, flush-fitting wall boxes.

Bonded safety earth cable

For safety reasons, a consumer unit has to have a thick earthing cable that's bolted to the caravan's chassis. This is normally covered with a yellow and green insulation sheath. Near the chassis connection there should be a warning label and this will bear words such as: 'SAFETY ELECTRICAL CONNECTION – DO NOT REMOVE'. If your caravan has a metal sink or washbasin, this should also be bonded with an earthing cable and fitted with a label.

Below left: A mains system in a caravan must include an earth bonding cable which is connected to the chassis and marked with a warning tag.

Below: In this example, an earth cable is bonded to a gas supply pipe and marked with a safety label.

Note
Any professionally built British caravan which displays a National Caravan Council badge of approval will have originally been wired to meet British and European Standards. However, if you purchase a pre-owned caravan it might include some owner alterations. For this reason you are strongly recommended to get a dealer or qualified electrician with knowledge of caravan 230V wiring to:

1 Check the installation.
2 Confirm that it is safe.
3 Rectify anything which is faulty.
4 Issue a dated certificate affirming its integrity.

Note: *Be aware that some DIY installations are wholly unsatisfactory*

Internal cables and 13-amp sockets

Inside a caravan, you are likely to find two or three 13-amp sockets fitted at convenient points. One of these is often allocated permanently for the refrigerator; however, some caravan manufacturers wire this appliance directly to a spur taken from the mains cable harness. Similarly a built-in battery charger is usually connected-up directly to the mains harness too. Either way, many owners often express the view that more sockets would be welcome in caravan installations.

There may be a permanently fixed 230V lamp too, although most illumination inside is provided by 12V lights that draw their supply from a caravan's battery.

The wiring inside a caravan should consist of flexible three-core cable that has been clipped in place at frequent intervals. You should *not* find the relatively inflexible 'twin and earth' flat PVC sheathed cable that's used for wiring in our homes. The reason for this is explained in the accompanying Technical Tip box.

ADDITIONAL PARTS NEEDED

You will also need the following items and may have to purchase them from a caravan accessory supplier:
☐ An approved hook-up cable.
☐ Adaptors if you want to couple-up to supply pillars abroad.
☐ An adaptor if you want to couple-up to a 13-amp socket at home.
☐ A system tester as shown at the end of 'Coupling-up procedures' (page 234).

 Technical Tip

Flexible three-core cable used inside caravans

For the technically-minded, the individual cores in cables used for the internal wiring should be 1.5mm^2 and made up of thin copper filaments as opposed to a solid copper strand. This construction provides cable flexibility, and that is important in a caravan on account of the vigorous 'shake-up' experienced during towing.

It is *not* good practice to install the flat 'twin and earth' solid-core cable used for fixed wiring in our homes. Solid-core rigid cable is more likely to become accidentally disconnected from screw connectors (e.g. in sockets) because of the relentless movement in towed caravans. If you've purchased a pre-owned caravan, check that flexible cable has been used inside; some fitters do not realise that touring caravans are wired differently from household installations.

Quality of hook-up cable

The girth of the required three-core flexible cable is conspicuously substantial. For the technically-minded, each of the three individual cables within the cover sheath (usually orange) should have a cross-sectional area of 2.5mm^2 and comply with British Standard/European Norm (BS EN) 60309-2. On the ends of the cable, industrial connections compliant with this BS EN standard include one that has brass pins for coupling to the site pillar, while the other has deeply recessed brass tubes for coupling to your caravan.

Although these connectors are weather-resistant, they're not intended for submersion in puddles. Summer downpours occasionally take us by surprise, which is why extra lengths of cable should never be linked together.

Note: Thinner cable must NOT be used for hook-up purposes. If you see connecting lead being sold at an unusually low price, it might be sub-standard. It has been alleged that some orange-sheathed products sold in the past have enclosed non-compliant 2.0mm^2 cable inside.

Mains hook-up cable is sold in 25m lengths with a plug and socket pre-fitted on either end. It has to comply with British Standards/European Norms.

Hook-up cable

A hook-up cable of 25m (plus or minus 2m) is now supplied as standard equipment with every new caravan. But that hasn't always been the case, so connection leads are also sold at caravan accessory shops. Regulations are very precise about hook-up leads, which must have an approved heavy-duty flexible three-core cable as described in the Technical Tip box 'Quality of hook-up cable'.

Adaptors

If you travel abroad, mains adaptors are often needed. It's appropriate to point out, however, that the industrial-style couplings used in Britain are now being fitted on new installations in many European

Far left: This short adaptor lead allows a British caravanner to couple up to a French supply pillar.

Left: The supply pillar on this holiday site in the Ardèche provides a two-pin French socket on the left and two British-style 'Euro' sockets on the front.

Many adaptors are needed when touring in mainland Europe; this one is for coupling to the traditional mains sockets in France.

This adaptor allows a caravan hook-up cable to be fitted into a domestic 13A socket; the portable RCD device shown here is recommended for safety.

countries. Sometimes these are referred to as 'Euro sockets'. However, on several sites abroad you may come across both types of socket fitted on hook-up pillars.

For the most part, however, you are likely to need an adaptor to suit supply sockets used in countries outside the UK. It will be many years before a universal standard is eventually established throughout Europe.

In addition, you may want to couple a caravan's hook-up cable to the mains supply at your home. For example, in the previous chapter it was recommended that a refrigerator is pre-cooled before leaving for a holiday and most owners like to do this using mains electricity from their house. By purchasing an adaptor to suit a 13-amp domestic socket, this coupling can then be achieved.

SWITCHES ON A CONSUMER UNIT

Irrespective of whether you purchase a new or pre-owned caravan, you should understand the function of the switches on a mains consumer unit. You will also be advised to operate these switches at several stages during the coupling-up procedure described later.

Consumer units may look different externally, and you'll come across both larger and smaller types according to the model of caravan and the extent of its mains supply facilities. Irrespective of the visual differences between units, the accompanying photographs show the key components you need to identify.

The purpose of each switch should be explained clearly in a caravan's owner's manual, but that sometimes gets lost. It is also extremely helpful if the switches are clearly labelled on the unit as well. Sadly that is often ignored and it is ironic that the accompanying photograph of a labelled

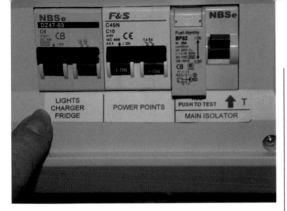

It is so helpful when the switches and test button on a consumer unit are clearly labelled like this.

consumer unit was taken in an imported German motorcaravan.

The Residual Current Device master isolating switch

Firstly look for the master isolating switch which forms an integral part of the residual current device, or RCD. This is effectively the 'life saver'. If you want to know how it operates, check the Technical Tip box.

The master isolating switch that forms part of an RCD operates in one of three ways:

1 You can switch off the supply manually.
2 The supply switches off automatically in milliseconds if there's a fault in the system. It is also activated if a user accidentally touches a live contact.
3 There's a test button that will cause the switch to disengage instantly when depressed – just as if a real fault had occurred.

Provided the unit is in full working order, any of these actions immediately disconnects the mains supply to the wiring and sockets *inside* a caravan.

Terminology
Whilst the term 'residual current device' has been adopted for several years, you will often see it referred to by its earlier names. For instance, in the past it has been referred to as an 'earth leakage circuit breaker' (ELCB) and also as a 'residual current circuit breaker' (RCCB). Some caravan handbooks have even used the terms interchangeably – which doesn't help clarity or consistency. Today, we should refer to this life-saving automatic cut-off device as an RCD to avoid ambiguity.

Pressing this test button simulates a fault and should immediately cause the master isolating switch to go into its OFF position.

(i) Technical Tip

How the RCD identifies a fault
A residual current device senses any imbalance in the current passing along live and neutral cables. An imbalance occurs if a leak or a short circuit from either cable runs to earth. This would happen, for example, if you were to accidentally touch a live component or cable. In the event of this happening, the consequent imbalance in current flowing along live and neutral cables is detected in *milliseconds* by the RCD, whose master isolating switch instantly 'trips out' automatically. This immediate termination of the supply can prevent a fatality, although a very brief shock may still be experienced when the live component is initially touched.

The two switches on the left inside this consumer unit are miniature circuit breakers or MCBs.

The miniature circuit-breakers

MCBs are a modern equivalent of rewirable fuses. In older houses, a rewirable fuse 'blows' (*ie* it melts and then breaks) when a fault develops in an appliance. However, in caravans – as in recently-built houses – there are MCB 'trip switches' instead; these are shown in the accompanying photograph.

Note that an MCB mustn't be confused with the similar-looking switch fitted on the RCD. Put simply, the principal function of the RCD that was described above is to prevent fatality through electrocution. In contrast, the purpose of an MCB is to prevent serious consequences, *eg* a fire, which might occur if there's a short circuit in either the wiring or one of the appliances being used.

Most caravan consumer units have either two or three MCBs depending on the complexity of the mains supply installation. If there are two MCBs, one is sometimes assigned to the fridge; the other serves the remaining 13-amp sockets. Be aware that you can operate the switches manually; in addition they will cut off a supply automatically if a fault is detected.

Note: *If your caravan's MCBs are not labelled, you can easily work out which appliances they respectively serve so that you can then mark them accordingly. When coupled to a mains supply, put all mains items into operation, then manually switch off one of the MCBs. Once you've checked which appliances then cease working, you'll know the MCB that controls their operation; repeat the test by switching off the other MCB(s).*

THE SUPPLY SOURCE

Hook-up pillars

A site supply is drawn from a hook-up pillar and the voltage in EU member countries has now been standardised. However, supply pillars don't follow a universal pattern and differ both in structure as well as the sockets they offer.

The accompanying photographs illustrate these dissimilarities, and the one shown on the opening page of the chapter includes TV supply sockets for aerial cables as well. At the base of this pillar there's also a locked door, and if the user overloads the supply a trip switch is activated and the site manager has to be notified. A member of staff will subsequently unlock the enclosure door and switch the system back on.

Other types of hook-up points are shown alongside.

Left: On this site in Wales, overload resetting switches are easily accessible, although it isn't intended that clients will operate them.

Above: A few hook-up pillars have 'pay-as-you-go' credit card swipe systems, but they're expensive to install and you won't see them very often.

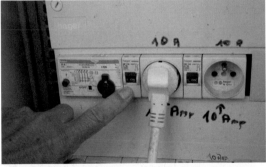

Left: Newly-built sites in France are fitted with the industrial sockets that we use in the UK. This older site still has traditional French sockets, for which British visitors need an adaptor.

Left: This French site offers different levels of supply (in amps) and the user-fee varies accordingly. The site warden inserts one of the switch blocks shown here to activate a visitor's chosen supply.

PUTTING A SYSTEM INTO OPERATION SAFELY

Confirming which appliances can be used

Before coupling-up to a mains supply, you should ask at the reception office how many amps are available from the site's hook-up pillars. For example, some site hook-up sockets offer no more than 5 amps whereas others offer 16 amps. To find the practical implications of this, refer back to the guidance and simple calculation given in the Technical Tip box 'Amps, volts and watts' at the beginning of this chapter.

Calculating which appliances will operate within your limit

To establish what appliances you can and can't run on your pitch, you first have to check the wattage of all your appliances. Here are some typical ratings taken from markings or labels affixed to appliances and from information given in their instructional manuals:

☐ Traditional mains light bulb: 60W.
☐ Flat-screen colour TV: 25W.
☐ Built-in battery charger (depends on battery charge level): 200–800W.
☐ Truma Ultrastore ten-litre water-heater running on mains: 850W.
☐ Dometic medium capacity RGE 2000 refrigerator: 135W.
☐ Dometic large RGE 400 fridge-freezer: 325W.
☐ Typical domestic pop-up toaster: 1,000W.
☐ Typical fast-boil domestic kettle: 2,500W (often called 2.5kW).

Then you need to decide which appliances will typically be running at the same time in order to total-up their respective wattages. When carrying out your calculation, don't forget that a fixed battery charger is usually working in the background and may not have an on/off switch. So include this item in your addition using a rough estimate of its wattage. It can only be an estimate because its consumption rate will vary according to the condition of the 12V leisure battery it's charging. If your battery is generally well charged, an estimate of 200W won't be far from the mark. If it's in a poor condition, the charger will be working hard to revive it so your estimate might be 500W.

Once the combined wattage of your working appliances is calculated, dividing the total by 230

establishes how many amps they will all be drawing from the hook-up supply. On some small rural sites whose hook-up supplies only offer 5 amps (maximum), you'll probably have to reduce the number of items that you were hoping to operate. However, on Club sites offering 16 amps there's much more scope.

Having to undertake these calculations might sound onerous, so for a quick check bear in mind that a site offering 5 amps allows you to run appliances whose combined rating doesn't exceed 1,000W. If the site hook-ups offer a maximum of 10 amps, the combined rating of your appliances mustn't exceed 2,000W. If you find that your demands are too great for your hook-up supply capability, take account of the fact that a 'three-way' refrigerator will run well on gas. Similarly, you can avoid using an electric kettle by boiling water on the hob. Your supply of electricity could then be prioritised – let's say to keep the 12V leisure battery in a good state of charge, to run a 230V lamp and to operate a colour TV. Naturally we all have different priorities when belt-tightening is needed.

If you do exceed your hook-up supply's capability, the site system will 'trip out', whereupon you receive no power at all. On some pillars you are permitted to reinstate the supply by resetting the supply switch yourself. However, on many sites you have to summon a member of staff to do this for you. Naturally, if the problem occurs when the reception office is closed this may involve a long wait.

Note: *On cold, dark, winter nights, a site's supply will be placed under heavy pressure, especially when all pitches equipped with hook-ups are occupied. Although an individual hook-up pillar might be able to provide a supply up to 16 amps maximum, a site's mains installation is not designed so that every pitch occupant can draw 16 amps at the same time. In consequence you may see warning posters that advise visitors to be sparing in their use of electricity. Disregarding this request may result in a site being plunged into darkness.*

If you feel uneasy about old hook-up pillars and a multitude of questionable cables, it may be safer not to use the supply.

COUPLING-UP PROCEDURES

Once you understand the way a caravan mains supply system is controlled and you recognise the supply limit from hook-up pillars on your chosen site, it's time to couple-up your caravan to the mains. This step-by-step checklist describes each task and gives the correct order of action:

Always make the connection with the caravan before coupling-up at the hook-up pillar.

☐ Have a look at the site hook-up pillar nearest to your caravan. Most pillars have several couplings and some might already be in use by caravanners on nearby pitches. If you find a multitude of doubtful-looking cables all around the hook-up, or have any concern about the safety of the supply itself, you might wisely decide not to couple-up your caravan.

☐ Check that all appliances in your caravan are switched off, and as a precautionary measure move the RCD switch to its 'off' position. Presuming the hook-up point looks sound, now carry out the following operations.

☐ Insert the female connector of your hook-up lead into the caravan inlet. That's the one on the lead that has the recessed brass tubes.

☐ Unravel the hook-up cable and work out a route for running it to the nearest hook-up pillar. Make

This shows how not to lay out your cable. Loops can trip other site users and the cable is immersed in a puddle after a heavy shower.

sure it lies flat on the ground and won't cause anyone to trip over when they're walking by in the dark. Also ensure that it doesn't go through low areas that might become puddles after unexpected downpours of rain.

☐ Before coupling to the hook-up point you'll see how much spare cable remains. Do not be tempted to leave it tightly coiled on a drum, because it might overheat when high-consumption appliances are in use. In severe cases the insulation might even start to melt. The correct procedure is to place spare hook-up lead in loose coils underneath your caravan.

☐ The remaining plug is referred to as the male coupling and you'll note that it has three brass pins within its moulded casing. The plug is pushed into the socket on the hook-up pillar, and on many hook-up installations the connection has now been completed. In other words, current will have reached your consumer unit.

☐ On other hook-up installations, the power doesn't start to flow until you rotate the coupling clockwise and hear a click. On the pillars where this is necessary, you'll see a red button near the socket and a label above. Unfortunately, however, the sun often bleaches out the label's instructions.

☐ Go to the consumer unit and check that the MCB switches are in the 'on' position. Then

This might look tidy, but never leave spare cable on a drum; put it in loose, open coils under your caravan.

The male plug is inserted into this free socket on a typical hook-up pillar found on many caravan sites.

Coupling and uncoupling is different on this type of hook-up and it is unfortunate that the instruction labels are sometimes missing.

To confirm that the master isolating switch 'trips-out' correctly, press the test button on your consumer unit.

The display of light emitting diodes (LEDs) on this tester indicates that an earth connection is at fault. The supply should not be used until this has been rectified.

move the RCD master isolating switch to its 'on' position.

☐ At this point it's always advisable to confirm that the automatic 'trip-out' function of the RCD is working correctly. So press in the small test button to verify that the isolating switch 'trips-out' instantaneously. Once this has been confirmed, reset the RCD switch to its 'on' position, secure in the knowledge that this all-important safety device is operating correctly.

Note: *If the master isolating switch doesn't react when you press the check button, do NOT use the mains system. Seek advice from a caravan dealer.*

☐ Now insert a test device into one of your caravan's 13-amp sockets. Products like the one shown alongside are sold at electrical dealers. When the socket is switched on, the illuminated LEDs can highlight certain faults in your system including a case of reverse polarity. With good reason, 'reverse polarity' can be a source of concern.

REVERSE POLARITY

In Britain, switches for wall sockets, lights and appliances are wired to the live cable. This means that when a switch is moved to its 'off' position, power can't reach an appliance at all. That's an important feature because it enables you to change a light bulb safely without having to switch off the entire 230V supply using the master switch that isolates your entire house.

Unfortunately the safety of the British system is lost if the live and neutral cables are wired-up the other way round. For example, a switch that controls the flow of current on the way *out* of an appliance certainly prevents the appliance from working. However, in such an arrangement an appliance or light socket remains live, even though it isn't operating. This could be dangerous.

The problem doesn't arise in mainland Europe because the usual practice abroad is to fit switches which operate on both the live *and* neutral cables. These are referred to as 'double-pole' switches and ensure that an appliance still doesn't become live even if the live and neutral feeds are wired-up in reverse. In fact on campsites abroad, it's not unusual to find that the supply at hook-up pillars has been connected the other way round. This is referred to as 'reverse polarity'.

As a result, British tourists abroad need to check mains polarity as soon as they couple-up at a site. Sometimes reverse polarity is indicated by a red warning light fitted to a consumer unit. Alternatively it can be revealed by means of one of the testers shown earlier. So what should you do in this situation?

☐ Many motorcaravanners acknowledge the potential danger and decide not to use the mains supply.
☐ Some recognise the fact that polarity-sensitive appliances may receive damage and that their appliances will remain live, even when switched off. However, they decide to use the supply in spite of the inherent risks involved.
☐ A few motorcaravanners have a pole-reversal component fitted retrospectively in their vehicle.
☐ Many owners get an electrician to prepare a reversal adaptor using a short length of hook-up cable complete with a plug that's wired the other way round and *boldly marked*. You can't purchase these, but when one is fitted into a site pillar that has been wired in reverse, the supply is duly rectified at source; your hook-up cable can then be connected next.

Technical Tip

Double-pole switching
Motorcaravans manufactured since 1994 have a double-pole switched RCD and double-pole MCBs – so the level of protection is improved. It is a pity that 13-amp double-pole switched sockets aren't fitted too. They are widely used abroad and can also be purchased in Britain. Their installation would add the final protection to motorcaravanners stopping on sites where the supply polarity's reversed.

If you often find that the polarity on site supplies is reversed, you can get one of these devices installed in your caravan.

Inside an RYD live/neutral changeover device, its connection block is clearly labelled.

The live and neutral cables in the socket of this French hook-up adaptor have been intentionally connected in reverse. Red and white tape reminds the user that it has been modified.

On this type of hook-up pillar, the coupling plug can only be withdrawn when a red button is depressed.

UNCOUPLING FROM A MAINS SUPPLY

When leaving your pitch, disconnecting a mains hook-up is essentially a reversal of the sequence given earlier. In particular, it involves:

1 Switching off all your appliances and the RCD switch on the consumer unit.
2 Withdrawing the plug from the site pillar to terminate the supply. Normally this involves a sustained pull, but on pillars whose sockets have red locking buttons you have to depress the button first to release the plug.
3 Withdrawing the plug from the caravan input socket. On a few types of input socket its release necessitates depressing a release lever. For instance, the socket pictured on page 223 has a release catch on its left side.

On damp mornings you'll want to dry-off the hook-up lead before coiling it up and stowing it away.

RUNNING MAINS APPLIANCES IN AN AWNING

If you want to run mains appliances in an awning, there are two options. Some caravans are manufactured with an external 13-amp socket which is housed in a weatherproof box. One of these can sometimes be fitted later by a caravan dealer.

Alternatively, a mobile supply unit manufactured by Powerpart is available through caravan dealers. This features a compact consumer unit with RCD and MCBs, three 13-amp sockets and a 25m length of hook-up cable. The advantage with this product is that it can also be used at home when working outdoors with DIY power tools and gardening equipment.

POWER FROM GENERATORS AND INVERTERS

Petrol generators

Modern portable generators are smartly designed, compact in size and much quieter than their industrial counterparts. However, they are surprisingly heavy, relatively costly to buy, and these leisure machines seldom provide as much current as you'd get from a site supply. To achieve that level of supply you would have to purchase an industrial generator and these models are costlier, heavier and noisier.

The output from portable leisure machines is typically from 650W (around 2.8 amps) to 2,000W (around 8.5 amps). Also be aware that generators often have two settings – 60Hz and 50Hz. To achieve a claimed 650W output you have to select the 60Hz setting; this provides a less stable supply that may not be suitable for operating sensitive appliances.

And a further warning. As the mains appliances in a caravan are switched on and off you'll often hear the generator engine altering its note. On many models this is accompanied by a brief irregularity in the output. A similar change of note can occur when a generator is first started up and is running on its choke. Only a few recent models, such as the Honda EU10i and EU20i generators, feature electronic systems that eliminate power irregularities.

Brief surges upset some types of electrical appliance, especially if you couple a generator to a caravan's mains inlet to run its battery charger. Most built-in battery chargers now feature 'switch mode' circuits, and supply irregularities can easily damage their electronic components. On account of this problem some generators have a 12V outlet for battery charging that will completely bypass the built-in charger in your caravan. You merely have to purchase a suitable coupling lead to fit the

Above left: Some caravans are fitted with an external socket so that items like this portable fridge can be operated in an awning.

Above: The mobile supply unit from Powerpart includes a fully equipped consumer unit and three 13-amp sockets for use in an awning.

Note

Circuitry in the most recent 230V portable generators from Honda includes a patented system referred to as 'inverter technology'. Models like the Honda EU10i and the EU20i employ this feature, which is claimed to eliminate power irregularities, unexpected surges and the attendant problems of damage to caravan appliances. The manufacturer also asserts that the delivered power is cleaner and smoother than electricity from a mains source.

The Honda EU10i produces a smooth, surge-free output on account of its 'inverter technology'.

Several leisure generators can bypass a caravan's fixed battery charger by using their own 12V DC output points.

This robust chain and lock is a wise purchase for securing this high-quality leisure generator. Thefts are not unusual.

generator's 12V outlet and take this directly to the terminals on your battery.

Good-quality generators are costly and there are often reports of them being stolen. Make sure you are able to secure a product you plan to purchase.

Also be aware that they must be covered when it is raining, but mustn't be used in an enclosed awning. Consider purchasing a purpose-made cover that's designed to allow the engine's exhaust fumes to discharge unhindered.

Finally, be aware that there has also been a recent influx of very cheap products imported from the Far East. If you intend to buy one of these, check that it's supported by a reliable after-sales, repair and spare parts service.

Inverters

When an inverter is connected to a 12V battery it will convert its 12V DC input into a 230V AC output. This can be useful, and even low-rated

Below right: The generator cover designed by Sew'n'So's provides good protection in rain and allows its exhaust fumes to escape easily.

Below: An unusual feature of the Sew'n'So's generator cover is the fact that it doubles-up as a useful carrying bag.

The Sterling Power-Q range of inverters from RoadPro starts with compact models like this, which will run low consumption products.

100W inverters will enable you to run a mains light bulb from a 12V battery.

However, the more you run through an inverter, the sooner your leisure battery will reach a state of total discharge. To give an example of this, if you were to buy a 250W inverter it typically draws more than 20 amps from a leisure battery. (250W divided by 12 volts = 20.8 amps). In other words, a 60 amp-hour (Ah) motorcaravan battery running only the inverter would be 'flat' in under three hours. In recognition of this, inverters often have low-voltage sensors that shut them down when a battery gets low enough to sustain damage.

Of course, a larger 90 amp-hour battery would work longer between recharges; the situation is also less acute when using an appliance that operates intermittently, such as an electric shaver. Similarly, if a compact 230V colour TV is used to show a half-hour episode of a favourite serial, a pure sine wave inverter might be the answer when using a site that's not equipped with hook-ups. On the other hand, long evenings of TV watching would soon leave you with a completely discharged battery. And that's why mains hook-ups are so popular.

Technical Tip

Inverter limitations
For sensitive equipment like TV sets, a 'pure sine wave' inverter is recommended, and these cost around three times the price of a 'modified sine wave' inverter. Inverters are complex products and one of the best explanatory guides is a leaflet supplied by Road Pro – telephone 01327 312233 or visit www.roadpro.co.uk.

CHAPTER THIRTEEN

USING 12-Volt
ELECTRICITY

Around 40 years ago, caravans were fitted with gas lamps. However, this changed when an Essex electronic specialist found a way to run a fluorescent light from a 12V battery. At first, the tow car's battery was used as the power supply. Then, a few years later, owners wanted to use this supply to run TV sets, stereo systems, heat distribution fans and extra reading lamps, and it immediately became clear that a caravan would need its own 12V battery. Overusing a car battery means you might not be able to get the engine started.

241

Wind generators send a trickle charge to a 12V battery – provided there's enough wind, of course.

The 12V system is soon ready for use after a few switches are checked on the main control panel.

The supply cables are clamped on to the live and neutral pillars of the leisure battery.

On the battery's live cable, you should see a fuse; this one is mounted in an airtight holder.

In modern caravans, putting a 12V system into operation is easy. Provided your caravan's leisure battery is charged-up and connected to its 12V supply cables, you go to the control panel and merely flick a few switches.

To get the best from a low voltage facility, it also helps to know something about the caravan's battery that's providing the power. There's also the wiring itself. So let's look at these items more closely.

The 12V circuit

Everything starts at the battery. Two cables have to be connected to its live (+) and neutral (–) pillars, and close to a leisure battery you will also see a fuse mounted in a holder. This should be connected to the live (red) cable, and protects the entire supply that follows. If you were to find that no 12V accessories were working, this fuse would be something to check.

At the start of a circuit, the thick supply cables resemble the trunk of a tree. Having drawn power from its source, the trunk later divides into branches. In the same way, a 12V supply divides at a control box and then takes separate pathways to convey current to different components.

The cable used for these individual branches is normally thinner than the cable used for connecting-up to the battery. However, its actual size is determined by the amount of power that different components require. For example, a water pump is a more greedy consumer of current than a light fitting, so a pump's supply cable needs to be thicker than one that's serving a lamp.

As a rule, a 12V supply is divided up into three separate circuits. These serve:

- The water pump.
- The lighting.
- Ancillary items like a TV socket, a heater fan and a radio/cassette player.

Note: *Each of the individual branches is usually controlled by a switch and a fuse of its own.*

The only other point to add is that most caravans have a secondary facility whereby 12V electricity for running indoor components can be drawn from the tow car's battery instead. This presumes that:

1 The caravan is coupled to the car.
2 The towbar installer has wired-up a link from the car battery to the multi-pin socket near the vehicle's towball.

In reality, when you're stopping at sites you only take power from a car battery as a last resort. Today's caravans are fitted with so many 12V accessories, a vehicle battery wouldn't last very long. So with the exception of a caravan's road lights, the remaining items of 12V equipment normally draw power from what is referred to as a leisure battery.

In summary, a caravanner must first decide which battery is needed to supply the power and secondly which accessories will be brought into use. This is achieved with the help of a control panel.

Control panels
In design and appearance, control panels differ in various ways. There was a period, for example, when they bore a large number of switches, a galaxy of indicator lights, an array of analogue gauges and a clock. These elaborate displays were reminiscent of the flight decks on aircraft and seemed wholly inappropriate amidst the soft furnishings of ordinary touring caravans.

Today the control systems are more sensibly restrained. Some are simple panels that bear labelled switches whose functions are self-explanatory. Others are more elaborate and present read-outs on liquid crystal display (LCD) screens. Provided you peruse their instructions with care, the information available on the screen even

On this simple panel, the rocker switch on the left allows you to choose which battery will provide the power; the gauge above shows its state of charge.

243

Battery selection switch
On many caravans there's a 'rocker-type' switch that can be set in one of three positions. When positioned in the middle, the 12V supply is switched 'Off'. The two other positions allow you to draw current from either the caravan battery or the car battery (presuming that you're coupled to the towing vehicle).

This simple control with its small pictograms is self-explanatory; for example, a tap image identifies the switch for the pump.

This control panel uses a liquid crystal display to show a wide range of features including temperatures, current consumption and the time.

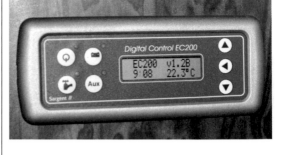

includes inside or outside temperatures, and the amount of drinking water left in a tank.

Other electronic gizmos are appearing as well. For instance, a recent Dometic roof-mounted air conditioning appliance comes equipped with a remote control handset. This even enables you to control its output when you're lying in bed; you'd have to decide if that's a feature you're likely to need.

To illustrate how 12V control panels differ, the accompanying photographs include several examples. Some control units include the fuses protecting the 12V accessories; in other caravans, fuses are fitted elsewhere. Notwithstanding these differences in detail, here are the controls to locate:

A high-quality roof-mounted air conditioning unit from Dometic is even supplied with a remote control handset.

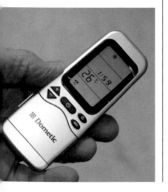

☐ The source switch which activates the supply of 12V DC electricity and determines whether it will be drawn from the caravan's 'leisure' battery or the tow car's 'starter' battery.
☐ Master lighting control switch. Although light fittings usually have their own switches, you can often turn them all out in 'one hit' by using a master switch. Typically this is positioned somewhere near the entrance door.
☐ Water pump switch. This is important to identify, especially if your caravan has a diaphragm pump rather than a submersible type. The reason for isolating a pump was given on page 191.

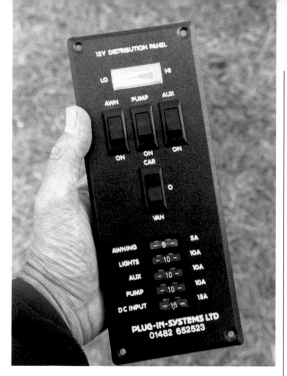

This simple control panel has separate switches for the external awning light, pump and other auxiliary circuits – together with fuses.

☐ Accessory master switch which controls the supply of electricity to accessories such as a radio/CD player, a 12V socket for a TV set, and heating system fans.

In addition to these controls it is normal to have a facility for identifying the charge level of your leisure battery. Some panels have a charge condition gauge; others have a warning light to indicate when a battery's charge level is low.

Now let's turn our attention to the source of the power. A basic understanding of leisure batteries is helpful because these are items that are not normally supplied when you buy a caravan.

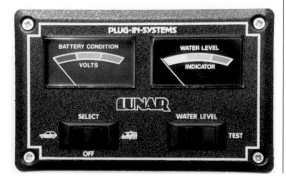

In this Lunar caravan, a 12V battery selector switch is supported by the gauge above, which indicates its charge level.

A leisure battery is constructed differently from a car battery. This Elecsol product is rated at 110Ah.

CARAVAN BATTERIES

A battery designed for use in a caravan, motorcaravan or boat is usually referred to as a 'leisure battery' and it is constructed differently from the batteries fitted in cars. Admittedly both products have a polypropylene case that houses lead plates and an electrolyte (either dilute sulphuric acid or an acidic paste). However, there are differences in the construction of the lead plates because car and caravan batteries have to perform dissimilar jobs. What's more, they don't do each other's jobs very well.

Different work patterns

A car battery has to provide a large amount of current to start an engine, but as soon as it fires-up the battery immediately receives a charge from the alternator. This is completely different from the work pattern of a leisure battery. In contrast, this has to keep low current appliances running for extended periods – often without the likelihood of receiving a recharge for a day or more.

If you use a car battery to perform the work carried out by a leisure battery, it soon needs replacing. That's because its lead plates are not suitable for the work regime described above. In contrast, leisure batteries are built with plates that *can* cope with repeated discharge/recharge cycles; accordingly they're often described as 'deep cycling batteries'. Not surprisingly, though, a leisure battery is unlikely to perform well if you use it for starting a car.

There is also another function that a leisure battery has to fulfil. Although its principal purpose is to run a caravan's accessories, it also acts as a buffer (*ie* a protection device) that absorbs any power surges that might come from a caravan's built-in battery charger.

To explain this further, when you've connected your caravan to a mains supply its built-in charger duly provides 12V DC electricity. This is not just used to recharge a battery: it also provides some of

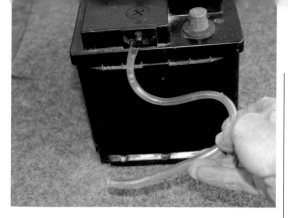

the power that can be used to run your appliances. Unfortunately, a charger's output isn't always smooth and even a small surge is liable to damage sensitive accessories. This is less acute when a leisure battery is wired into the circuit because it has the effect of smoothing out irregularities. In consequence, a 12V supply that has been augmented by the output from an onboard charger is then more stable.

Lead-acid or gel leisure batteries?

Most caravanners purchase what is commonly described as a 'wet' lead-acid battery. These popular purchases have removable screw caps on the top, and inside each cell you can see a fluid. This is referred to as the electrolyte and it consists of a dilute solution of sulphuric acid. This type of battery also has a ventilator tube, so if a mix of hydrogen and oxygen is created during a heavy charge, the gas can be safely dispersed outside.

The alternative is a gel battery in which the electrolyte is an acidic paste. Each cell is sealed and nothing leaks out if you turn the casing upside down. Since this type of battery has to be charged at a lower voltage than a 'wet' battery, it won't produce gas and therefore doesn't need a ventilation tube.

Technical Tip

Charging gel batteries
Some manufacturers of gel batteries state that the maximum charge level for their products is 14.2V. Others give a limit of 14.4V. Owners might wish to check this.

Gel batteries are occasionally used in caravans. They have no liquid to spill and don't create gas if charged correctly.

Gel batteries are obviously the preferred product for use on jet skis and quad bikes because they occasionally roll over. Presumably it's for safety reasons that they are now being fitted on some imported caravans too. However, many battery engineers point out that from an electrical viewpoint, a lead-acid product is a better performer than its gel counterpart. It is usually much cheaper as well. With those points in mind, many UK caravanners opt for 'wet' lead-acid batteries and make sure there are ventilation facilities to deal with the release of gas during charging.

Battery capacity

The external dimensions of batteries differ and this is often related to their capacity, which is rated in amp hours (Ah). The greater an Ah rating – marked on its label – the longer a leisure battery provides power before it needs recharging.

Owners who normally stop at sites equipped with 230V hook-ups usually find that a 60Ah battery is adequate. At the other extreme there are owners who seek as much self-sufficiency as possible and prefer to stop at remote farm sites where mains power is seldom supplied. Similarly there are caravanners who enjoy touring in winter when daylight hours are short and fan-driven heat is essential. In those instances, it is necessary to fit a leisure battery with a higher Ah capacity.

In practice, many owners of modern caravans find that their leisure battery becomes discharged after only a couple of days. If that's the case, a 110Ah battery provides power for much longer, although the greater the Ah capacity the longer it takes to recharge it from flat. Also be aware that a caravan battery locker sometimes offers insufficient space to accommodate products with a high Ah capacity.

Caravan battery locations

The Safety Tip panel on page 253 explains that a battery often gives off an explosive gas when it's being charged. This is why modern caravans have

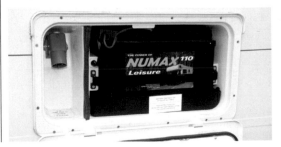

This 110Ah leisure battery just fits into the purpose-made battery box fitted in a Bailey Ranger caravan.

Although a rigid tray is less likely to get damaged, some batteries are now installed with a protective bag.

a purpose-built box with an outlet so that gas can escape. In practice, these outlets are often discreetly located to maintain protection from the weather.

To provide security there should also be clamps or straps to ensure that a battery doesn't topple over and spill its corrosive acid. Recent battery boxes also include a plastic tray that encloses the lower part of a battery's casing. As long as these purpose-built boxes are sufficiently capacious to house a higher capacity (Ah) battery (if needed), the arrangement is hard to fault. It's certainly a great improvement on previous practices.

There was a time in the 1980s, for example, when some caravan manufacturers provided a storage cage for a battery which was fitted in the gas locker compartment. This is potentially dangerous because gas control valves occasionally develop a leak. Equally, when you couple a connection to a battery terminal you sometimes create a small spark, so an accumulation of leaking gas could conceivably be ignited by a spark from the battery. That's why batteries and gas cylinders *must* be kept well apart.

The problem of sparks at battery terminals is another reason why clamping devices are better than crocodile clips for making a connection. They are less likely to create a spark if nudged accidentally and seldom spring off unexpectedly. To save the bother of using a spanner, some caravanners use coupling products that have a spring-loaded clamp. However, their contact surfaces must always be clean.

Before the advent of purpose-made battery boxes, many owners used to keep their leisure battery in a blanket locker; others used the bottom of a wardrobe. Either way, a battery stowed in these locations must be effectively secured so it cannot fall over in transit. Then there's the matter of ventilation. A caravan manufacturer is most unlikely to have fitted a high-level ventilator in a wardrobe or bed box, so a plastic ventilator tube is essential. If fitting a battery in an old caravan, it is often

Spring clamps are made to clip on to battery pillars, but the contact surfaces need periodic cleaning.

To fit a battery in an older caravan, it's often wise to purchase a purpose-made battery box for mounting inside a locker, like this.

wise to purchase a purpose-made battery box with sealed lid to screw down in a locker indoors. However, it is also necessary to create an outlet hole through a caravan's floor for the flexible gas escape tube.

As a point of interest, a few readers might purchase a second-hand caravan complete with a TP2 battery box. This once-popular accessory is a plastic carrying box that also houses a purpose-designed battery charger at one end. The TP2, however, is no longer made.

Life between charges

The length of time that you can run a battery before it needs recharging is partly determined by its amp-hour capacity. But that is only one of many considerations. For instance, there's a huge difference between caravanning in summer with long hours of daylight and caravanning in winter. During December's dark evenings, many hours are often spent around a TV with a 12V fan blowing warm air and lights in full use.

Provided there's a restrained use of 12V accessories, a fully-charged 60Ah battery meets most caravanners' needs during a weekend in summer. Needless to say, a 75Ah battery contains more power and a 110Ah battery will last even longer.

Of course, none of this matters one jot if you nearly always use pitches with mains hook-ups and your caravan's got an efficient built-in charger. Moreover, most fixed battery chargers can be left permanently running. This means that when you are using battery-operated appliances, the battery's output is matched by the charger's input. It's true that older 'pre-electronic' chargers are best switched off when a battery has achieved a full charge, and that's something that you should check either with a dealer or the charger manufacturer.

In contrast, if you seldom stop at sites that have mains hook-ups you'll be entirely reliant on the battery for a supply of electricity. However, calculating a battery's likely performance period before needing a recharge can be an exacting task. As a further complication, temperature plays a part and so does the age of your battery.

Battery manufacturers also emphasise that you should never run a leisure battery to the point where it's absolutely flat. In fact, a battery is claimed to last many more years if you start recharging it as soon as its charge level drops to 50%. Whether the majority of owners heed this advice is anyone's guess.

Let's also return to that matter of a battery's amp-hour (Ah) rating. The figure quoted by manufacturers and marked on a label relates to its performance in an ambient temperature of 25°C (77°F). In reality there are many 24-hour periods in the UK when the temperature is much lower than that. The accompanying Technical Tip panel indicates the significance of temperatures and the effect that they have.

Lastly, if you use a battery to run a lot of appliances simultaneously, this obviously hastens the time when a recharge is needed. But it's worse than that, because a high demand in a short space of time also reduces an Ah rating even further. To highlight this, some battery manufacturers even quote different Ah figures on their battery labels to acknowledge this phenomenon.

Checking battery charge level
The control panel in modern caravans usually provides information about a battery's charge condition. To get a true picture, however, bear in mind that if the battery has just been receiving a charge – either when you've been towing or when a mains charger has been coupled – it should be left to settle for at least four hours before the reading is taken. Certainly after a long charge on a workbench, a truer picture is obtained if you wait 12 or even 24 hours. This is because older batteries look misleadingly good when the charger is first disconnected, but subsequently lose their charge

Temperature effect on a battery's output
The stated Ah capacity of a battery presumes that there is an ambient temperature of 25°C (77°F). One well-respected battery manufacturer states that for every drop of 1°C below that figure, there's a 1% reduction in its performance capability. So at 0°C, *ie* freezing point, the nominal Ah capacity is reduced by 25%. This means that a battery nominally rated at 60Ah effectively becomes a 45Ah battery at 0°C. Bearing this in mind, a battery mounted in an external locker performs less well in cold conditions than an identical one fitted indoors.

This label indicates the effect that a high rate of discharge over a short period of time will have on a battery's Ah capacity.

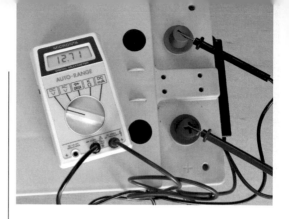

The reading of 12.71V displayed on this digital voltmeter reveals that the battery is fully charged.

quite quickly even without being put into use.

Notwithstanding the warning light systems fitted on many caravan control panels, a more accurate assessment of condition is achieved by putting a voltmeter across a battery's terminals. Readings from a voltmeter are interpreted in the accompanying panel. Suffice it to say, a product that we refer to as a 12V battery carries a rather inaccurate title. If a voltmeter registers 12V, the battery is discharged. In a fully charged state, it should read 12.7V.

Looking after a leisure battery

In view of the cost of a leisure battery, always take heed of the manufacturer's advice. Here are some of the ways to get the best from a battery:

1 A battery's electrolyte should be checked periodically, but do *not* smoke when carrying this out. The inspection involves removing the caps

Technical Tip

Approximate indication of a battery's state of charge

Voltmeter reading	Approx charge state
12.7V or over	100%
12.5V	75%
12.4V	50%
12.2V	25%
12V or under	Discharged

Note
1 *Some electrical specialists point out that this information should only be taken as an approximate guide.*
2 *Remember the advice about letting a battery rest for four hours or more after a charging period in order to get a more accurate reading.*
3 *Make sure every 12V appliance is 'Off' when taking a reading. This should include the clock, which sometimes gets overlooked.*

To ensure that its lead plates were immersed in electrolyte, de-ionised water was added to this battery.

Emission of an explosive gas

When a battery is charged at a high rate, it creates an explosive gas (a mix of hydrogen and oxygen) that often lingers around the cells, even after charging ceases. Make certain that no one nearby is smoking when a charger is disconnect from the terminals. When batteries explode the casing often disintegrates, and acid can easily get splashed in your face. Explosions also occur if there's a flame nearby – such as a pilot light on a gas appliance.

The gas normally only forms when a charging voltage exceeds 14.4V but it *can* be emitted at lower voltages if a battery cell is faulty. For this reason, always ensure there are *no* naked flames or a source of sparks near a battery when it's being charged or its cells are being checked.

Also note that this gas is lighter than air – so if a battery is fitted in a sealed compartment, there must be a high-level outlet to allow escaping gas to discharge and disperse outdoors. Alternatively, if a leak-proof tube and connecting elbow can be coupled to a battery, this may be routed down through the floor since gas will be forced downwards under pressure.

over each cell and checking the level of acid inside. The electrolyte, as it's called, should just cover the lead plates that you can see in each cell. If the level has fallen in one or more cells, top-up where necessary with de-ionised water. This is sold at car accessory shops.

2 If a lead acid battery is left in a discharged state for a day or more, it will often be irreparably damaged. Attempts to recharge it may prove fruitless.

3 Avoid running a battery until it is completely flat. As stated earlier, always start recharging a battery when the control panel indicates that it's in a low state rather than after it's been used to the point of exhaustion.

4 When you want to remove a battery from its locker, always disconnect the negative terminal first. Equally, when you're installing a battery, connect the negative terminal last.

5 Sometimes you find that the terminals on a battery get covered with a white powdery substance. To prevent this forming, lightly smear the terminals with grease or petroleum jelly (Vaseline).

To prevent a deposit forming on the battery terminals, coat them with a thin film of Vaseline or grease.

Charging a leisure battery
Using the tow car
When you are towing a caravan, some of the charge from the tow vehicle's alternator should yield a small input for the leisure battery. Since this isn't a particularly high input, it's referred to as a 'trickle charge'.

In some caravans the wiring is such that you have to put the battery selection switch on the control panel to the 'car' position in order to receive a trickle charge from the car. Guidance on this should be given in the caravan's Owner's Manual. Failing this, tow your caravan to a service centre and get an electrician to put a voltmeter on the battery's terminals. When the engine is started there should be a distinctly higher reading – say 13.8V – at the battery. This increase from the resting voltage of the battery (12.7V if it's fully charged) indicates that the alternator's replenishing charge is reaching the battery.

On the other hand, if the battery remains at 12.7V or lower then alter the position of the selection switch, restart the engine, and ask the electrician to take another reading. One way or the other there should be a clear rise in voltage when the engine is running. If this is not the case, an electrician would then take a reading at the 12S or 13-pin socket at the back of the car to confirm that the towing electrics have been wired up correctly. Sometimes the fault is in the car rather than the caravan.

Using a hook-up on a site
If you use a mains hook-up, the caravan's built-in charger will keep the battery in a good state of charge. As mentioned already, some chargers can be left on all the time and electronic circuits prevent them from overcharging a battery. This kind of circuitry can also detect when a battery is fully charged, whereupon the charger goes into 'sleep mode' and ceases giving a charge current.

Fixed battery charger
Some chargers installed in caravans have an on/off switch but many start operating automatically as soon as a 230V supply is connected.

Not only does the output from one of these devices charge the leisure battery; it provides a 12V supply to run the indoor accessories as well. These two functions operate simultaneously and that's why built-in chargers are designed not to yield more than 13.8V. The restriction means a battery won't start 'gassing' either and it's well within the 14.4V limit for charging a gel battery. Of course, it will make your 12V lights glow more brightly, but it's unlikely to cause them to fail.

Portable stepped chargers
Unfortunately, lead-acid batteries respond better when recharged with an initial input around 15V or more, followed by a gradually reducing charge. This causes an emission of gas and a battery's cells need topping-up more often. However, periodic 'gassing' extends the life of a battery.

In order to meet this need, some electrical specialists are manufacturing portable chargers which offer 'stepped charging' regimes. Their electronic circuits are able to evaluate a battery's condition and also to monitor the battery's progress while the charging process takes place. For example, a charging regime might commence with a boosting output of 15V that then tapers off as the battery responds. That is just what many batteries need. However, you wouldn't want your caravan's *built-in* charger to start at 15V, because it is usually running 12V appliances at the same time, many of which could get damaged.

That is why many owners disconnect a leisure battery from the 12V circuits in their caravan and transfer it to a bench. Using a portable charger from manufacturers like CTEK, they can then provide a charge regime that suits a battery best.

Note: *Further technical information on batteries and charging are dealt with in* The Caravan Manual *(4th Edition), also published by Haynes.*

Trickle chargers
These products are designed to keep a battery (which is already in a good charge condition) fully maintained by providing an occasional input of power when it's needed. Trickle chargers are used by many owners of vehicles that have to be parked for extended spells, like classic cars, motorcycles in

On this 1990 Compass caravan, the built-in charger was located in an external locker and had to be switched into action.

255

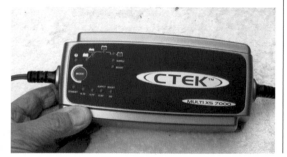

Portable stepped chargers like this CTEK product offer different charging modes to suit different types of battery and different operating situations.

The Carcoon trickle charger was designed to keep the batteries in classic cars up to scratch, but many caravanners now use them as well.

winter – and caravans too. Most products can be left permanently connected to both the mains supply and the battery because their electronic circuits monitor voltage and activate charging only when it's required.

Solar and wind generators
Neither of these products is cheap to buy and purchasers don't necessarily have them fitted with the hope of saving money. When conditions are right, both are able to provide a battery with a trickle charge, thereby helping to extend a battery's output before it needs a renovating recharge.

Wind generators are often fitted on boats and work best in exposed places where prevailing winds are strong. In large oceans they are a great asset. However, their use in caravanning venues is less convincing.

As regards solar panels, these only need light, although they perform best in bright sun and clear skies. Some caravanners use portable panels and have to take care that they don't get stolen. Other products are permanently installed on the roof and semi-flexible versions are remarkably light.

Portable solar panels have the advantage that they can be moved to track the sun; but you have to make sure that they don't get stolen.

To give an example of current output, a 70W

Semi-flexible panels can be easily bonded to the roof and are much lighter than the versions protected with heavy-duty glass.

flexible solar panel that costs around £450 (plus fitting charges) can yield approximately 3 amps in a sunny position on a clear day. The output might be higher at midday but would be considerably less when it's raining and dull. In one hour of favourable light, its coupled battery might therefore receive 3 amps. However, 3Ah represents only a small fraction of the capacity of a 65Ah battery.

So there aren't dramatic achievements, but during an eight-week test conducted in the Midlands between mid-July and mid-September 2007 the author's roof-mounted 70W panel produced a logged total of 540 amps. The yield would be considerably less in the shorter daylights hours of winter, but this test proved that solar panels *do* make a useful contribution.

Using a portable generator

These products are compact and useful but they are also heavy and rather costly. Many models also provide an irregular output, and fluctuations can damage the circuits in 'switched-mode' electronic chargers that are fitted in the latest caravans. The subject of generators was discussed in more detail in the previous chapter, so check the advice given there.

ECONOMY MATTERS

Recognising that the demands placed on a leisure battery are greater now than in the past, efforts are being made to introduce less power-hungry appliances. Lights, for example, have been brought under scrutiny.

In the late 1960s caravans were fitted with gas lamps, and when tungsten 12V car bulbs were tried it was decided they drew too much current. However, the move away from gas gathered momentum when fluorescent lights were invented that could operate using a 12V supply. This was a turning point, and by the early 1970s gas lamps were phased out and fluorescent lights took their place.

A panel must be connected with a solar controller; some versions display features like the amount of current being received and battery condition.

257

Interior lights that use a traditional tungsten filament bulb usually take more current than a small fluorescent strip light.

The bright, warm light from a halogen lamp is fine but these products take quite a lot of current. They also get very hot and the bulbs don't tolerate current irregularities.

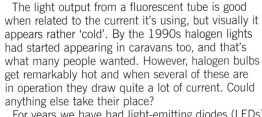

The light output from a fluorescent tube is good when related to the current it's using, but visually it appears rather 'cold'. By the 1990s halogen lights had started appearing in caravans too, and that's what many people wanted. However, halogen bulbs get remarkably hot and when several of these are in operation they draw quite a lot of current. Could anything else take their place?

For years we have had light-emitting diodes (LEDs) as the indicator lamps on electronic appliances. Stereo players, CD players and dozens of products have red or white LEDs on their fascias. But these tiny components were costly – until products started being produced, in volume, in the Far East.

By assembling a cluster of LEDs in red, white or orange you get good illumination without drawing much current. In fact LED light units draw considerably less current than a comparable output from a halogen bulb. Furthermore, an LED doesn't get hot either and individual examples usually last for many years. In consequence, LED light units are now used in caravans and as exterior lights on cars, caravans, buses and boats. On the 2010 Bailey Pegasus Caravan, for example, a string of LEDs even appears in the grab handles. A drive for economy has undoubtedly helped these devices gain a foothold, especially when there's a limit to what a leisure battery can supply.

These LED lights consume little current, don't get hot, last for many years and this example can even be fitted into some holders as a replacement for a halogen bulb.

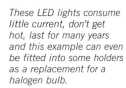

Road lights using LEDs were being fitted on 2009 motorcaravans and have also been used on touring caravans.

When the Bailey Pegasus was introduced at the end of 2009, red LED lights were fitted in the rear grab handles; white ones were fitted at the front.

END OF SEASON

If there are long periods when your caravan remains unused, you should still arrange to keep the leisure battery charged. To do this, many owners take it out of the caravan and put it on a bench at home near a charger. However, this means that if your caravan has an electronic alarm powered by the battery it will then be disarmed.

When bench-charging at home, ensure that no one smokes near the battery and check there are no naked flames (eg a pilot light) nearby. Several portable chargers will keep a battery in good condition and examples were mentioned earlier.

CONCLUSION

Older caravans were far more simple and a lot less sophisticated. For use in warm places in the summer when the evenings are light, it is hard to justify the expense of having an elaborate 12V supply system supported by a costly leisure battery.

On the other hand, today's modern caravans can be used all year round and offer all sorts of comfort features. Few owners could do without electric water pumps, twinkling spotlights, fluorescent ceiling lamps, a TV supply socket and a warm-air distribution system. But this means you're hugely dependent on a good 12V supply, so the leisure battery needs to be kept in a good state of charge, even when the caravan is parked for long spells.

CHAPTER FOURTEEN

GAS

The most popular fuel used in caravans for cooking and heating is liquefied petroleum gas, or LPG as it's usually called. It is available in Britain and abroad in cylinders that are sold in various sizes. Less pleasing is the fact that there's little standardisation in cylinder couplings. That aside, LPG is a good fuel – although it is highly flammable and needs to be treated with care, respect and understanding.

261

When the temperatures fall in winter, propane gas performs far better than butane.

Remember that LPG is highly flammable. It also has the potential to create explosions, which contributed to its development as an alternative fuel for road-going vehicles. In Europe, many cars currently use LPG as their main fuel.

Although caravanners have to learn how to use LPG safely and change cylinders when necessary, that is all that an owner is required to do. Do not attempt any work on your supply system, its components or its gas appliances. Tasks of this kind should always be entrusted to a competent gas engineer who has received formal training in the use of LPG in leisure vehicles. The Gas Safety (Installation and Use) Regulations 1998 provide further guidance on this subject.

It is also a statement of the obvious that this type of gas has to be used with the greatest of care. It also confirms why a caravanner is strongly advised to know something about LPG's characteristics, the way it can be safely used, and precautionary measures to take in the event of a leak.

If you detect a leak and the escaping gas hasn't ignited, the advice usually given is to:

- Put cigarettes out at once and extinguish any naked flames.
- Shut off individual gas control taps indoors.
- Close the valve on the supply gas cylinder.
- Open all windows, internal doors and the main entrance door.
- Check if the leak seems to come from a gas cylinder valve.
- Remove a suspected faulty cylinder from the gas locker.
- Put a faulty cylinder in a well-ventilated space outdoors.
- Consult a gas supplier regarding the safe collection of a leaking cylinder.

If there's any element of doubt relating to safety, do not remain in your caravan. Depending on the weather, however, you might choose to use the caravan as long as you cease using the gas system and any gas-operated appliances.

Safety when fitting and removing gas cylinders

When changing a cylinder, make sure there are no sources of gas ignition anywhere nearby. An electric heater, a gas water heater, pilot lights on an instantaneous water heater, an outside barbecue, a gas-operated portable awning lamp and so on should be extinguished if their proximity could lead to ignition. Equally, no one should be smoking nearby.

SWITCH OFF THE CYLINDER YOU WANT TO CHANGE. If you have an approved twin-cylinder coupling device with a manual or automatic changeover valve (described in the final section of this chapter), it *is* permissible to let the active supplying cylinder remain switched on. But you should still turn off the cylinder you want to change – there may be a small amount of gas still remaining, even if it's not sufficient to run the caravan's appliances properly.

A gas cylinder is one of several important items that's not included when you purchase a new caravan. However, it's not difficult to obtain a cylinder of liquefied petroleum gas (LPG), or to purchase an appropriate regulator if the caravan doesn't have one fitted. Once these two items are in your possession, all that remains is to couple-up, turn on the cylinder and enjoy the benefits of a clean, convenient fuel. But is it really as simple as that?

To begin with, anyone using LPG must be absolutely certain that they are handling the product safely. Linked to that is the importance of having an understanding of its characteristics.

Caravanners have to couple-up and turn on their gas cylinders themselves.

Technical Tip

Terminology
Terms that are ambiguous or inaccurate should be avoided when dealing with LPG. For example:

1 Some people wrongly refer to LPG as 'liquid' petroleum gas, which is a contradiction because a gas is a gas and a liquid is a liquid; gas engineers correctly refer to it as 'liquefied petroleum gas'.

2 You will often hear caravanners state that they need another gas 'bottle', and that can certainly confuse a new owner. Beer might be sold in bottles but LPG is sold in purpose-made 'cylinders'.

3 A cylinder is usually connected to a system using a flexible 'coupling hose'. Sometimes this is rather confusingly referred to as a 'pigtail' – a term also used by towbar fitters for a linking connection near a towball. The term 'pigtail' is therefore avoided in this chapter.

4 With the exception of stainless steel flexible pipes used for coupling-up, a coupling hose in a gas system is made of synthetic materials that include rubber. However, to call it a 'rubber hose' would be ill advised, because that might tempt someone to try coupling-up with an ordinary piece of rubber hose they found in their garage. Only approved coupling hose should be used which complies with current standards.

5 Coupling hose is available in Low Pressure (LP) and High Pressure (HP) varieties, as marked on the sides. The correct choice of hose is important, as described later.

For the sake of clarity, the terminologies preferred by gas specialists will be used in this chapter.

Only approved coupling hose should be used. The markings here confirm that this is high-pressure hose that left the factory in September 2008.

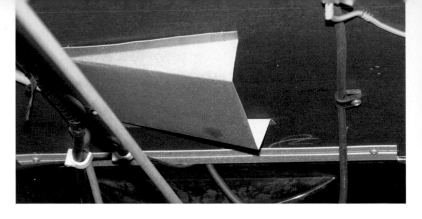

Never cover the drop-out holes in a caravan, which are formed so that leaking gas can escape. On the underside of the floor, this one is fitted with a draught shield.

CHARACTERISTICS OF LPG

An understanding of LPG's characteristics helps to reinforce why precautionary measures must never be treated lightly. Note the following points:

- ☐ In its natural state, LPG is *not* poisonous.
- ☐ Caravanners use two types of LPG – butane and propane.
- ☐ LPG does *not* have a smell, which means that leaks might not be noticed.
- ☐ To warn of leaks, distributors add what is called a 'stenching agent'.
- ☐ LPG is denser than air and if a leak occurs the gas sinks to the lowest point.
- ☐ LPG reacts with some chemicals, which means that jointing compounds, pipes and coupling hose must be products that are specifically intended for use with butane and propane.
- ☐ The gas escape outlets in a caravan are called 'drop-out holes' and should never be covered up.
- ☐ When using an appropriate regulator, the gas appliances installed in British caravans run on butane or propane without requiring any adjustments.
- ☐ Since LPG is highly flammable it must be stored in accordance with the LP Gas Association Codes of Practice.

STORAGE

At points of sale

Retailers and site operators supplying gas have to comply with strict rules when storing and handling LPG cylinders. For example, on rare occasions cylinder valves have become faulty and leakage occurs. Noting the earlier point that the gas is denser than air and sinks to the lowest point,

storage facilities must allow leaking gas to disperse safely. That's why mesh cages are normally used and situated outdoors, well away from any potential source of ignition.

In your caravan

Manufacturers have to comply with strict specifications and gas cylinder lockers must have low-level drop-out holes. The most common place for a cylinder locker is at the front of a caravan. However, caravans built by Avondale usually have lockers situated on one side and close to the axle.

A storage locker should also offer a minimum of 30 minutes' fire resistance. However, in view of caravan structures some experts regard compliance with this expectation as unreasonably hard to achieve.

External access is required too, and the locker should be totally sealed from the living area. However, there have been models built in the past where a small hatch inside the caravan at the front enables a user to reach into the gas locker to close or open a cylinder valve. That was not considered good practice and the idea was dropped soon after its introduction.

In addition, a gas cylinder locker must never be used to accommodate a battery, contain fuses, include a light or be used as a routeway for electrical cabling unless it is wholly sealed in a conduit. Anything that could create a spark is considered dangerous, although a few models now have recessed, sealed and covered niches that contain light-emitting diodes for illumination.

A robust and reliable way of securing cylinders in an upright position is also crucially important, recognising that bumpy roads pose a challenge to any fixing system.

At home

During a long lay-up period some owners remove their cylinders, but it is not safe to store them in a house. In fact the worst place of all is in a cellar,

Site operators often supply gas cylinders, but storage regulations have to be strictly observed.

Unlike the majority of caravans, models from Avondale are usually fitted with a gas cylinder locker on one of the side walls.

Don't make this bad mistake. The gas cylinder has been stored alongside a can of petrol and a 12V battery that could create a spark.

266

since this is normally devoid of low-level ventilation outlets. In the event of a cylinder valve developing a leak, the heavier-than-air gas then has nowhere to escape, so it accumulates around the lowest parts of the floor.

A garage is often unsafe too, especially if it's used for a car, to store a petrol can and to charge a battery. It's better to store a cylinder externally in a weather-protected and well-ventilated position.

TYPES OF LPG

Two different types of LPG are used by caravanners in Britain. One is called butane, the other is propane, and their respective characteristics need to be recognised.

It can be extremely dangerous to lay a cylinder on its side. If a tiny amount of liquefied gas seeps through a leaking valve it will change into a large volume of gas.

Always keep a cylinder in its upright position
It is not unknown for valves on cylinders to develop a small leak. For instance, if grit or grass gets caught in the spring-loaded steel ball that forms the seal on a Campingaz cylinder, the obstruction may lead to a seepage of gas. Sometimes you can even hear a faint hiss.

The problem is usually solved by taking a Campingaz cylinder outdoors, checking that there's no flame nearby and depressing the ball very briefly with a small screwdriver. A sharp blast of escaping gas occurs instantaneously and usually dislodges the obstruction, whereupon the steel ball reseats itself correctly.

The valves on other types of cylinders can also develop leaks and it's therefore extremely dangerous to lay a cylinder on its side. A tiny drop of liquefied butane gas trickling from a cylinder resting on its side will multiply in volume around 233 times as it converts into a gas. The increase in volume of propane is approximately 274 times greater. The potential hazard of this is clearly apparent.

Butane

Key points about butane:

☐ It is widely sold throughout Europe. There are many suppliers, many different sizes of cylinder and (unfortunately) many dissimilar connecting systems.

☐ It has a higher calorific value than propane and since it burns at a slightly slower rate it's a more efficient heat producer.

☐ It presents problems in cold conditions because it doesn't change from its liquefied state into a gas. This occurs when temperatures fall to –2°C (around 29°F) at atmospheric pressure. Accordingly, butane is *not* the preferred gas for winter use or for visits to cold regions.

☐ It is heavier than propane. Taking the smallest cylinder sold by Calor Gas as an example, the propane version holds 3.9kg (8.6lb) whereas an identically sized cylinder filled with butane holds 4.5kg (10lb).

☐ A small volume of liquefied butane converts to a very much larger volume of gas. The difference is about 1:233.

In Britain, butane supplied by Calor Gas Ltd and by Campingaz is sold in blue cylinders.

Propane

Key points about propane:

• This is the preferred winter fuel because it changes from a liquefied state into gas in temperatures as low as –45°C.

☐ Outside the United Kingdom, it is harder to find propane in portable cylinders for leisure activities, although 11kg and 13kg propane cylinders are available in France, Italy and Spain.

☐ Some processing companies add a small amount of propane to their butane cylinders in order to improve cold-weather performance.

At one time the butane cylinders from Calor Gas were light green but nowadays they are always painted blue.

Technical Tip

When temperatures fall, the rate at which liquefied butane changes to gas decreases progressively. So, even though the temperature in a gas cylinder locker might still be above freezing point, a significant reduction in the output of gas often becomes apparent, especially if you're cooking a meal and trying to run a space heater and water heater *at the same time*. On noting a lower than normal flame on the hob, many caravanners wrongly presume that the cylinder is nearly empty and fit a replacement prematurely.

Propane gas, which is sold by Calor Gas in red cylinders, is able to convert from its liquefied form in temperatures as low as –45°C.

☐ It is lighter than butane in its liquefied state. If you check two cylinders of identical size, you'll see from markings on the side that the propane one holds less in weight than butane.

☐ A small volume of liquefied propane converts to a very much larger volume of gas. The difference is about 1:274.

☐ It has a vapour pressure that is considerably greater than butane. Note how this affects the type of gas regulator required as described later in this chapter.

☐ The 'off-take' rate of a propane cylinder permits it to run more gas appliances simultaneously than a butane cylinder. This is similarly beneficial when running appliances like a high-performance space heater that consumes a large quantity of gas.

In Britain, propane supplied by Calor Gas for caravanning is sold in red cylinders; the Calor Gas propane 'Patio Gas' cylinders are green. BP Gas Light propane cylinders are green and white.

WHICH GAS SHOULD YOU USE?

Having considered the differences between butane and propane, you will immediately appreciate why caravanners who only go away in the summer usually keep to butane. In contrast many year-round caravanners use propane all the time. Others run both types of gas, but the different cylinder couplings need to be recognised. For example, owners of caravans manufactured pre-1 September 2003 will need two cylinder-mounted regulators to suit the types of gas being used.

On later caravans there's a wall-mounted 'universal' regulator that's designed to operate with either gas. However, this necessitates the purchase of both a butane and a propane connecting hose because the respective cylinder couplings are different.

Some owners use both butane and propane gas; on pre-1 September 2003 caravans this means that two cylinder-mounted regulators will have to be purchased.

Calor is the most commonly used gas in the UK. In addition to the company's wide variety of cylinders you also have a choice of butane or propane gas. You will also find that many dealers allow you to exchange an empty butane cylinder for a full propane one, and vice versa. Irrespective of these options, caravanners soon decide which products they like best and their preference is often determined by seasonal issues and destinations.

Large cylinders used outside a caravan can cause damage if knocked over; the caravanning clubs strongly discourage this practice.

THE RANGE OF SUPPLIER-FILLED CYLINDERS

In the UK several specialists sell gas cylinders to leisure users, and the introduction of owner-refillable portable cylinders has also been well-received by many caravanners.

In this competitive field, Calor products are used in both the UK domestic *and* leisure markets. For instance, large cylinders are supplied to homeowners for their daily domestic needs, although Calor's 19kg propane products are too heavy and bulky to transport in touring caravans. Remember, too, that a cylinder should never be transported horizontally in case liquefied gas was to seep through its valve mechanism. Equally, a gas cylinder should always be mounted securely in a caravan gas locker. Standing a cylinder outside a caravan is potentially dangerous and the practice is strongly discouraged by caravanning clubs.

In spite of the popularity of Calor Gas in this country, the company's products are not available abroad. In contrast, Campingaz is available in over 100 countries worldwide and cylinders are available in most European countries. But there are exceptions: Campingaz is not available in Finland or Sweden and is seldom stocked in Norway.

Also bear in mind that Campingaz cylinders only

The largest Campingaz cylinder, referred to as the 907, only holds 2.72kg of butane. The small one on the right is really only suitable for running a camping stove.

Two sizes of BP Gas Light are currently in production and their composite plastic containers are claimed to be half the weight of an equivalent-sized steel cylinder.

The Calor Lite cylinders are made using recyclable steel and are fitted with an internal float mechanism that operates a level-indicator needle.

contain butane, which can present a problem for winter caravanners. It is believed that a small amount of propane is added to improve performance in cold environments but this strategy is not revealed on the cylinders' markings. Furthermore, only the 907 cylinder is suitable to meet the typical consumption requirements in modern caravans. This is the *largest* cylinder in the Campingaz range and it only holds 2.72kg of butane: even the *smallest* butane cylinder in the Calor Gas range holds 4.5kg of butane.

Notwithstanding the long-standing use of Calor Gas and Campingaz in Britain, the choices increased further when BP introduced 'Gas Light' cylinders in 2006. These are being marketed in conjunction with Truma UK, and the corrosion-proof cylinders made of a composite plastic containing glass fibre are claimed to be half the weight of steel cylinders of equivalent capacities. Part of its structure is semi-transparent too, so you can see the level of the LPG inside.

Two sizes of BP Gas Light cylinders have been introduced and these hold 5kg and 10kg of propane respectively. However, some caravan lockers are not able to accommodate the larger product, which is 587mm high; both have a diameter of 305mm. As regards coupling-up, Gas Light cylinders have a 27mm clip-on valve and many owners need to purchase an adaptor in order to use these products.

In response to the BP weight-saving initiative, Calor subsequently launched a new lightweight cylinder in autumn 2007. Known as the Calor Lite, this is filled with propane; it is made using recyclable lightweight steel and fitted with plastic handles. The Calor Lite cylinder is also fitted with a level-indicator that uses the float mechanism introduced in 2005 for use with the Company's 'Patio Gas' propane cylinders.

Though slightly taller, Calor Lite 6kg cylinders are otherwise the same dimensions as existing standard 6kg Calor Gas cylinders; they also employ the screw-thread 'pole' couplings fitted on the Company's current 3.9kg, 6kg and 13kg propane cylinders.

The alloy collar on this Calor Gas cylinder indicates that its empty weight is 17lb 6oz. This converts to 7.88kg, and the weight of the gas it contains is 6kg.

When filled with 6kg of propane, a Calor Lite cylinder weighs a total of 10.52kg.

By comparison, the alloy collar on Calor's equivalent 'heavy' cylinder records a tare (*ie* cylinder-only) weight of 17lb 6oz – *ie* 7.88kg – and when added to the gas content (6kg) totals 13.88kg. In other words the new Calor Lite cylinder is 3.36kg (about 7.4lb) lighter than its big brother, which is a significant saving in weight.

Technical Tip

Cylinder sizes

The weight in kilograms with its approximate equivalent in pounds relates *only* to the gas itself. On Calor products this is clearly marked on the cylinder. It does *not* relate to the total weight of both the cylinder and its gas content.

Calor products

3.9kg (8.6lb) propane } Same external
4.5kg (10lb) butane } size of cylinder

6kg (13.2lb) propane } Same external
7kg (15.4lb) butane } size of cylinder

13kg (28.7lb) propane } Same external
15kg (33lb) butane } size of cylinder

19kg (41.9lb) propane

6kg (13.2lb) propane Calor Lite cylinder (introduced 2007)

Calor gas butane cylinders are painted blue. Calor gas propane cylinders are painted red.

Note: *The larger cylinders, notably 13kg propane, 15kg butane and 19kg propane, will often be found in use on permanent pitches but are normally too large for safe transport. Caravan locker compartments are not designed to accommodate cylinders of these sizes and it has already been emphasised that a cylinder should never be transported on its side.*

Campingaz products

0.45kg (1lb) butane
1.81kg (4lb) butane
2.72 kg (6lb) butane

Campingaz cylinders are painted blue.

Note: *Only the Type 907 Campingaz 2.72kg butane cylinder is a practical proposition for the caravanner. The two smaller cylinders are really intended for camping use only.*

BP Gas Light cylinders

5kg (11.02lb) propane
10kg (22.04lb) propane

BP Gas Light cylinders are coloured green and white.

Gaslow owner-refillable cylinders

6kg (13.2lb) propane
11kg (24.3lb) propane

Gaslow cylinders are coloured yellow.

The Calor Lite cylinder is fitted with a small gauge that shows how much gas is left. On this cylinder, the needle indicates that it's completely empty.

The gauges from Gaslow indicate a cylinder's state-of-fill when appliances are in use; they are also used to indicate if there is a leak in a gas supply system.

The Truma Sonatic device uses ultrasonics to establish how much gas there is in a popular-sized Calor Gas cylinder. The information is shown on a small display screen.

It is helpful to weigh a new cylinder on some scales and to note the findings. Further checks reveal how much gas remains after it has been used.

How full is the cylinder?

Finding out how much gas is left in a part-used cylinder isn't easy unless you use a Calor Lite cylinder, which has a gauge, or a BP Gas Light cylinder, which has translucent sides. To assist owners of other cylinders, several products are made which can reveal a cylinder's 'state-of-fill'. For example, Gaslow gauges are useful purchases, although they only tell you a cylinder's state-of-fill when an appliance is actually in operation – *ie* when gas is being drawn from the supply.

In contrast the Sonatic system from Truma uses ultrasonics to check a cylinder's state-of-fill, and its findings are relayed to a liquid crystal display mounted inside the caravan. At present, however, the Sonatic is only available for operation with Calor Gas 7kg butane or 6kg propane cylinders.

A simple but effective alternative is to weigh a freshly purchased cylinder on your bathroom scales in order to establish the combined weight of both the cylinder and its gas contents. Since the weight of gas in a new cylinder is often marked on the side, you can then calculate what part of the total weight is represented by the cylinder itself. In addition, whenever you recheck the total weight after some of the gas has been drawn off, it's then easy to work out how much gas is remaining.

OWNER-REFILLABLE CYLINDERS

The sale of refillable cylinders has become a contentious issue on safety grounds. For example, liquefied gas is delivered from many forecourt pumps at some force and any spillage on your hands leaves painful injuries. There are other safety issues too, just as there are when petrol is dispensed by a member of the public into a portable can.

Also be aware that a gas vessel should never be filled more than 85–87%, which is why it should be fitted with a European Pi approved filler valve. This device automatically shuts off the gas as soon as a tank or cylinder reaches its 80% limit. Some refillable portable cylinders *do* incorporate an approved, automatic cut-off device: others don't, and the user is expected instead to watch the rising level of the liquefied gas through a sighting zone in the side of the cylinder. This can be difficult. Controlling a fast-filling fuel dispenser with accuracy may prove challenging, and overfilling can have disastrous consequences. The situation is especially dangerous if you drive with an over-full cylinder in your caravan, because a change in air pressure can cause its contents to expand.

Not surprisingly, gas specialists became very concerned about the introduction of refillable gas cylinders that were not equipped with automatic safety cut-off valves. In acknowledgement of this and other concerns, a statement published by the LP Gas Association (IS24, June 2007) expressed the views of its members very clearly. The LPGA document asserts that permanently fixed gas 'vessels' intended for heating and cooking 'may be permitted to be re-filled at autogas refuelling sites *provided* they:
☐ remain in situ for refilling; and

273

The 6kg and 11kg refillable propane cylinders from Gaslow are fitted with an over-pressure relief valve and an automatic shut-off device to prevent overfilling.

☐ are fitted with a device to physically prevent filling beyond 80%; and
☐ are connected to a fixed filling connector which is not part of the vessel.'

– in other words, appropriately installed tanks are deemed acceptable. So, too, are the specially-made cylinders sold by Gaslow, provided they are permanently installed and connected to an autogas filler point using Gaslow's stainless steel pipe. This filler should also be a permanent fixture mounted on the caravan. The components in this system carry a 15-year warranty, at which point the cylinder (which is marked with a date) must be exchanged.

Of course, not everyone wants to spend a three-

(i) Technical Tip

The Gaslow refillable system

In response to the safety concerns described in the text, Gaslow, a long-established gas specialist, has designed a safe, caravan-specific owner-refillable installation. Products available from Gaslow include yellow portable cylinders, which are installed to act like the fixed tanks sometimes used on motor caravans. With capacities (in gas weight) of 6kg and 11kg respectively, these carry a 15-year warranty; after that period they can be replaced for a small fee. The cylinders are manufactured with a European Pi-approved filler valve that shuts off automatically when the gas vessel is 80% full. They also have an over-pressure release valve. Other components in a Gaslow installation kit include:

- a 0.6m length of semi-flexible, rubber-free, stainless steel pipe; and
- a filler coupling for mounting externally on the wall of a caravan. This is the type used on many LPG converted cars.

When the fitting work is carried out, a cylinder (or cylinders) must be installed in the caravan's locker and fixed permanently in place. A cylinder also has to be coupled-up to a wall-mounted filler, using the stainless steel pipe provided. Three optional filling adaptors are also available as 'extras' from Gaslow, to match different European coupling systems.

To refill a cylinder in a Gaslow installation, the caravan has to be towed to a fuel station that's equipped with LPG pumps. Since this can sometimes be inconvenient, some owners pair a Gaslow product with a dealer-exchange cylinder. Various combinations of cylinder are permissible and Gaslow also supplies manual and automatic changeover regulators.

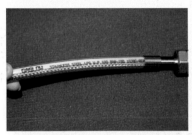

An installation kit from Gaslow includes a 0.6m length of rubber-free, semi-flexible stainless steel tubing that carries a 15-year warranty.

One of these filler couplings has to be fitted externally on a caravan. This is the same type as is used on many cars that run on LPG.

figure sum to have a tank or a fixed cylinder system installed, but safe and easy-to-use systems are now available. Moreover, a Gaslow system can often be uninstalled, transferred, and refixed in another caravan without requiring major alterations. But is an owner-refillable system worthwhile?

Perhaps the main attraction is the fact that gas drawn from an LPG pump at a filling station is considerably less expensive than gas supplied with an exchange cylinder. In other words, an owner who goes caravanning regularly, especially in winter, might purchase a sufficient quantity of gas to recuperate the cost of a refillable cylinder and its installation quite quickly.

There are also advantages if you travel abroad; Autogas stations supplying gas-powered cars dispense propane which is the chosen fuel of many caravanners. Sometimes a coupling adaptor might be needed but these are available from gas specialists.

REGULATORS

A regulator is an essential component in a caravan's gas supply system. Its function is to ensure that gas is supplied to appliances at a consistent and appropriate pressure regardless of whether the supply cylinder is brimful or approaching exhaustion. The pressure of gas in a cylinder is also affected by changing temperatures and that's another reason why a regulator is needed.

Inside its casing there's a diaphragm that stabilises the flow of gas and delivers it at the pressure required by the gas appliances. It's essential that a regulator is protected from the weather because its diaphragm relies on a tiny breather hole in the casing, which mustn't get blocked. If rain is able to enter this hole during cold spells in winter, it could freeze, thereby upsetting the diaphragm's operation.

Technical Tip

If you ever get a frightening tall flame on a stove burner, this is 'over-gassing', which is usually caused by a faulty regulator. The condition typically occurs when the breather hole on a regulator gets blocked.

The diaphragm in a regulator cannot operate properly if the tiny breather hole in its casing gets blocked with dust or frozen water.

Technical Tip

What is the age of your caravan?

An important change to gas supply systems came into effect on 1 September 2003. This revision introduced a new working pressure for caravan gas systems and prompted alterations to regulators and coupling hose.

Some readers will own a caravan built *before* that date; others will own one built *after* that date. Since this has significance with regard to your gas system both types are described here.

A number of newer caravans fitted with the revised installation have also suffered from gas starvation, damaged regulators and poorly performing appliances. An explanation for this and the way to cure problems are described in the sections that follow.

This butane regulator with its own gas control knob is purpose-designed to fit the connection on a Campingaz cylinder.

Apart from the need to keep a breather hole clear, there is nothing in a caravan's regulator to service or adjust. Accordingly its casing is sealed and a regulator normally gives unfailing service for several years. Opinion is divided in respect of making a routine replacement. Some specialists stipulate every five years; others quote ten years – or at any time when it shows evidence of wear and damage.

Changes to systems

For many years it has been necessary for anyone buying a caravan to purchase a regulator to match the type of gas cylinder they want to use. It stands to reason that if a regulator is designed to be mounted on top of a cylinder, the respective couplings have to match. In addition, a different regulator is needed to fit a cylinder containing butane from the regulator needed to fit a propane cylinder.

Unfortunately for those caravanners who tour widely throughout Europe, the huge variety of cylinder connections means that an array of regulators or adaptors might have to be purchased.

When travelling in Europe and using different types of cylinder it's often necessary to purchase coupling adaptors. Here are three of the more popular ones sold by specialists like Gaslow:

The push-on adaptor for BP Gas Light cylinders, which permits connection using a Calor-type threaded cap nut.

This adaptor is often needed for Spanish cylinders. Others are available for Norway, Portugal and the Republic of Ireland.

If you don't have a regulator to fit a Campingaz cylinder, this adaptor allows you to couple-up to one that has a threaded cap nut.

There have also been problems for companies importing and exporting caravans. In Germany, for example, gas appliances installed in caravans and motorhomes used to be manufactured to run at the higher pressure of 50mbar. In Britain, however, appliances were fitted to run on 28mbar (butane) and 37mbar (propane) without needing adjustment.

It became increasingly clear that standardisation of products and practices was needed in European Union member states. New European Norms were therefore published in 2001 (BS EN 12864) and 2002 (BS EN 1949), and these made radical changes that affected both regulators and cylinder coupling arrangements. The new standards were implemented by UK manufacturers on 1 September, 2003.

Recognising the fact that some readers own or intend to purchase a caravan built before autumn 2003, the earlier systems need to be explained. So, too, do the gas systems installed in post-2003 models.

Systems in caravans built before 1 September 2003

As mentioned already, mounting a regulator directly on top of a supply cylinder has been customary practice for many years. In addition, cylinder-mounted regulators have to match the type of gas and the style of coupling. To eliminate any chance of fitting an incorrect regulator, a propane cylinder always has a different coupling from a butane one.

On some butane cylinders there's a push-fit arrangement; on others there's a threaded coupling and you need to tighten this using a spanner.

Remember, too, that Calor Gas screw-type couplings have a *reverse thread*. So forget the usual convention for threaded fixings. To carry out

Since the gas appliances fitted in a caravan have to be compatible with its installed gas supply system, gas specialists state categorically that anyone owning a caravan built before 1 September 2003 must not attempt to install the regulators and supply arrangements used for models built after that date.

277

Regulator spanner
Coupling a regulator to a Campingaz cylinder doesn't need a spanner; equally, a regulator to suit Calor's clip-on system doesn't require special tools either. However, all the Calor Gas propane cylinders, together with Calor's 4.5kg butane cylinders, require a spanner to tighten up the regulator connection. Accordingly, open-ended spanners are sold at caravan accessory shops.

But be warned. If someone else coupled your regulator using a plumber's wrench and unnecessary zeal, a Calor spanner isn't likely to be tough enough to loosen it when your cylinder needs changing. That's not something you want to discover when it's dark, cold, and pouring with rain.

Calor Gas sells an inexpensive spanner for tightening regulators that are attached using a threaded cap nut.

Procedure when fitting and removing gas cylinders

NEVER COUPLE OR UNCOUPLE A GAS CYLINDER NEAR A SOURCE OF IGNITION LIKE A FLAME OR A LIT CIGARETTE.

1. *Campingaz cylinders*
Since there's a screw thread on top of a Campingaz cylinder, it means that when the regulator or adaptor finally loosens a small quantity of gas usually hisses out while the valve ball reseats itself. So act promptly to complete the disconnection. The same thing occurs very briefly when connecting a new cylinder.

In view of this brief moment of leakage, you might prefer to lift a Campingaz cylinder out of the locker while making the connections. It also helps to hold the regulator and to rotate the cylinder itself, rather than the other way round which merely twists the connecting hose.

2. *Screw-thread Calor cylinders*
1. When connecting and disconnecting a cylinder, always make sure first that the cylinder's handwheel is OFF – *ie* turned fully clockwise (this has a conventional right-hand thread).
2. When a new Calor butane cylinder is supplied, it normally has a small black cap over the threaded outlet. Remove this by turning it CLOCKWISE when looking at its dome (the coupling has a left-hand thread). Keep it for when you return the empty cylinder.
3. When a new propane cylinder is supplied, it has a small black plug in the coupling. Remove this with a large slotted screwdriver, turning it CLOCKWISE when looking at the slot (the coupling has a left-hand thread).
4. Check the connection surfaces (whether it's a butane or propane cylinder) to confirm they're clean and unobstructed. Then offer-up the threaded coupling. Hand-tighten it first, turning it ANTI-CLOCKWISE, and complete the job using an open-ended spanner. Since they don't have a washer, propane couplings have to be tight.
5. Turn on the gas cylinder's hand-wheel, checking immediately for a hiss or smell. For a more thorough DIY test, apply a proprietary leak-detecting fluid or a prepared mix of soapy

Low-pressure hose is only fitted when a regulator is directly coupled to a cylinder. This should be tightly secured to the regulator's ribbed nozzle using a hose clip.

a coupling exercise you have to rotate the nut anti-clockwise to couple your regulator to a Calor Gas cylinder and vice versa if you want to remove it.

One of the implications of fitting a regulator directly to a cylinder is the fact that gas pressure is immediately reduced and it can then be fed to a caravan's fixed copper pipes using a short length of approved *low-pressure* (LP) hose. This will be marked on the side, together with the date when it left the factory. It can also be coupled satisfactorily to the main supply pipe and the regulator using good-quality hose clips.

During an annual habitation service, the short length of low-pressure coupling hose will be replaced. Get this done even earlier if a hose shows premature wear or distortion, particularly near the clipping points.

This coupling system, which has been used for many years, has much to commend it – apart from the fact that regulators have to be cylinder-specific. However, regulators for cylinder mounting are not unduly expensive and (at the time of writing) are often sold for less than £10.

water to the coupling areas. Then look closely for bubbles, which signify an escape of gas.

6. When returning an empty cylinder to a supplier, the plastic cap (butane) or plastic plug (propane) should be refitted.

3. Clip-on Calor cylinders

No tools are needed to connect or disconnect this type of coupling. Furthermore, there isn't an ON/OFF turn-wheel; instead, the ON/OFF control is an integral part of a clip-on regulator or adaptor. On the regulator shown alongside, a retaining collar won't permit disconnection until the tap is turned OFF.

Preparing a new cylinder – Rotate the orange cap so that its arrow points towards the opening in the cylinder shroud. Remove the cap by pulling on the plastic strap and lifting as you do so.

Attaching a clip-on regulator – The retaining collar is lifted up with the thumb while the regulator is pushed down onto the cylinder connection.

Switching on the gas – Once the regulator has seated properly and the retaining collar has been lowered you can rotate the operating tap to the vertical ON position.

Disconnecting a clip-on regulator – The design of a clip-on regulator intentionally ensures that the release collar can only be pushed upwards when the turn-tap is in its OFF position.

When a cylinder is exhausted the orange cap is pushed back onto the coupling.

 Technical Tip

Neither propane screw couplings nor Calor clip-on couplings have sealing washers. However, if you use a screw-on butane regulator to suit Calor's 4.5kg butane cylinder, it has a washer that *must* be changed regularly. A packet of three washers costs pennies rather than pounds. Some caravanners think they can reuse the washer fitted in the screw-on cap that's supplied with a refilled 4.5kg cylinder. *Don't!* It's not made of the correct compound and will soon be the source of a leak.

The washer fitted to a butane regulator that's attached to a cylinder with a threaded cap nut needs replacing periodically.

To avoid purchasing a packet of washers, some caravanners use the washer from this plastic cover. However, it is not suitable for the job.

279

280

Wall-mounted 30mbar 'universal' regulators fitted in Avondale's gas lockers are from Clesse and are usually mounted high in the compartment as recommended.

Many caravans have Truma 30mbar 'universal' regulators. Note the high-pressure flexible hose with factory-fitted connectors for coupling-up to a cylinder.

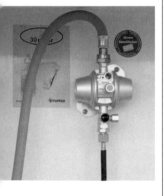

Some German caravans are supplied with a 30mbar regulator designed for connecting directly to a cylinder in place of a wall-mounted product.

Systems in motorcaravans built after 1 September 2003

The publication of new European Norms/British Standards prompted changes to gas regulators, and the type of hose used to couple-up to cylinders. Here are some of the main innovations:

☐ A new design of 'universal' regulator was developed that would operate using either butane or propane.

☐ A new standardised working pressure of 30mbar was introduced. Gas appliances now being installed are set to work at this pressure and are labelled accordingly.

☐ The new 30mbar regulators are almost always fixed on the wall or ceiling of gas cylinder lockers, thereby forming part of a caravan's factory-installed supply system. This practice means that regulators now receive manufacturers' soundness checks, together with the rest of the installation, before leaving the factory.

☐ The only component which a new owner has to purchase is a factory-made *high-pressure* coupling hose with crimp-fit connectors. These connectors are important and the types of hose clips hitherto used on low-pressure hoses must *not* be fitted.

☐ High-pressure hoses with different couplings are now manufactured. Whereas the connector for coupling to a wall-mounted regulator is standard, the connector on the other end has to suit the owner's choice of gas cylinder.

☐ Although there are coupling hoses to suit most types of cylinder connections used throughout Europe, a few systems require the owner to purchase an adaptor.

☐ Notwithstanding the benefits offered by wall-mounted regulators, a few German manufacturers continue to supply cylinder-mounted regulators instead. Although these are 30mbar 'universal' regulators handling both butane and propane, their connections have to suit the owner's preferred type of cylinder.

During servicing operations, technicians inspecting poorly performing gas appliances found that an 'oily liquid' was contaminating regulators and affecting the gas supply.

Problems with the new system

The change to wall-mounted, butane/propane 30mbar regulators together with a high-pressure coupling hose offers improved convenience when travelling in Europe. However, since the introduction of this system there have been several incidents where caravanners have experienced gas blockages and consequent problems with appliances.

There have also been reports of an 'oily liquid' appearing in gas supply pipes as shown in the accompanying photograph.

Intense investigation and laboratory analysis of the curious liquid has revealed that it contains a plasticising agent. It subsequently transpired that this was the product used in the manufacture of flexible rubberised hoses.

Investigators were also mindful that the high-pressure hose linking a cylinder to a wall-mounted regulator was providing a pathway for gas flowing at *cylinder pressure*. In older installations, the hose handles gas at *lower pressure* because the regulators are mounted directly to the top of its supply cylinder.

It was subsequently found that when appliances were not being used, condensation sometimes developed in the high-pressure gas hose that couples a cylinder to a wall-mounted regulator. If plasticising compounds then percolate (*ie* leach) out of a hose's material and mix with this condensate, the product is almost certainly the mysterious 'oily liquid'. Furthermore, if this contaminated condensation then trickles down a sloping hose into a regulator, it would undoubtedly interfere with the operation of its diaphragm. It was concluded that this must account for the reported problems of gas blockages and failing regulators.

A document published in January 2007 by The National Caravan Council (NCC) described the findings of investigations in some detail. The advice subsequently sent to dealers was to check that an installed regulator is mounted *higher* than the outlet of the gas supply cylinder. If that isn't

This regulator is mounted high in its gas locker and has a short extension pipe at the top with an elbow, thereby creating a marked downward slope on the coupling hose.

the case, qualified installers have been advised to raise the regulator so that the coupling hose would slope down to the cylinder itself. To gain height, extension outlets and elbow joints are often fitted too. This means that any condensation flows back to the cylinder instead of entering and upsetting the operation of the regulator.

To provide further protection, Gaslow has also introduced couplings that comprise a semi-flexible stainless steel ribbed pipe covered with a braided steel sheath. This is completely free of plasticising compounds and acts as a logical alternative to traditional rubber-composition coupling hose.

Time will tell whether these recommended measures will end the blockage issue and The National Caravan Council concedes that the phenomenon was totally unexpected. The published document affirms that there is no inherent fault in either the gas or the individual components in post-2003 systems. It is also interesting to acknowledge that blockages don't seem to occur in the earlier systems that employ cylinder-mounted regulators.

Changeover systems

A caravan's gas locker has space to accommodate *two*

Below right: To eliminate the possibility of a plasticiser acting as a contaminant, Gaslow has introduced flexible stainless steel coupling pipe that is entirely free of rubberised compounds.

Below: If an owner of a recent caravan wants to couple to a propane cylinder, this stainless steel coupling from Gaslow has a hand-wheel tightener so that a spanner isn't needed.

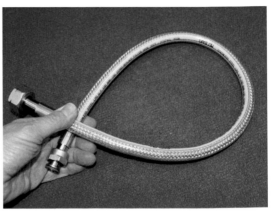

This caravan is fitted with a manual changeover system. High-pressure hoses from the two cylinders link with the regulator, and the hand-wheel valves on top of the cylinders determine which one supplies the gas.

283

gas cylinders. Most owners ensure that two cylinders are duly fitted, and some caravanners have a manual or an automatic changeover device fitted as well.

When a supply cylinder runs out, this permits a hasty switchover because it eliminates the need to uncouple and reconnect hoses. Several products are manufactured and there are changeovers to suit a variety of combinations including:

☐ Systems conforming to earlier British Standards with cylinder-mounted regulators.
☐ Post-2003 supply systems with a 30mbar wall-mounted regulator.
☐ Post-2003 supply systems with a wall-mounted regulator and supplied by a pair of Gaslow's refillable cylinders.
☐ Post-2003 supply systems with a wall-mounted regulator and supplied by one Gaslow refillable cylinder paired with one normal propane cylinder.

As stated earlier, LPG is certainly a convenient product to use but it helps to have good understanding of the many types of gas supply components. That, in turn, enables you to get the best from a caravan's system.

Some caravanners have an automatic changeover device fitted so that a switchover from an emptied cylinder to its partner is carried out without owner-intervention.

CHAPTER FIFTEEN

COOKING
AND HEATING
APPLIANCES

Following on from the earlier chapters which describe mains electricity and gas systems in caravans, this chapter looks at cooking and heating appliances. Many different products have been fitted in the last 30 years and it would be impossible to provide detailed operating instructions relating to individual appliances. However, there are some general issues to note that are discussed in the sections which follow.

285

The array of kitchen appliances in this 2010 Bailey Pegasus shows how well-equipped many modern caravans can be.

Like many high specification modern caravans, this Bailey Pegasus has a four-burner hob.

On the Avondale Landranger 6400, the gas isolation valves are clearly labelled.

At one time, LPG was merely used to run a small hob and a couple of wall-mounted gas lights. With only two burners on many hobs, the preparation of a meal called for some forethought – but few caravanners complained. It would have been unthinkable in those days to envisage the level of provision that is commonplace today. Many modern caravans offer four-burner hobs and a few include an electrically-powered hotplate.

However, when the number of gas-operated appliances increased, caravan designers realised that the supply system had to adopt practices similar to those used for electrical wiring. In this arrangement a main trunk route comes from the cylinder regulator, which then sub-divides into branches to provide separate supplies to individual appliances. There also has to be a control facility in order to isolate different gas appliances.

To achieve this, today's caravans have a series of gas isolation valves that control the flow serving each of the branches. These are usually well labelled and the information is normally reproduced in the caravan's owner's manual. If a manual is missing, you can often follow the route of the pipes, albeit on your knees, with a torch and maybe a mirror as well. Having established what each pipe seems to serve, you can verify your observations by igniting appliances individually and then closing off the valves. When you have identified the appliances being served by the different valves, it's then just a matter of marking them with adhesive labels.

Not that gas is the only fuel used for cooking and heating in caravans. Mains electricity also plays an ever-increasing part and recent experiments in space heating have used a small tank for diesel fuel as well. Now let's look at the all-important subject of safety.

Gas specialists like Calor Ltd sell carbon monoxide detectors that emit a warning if a dangerous situation develops.

SAFETY

When you buy a new caravan, its gas appliances will have been installed in accordance with the regulations applicable to LPG appliances in leisure vehicles. Documents provided with a purchase should verify their compliance, and certification papers are often signed by the LPG gas specialist who inspected the installation.

Things are seldom as straightforward when you purchase a second-hand caravan. Ideally, a pre-owned caravan will be supplied with a recently signed and dated certificate to confirm the integrity of the supply system and its appliances. A good service centre can arrange for this to be carried out prior to the sale and signed/dated documents will give a purchaser assurance that the gas system is in safe working order.

That's the 'ideal world'. In reality it's not unusual to find that this certification is missing and then it's up to you to have the checks carried out before putting your newly acquired caravan into commission. It only needs something like the gas/air mixture to be out of adjustment on a hob and there's a risk that carbon monoxide will be emitted. Since this can have disastrous consequences, always have your appliances checked and serviced regularly.

Bearing in mind the potential danger of carbon monoxide poisoning, some caravanners fit a battery-operated detection device. These are sold by specialists like Calor Gas and products can also be found on sale in many DIY stores.

When a caravan is built, its manufacturer also has to make provisions for possible gas leaks. These have to serve both the supply system and individual gas appliances. This is why there are several low-level ventilators in caravans, often referred to as 'drop-out holes'. Since LPG is heavier than air, these ventilators allow leaking gas to escape to the outside.

Unfortunately, some owners find that 'drop-out' gas escape vents cause draughts so they cover them up,

Never cover or restrict the opening of a low-level gas escape vent – which is often called a drop-out hole.

To light hob burners on many imported caravans you need a hand-held igniter like this Zippo device.

288

Flame-failure device operation

So how does a flame-failure device (FFD) work? In simple terms, the metals used for its probe respond to heat, interact and create a small electrical current. This is conveyed to the gas control itself and the supply is powerful enough to open an electro-magnetic valve. Hence:

- When the probe is hot, gas flows to the burner.
- If a burner blows out, the probe becomes cold whereupon a spring shuts off the valve. At that point, gas can't get to the burner.
- Pushing in the control knob when you're lighting a burner merely overrides the electro-magnet and holds the valve open, thereby allowing the probe of the FFD to get hot.

If an FFD fails, get the appliance checked by a qualified specialist in LPG installations. Never prop open the control with a stick or peg.

The small probe indicated here is part of the flame-failure device; to the left is a spark igniter.

which is extremely unwise. If these vents *do* lead to uncomfortable draughts, it's usually possible to fit a deflector below the floor as shown on page 264. This can shield a ventilator without affecting its function or reducing its dimensions.

Now let's look at some individual gas appliances.

HOBS AND GRILLS

Gas hobs have been a standard fitment in British caravans for a long time. As mentioned already, some models are fitted with two or three burners; others have a complete set of four.

In addition, many models offer automatic spark ignition which means that neither matches nor a hand-held igniter are needed. However, it is interesting that hobs installed in caravans imported from abroad are less likely to have a built-in spark igniter.

Whereas an igniter is a convenience item, a flame-failure device (FFD) is obligatory on recent models. Its function is to ensure that the gas supply to a hob's burners is automatically terminated if its flame gets blown out. To achieve this, a small probe is angled into the path of the flames and when this gets hot it automatically holds open the gas supply.

However, its operation means that when you initially light a burner, you have to depress the control knob for several seconds to override the control mechanism. This gives the probe a chance to heat up.

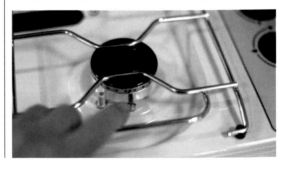

British caravanners usually expect to find a grill installed under a hob or within an oven, whereas many imported caravans don't have one.

As regards grills, these are normally only fitted to British caravans. Few Continental manufacturers fit a hob that embraces a grill in its design and it seems that caravanners from other European countries seldom use them. We can only presume they haven't discovered the pleasures of toast.

In recognition of our expectations, some importers of foreign models fit a separate grill unit as soon as every caravan is delivered to Britain. Other importers insist the manufacturer abroad makes special export models to suit British tastes.

Finally, please read the Safety Tip panel below on 'Hobs, heating and ovens'. It is most important.

Hobs, heating and ovens

- Never use a hob (or an oven) to act as a space heater. There are some kitchen layouts where heat rising from a burner that hasn't been covered by a pan is sufficient to cause damage to the locker or shelf above.

- If the gas/air mix on a hob or oven is slightly out of adjustment, there's a possibility that small quantities of carbon monoxide are present in the products of combustion. If you find that the undersides of cooking implements become badly covered with soot, this indicates that the flame is incorrect. Get the hob checked by a qualified gas specialist at once.

- Never close the glass lid of a hob when its burners are still hot. Furthermore, if your hob is mounted close to a side wall, remember to lift up its safety heat shield.

A hob should never be used as a space heater for several safety reasons.

If a hob isn't covered with a pan, lockers above a burner might get dangerously hot. The clearance being measured here has to comply with safety regulations.

Some hobs are mounted close to a plywood internal wall, so they have a heat shield that must be lifted before the burners are lit.

This capacious caravan oven manufactured by Dometic even includes a rotisserie-spit facility.

To suit caravanners who don't want a full-size domestic cooker, this 2007 Avondale caravan is equipped with a smaller and lighter appliance.

GAS OVENS

Although it's difficult to know if many owners use an oven regularly, modern caravans nearly always have one, whether it's wanted or not. Most full-size cookers are smart and efficient but they are also heavy, thereby taking up a significant part of a caravan's payload allowance.

Weight aside, if you bake cakes or like to cook a traditional Sunday lunch on holiday, a domestic-size 'cooker and oven' is obviously important. Whether it's worth having one just to heat a meat pie or to reheat fish and chips is debatable. With that in mind, some manufacturers fit lighter and less elaborate appliances.

The level of provision obviously differs but whatever caravan you purchase please note the points mentioned already about safety and servicing.

MICROWAVE OVENS

Compact microwave ovens are fitted in many caravans in the mid and upper price ranges. Once the cost of these appliances started falling, several caravan manufacturers decided to install them. It is patently clear that the inclusion of a microwave oven impresses many potential clients and acts as a purchasing incentive.

However, in practical terms these appliances only operate on 230V, and cooking times are normally longer than they are in the microwave ovens used in our homes. That's because site hook-ups only have a limited supply of current and microwave ovens, especially during the initial start-up phase, consume a lot of power. In consequence the models fitted in caravans have lower wattages, thereby affecting their 'cooking time' performance.

As regards the installation, most manufacturers build an oven into a head-height locker. For some people the appliance can then be quite hard to reach, and if you are removing a mug of hot coffee,

great care is needed to ensure that its contents aren't spilt.

Ventilation is important too. An appliance mustn't be allowed to overheat and generous ventilation is needed around its casing. If you compare different installations you will find that some caravan manufacturers fit more air escape outlets than others. It is certainly annoying when the safety mechanism of an appliance trips-out automatically because it is getting too hot.

Finally, there are many caravanners who prefer to use remote sites that don't offer hook-up facilities. To obtain a 230V supply, some then purchase a portable generator to run mains appliances like a microwave oven. Unfortunately they subsequently find that their generator isn't powerful enough to operate this appliance.

The problem arises from a misunderstanding. Naturally, you'd imagine that a 1kW (*ie* 1,000-watt) generator ought to be able to run a 650W microwave oven. But it probably won't, for this reason: a microwave oven's rating of 650W refers to its *output* (or 'cooking power'), which is far less than the *input* it needs. As a rough rule of thumb, you have to double the quoted output and then subtract 10% to ascertain the required input needed from a supply source such as a generator. In other words, a 650W oven needs an input of around 1,170W – and that's more than the maximum output given by a 1,000W (1kW) portable generator.

There is no doubt that microwave ovens can be useful appliances, but operating them in a caravan is not always as straightforward as it might appear.

SPACE HEATERS

The term 'gas fire' has long been superseded for good reason. Moreover, the word heater is insufficient because modern caravans are fitted with two completely different heaters. One's a water heater whereas the other heats the living space.

If a microwave oven is installed in an enclosure that doesn't have adequate ventilation, its overheat trip switch will be triggered.

This display of a room-sealed heater shows how both the air intake and flue are coupled-up to an outside wall.

Exposed-flame gas fires

If you buy an older caravan fitted with a gas fire that has exposed flames and which isn't coupled to a permanently installed flue, get it removed and scrapped at once. It could cause a fatality, and if it hasn't been checked by a qualified specialist in LPG appliances, do not use it.

Behind the removable front on this Carver space heater you can see the finned heat exchanger which releases heat from the burners to the living area.

Gas fires

In the early 1970s, many owners had optional gas fires installed. Even in the 1980s, some caravans were equipped with a gas outlet mounted on the floor. Portable gas fires were sold for coupling up to these gas points using a flexible hose – this was simply pushed on to the ribbed nozzle of the outlet and clipped in place. That is no longer permitted.

In the past, many fires were lit using a match, and the problem of carbon monoxide emission – described above with regard to hobs – was potentially a source of danger. So these products are no longer fitted for safety reasons. Furthermore, if anyone purchases an older caravan and finds that an old-style open-burner fire is installed, they are strongly advised to have it removed by a gas specialist and replaced with a room-sealed space heater.

Room-sealed space heaters

Room-sealed heaters have the following features:
- [ ] A modern space heater in caravans is permanently installed; it is never a free-standing, movable unit.
- [ ] Its gas burner is situated within a sealed enclosure which is referred to as a heat exchanger.
- [ ] A feed duct or specially constructed inlet draws oxygen into the enclosure from *outside* the caravan.
- [ ] All products of combustion are returned directly *outside* via a flue system.
- [ ] As the heat exchanger gets hot, it warms up the air around it.
- [ ] Heat exchanger enclosures are designed to release heat efficiently – that's why they often have fins on their outer surface. These look reminiscent of air-cooled motorcycle engines.
- [ ] Provided it is regularly serviced, a room-sealed heater can usually be left in operation all night. However, you should confirm that this is the case by checking the owner's manual, or seeking advice from a dealer.

From this description you will note that the entire burning process is completely sealed off from the interior living area of your caravan. However, it stands to reason that a fully enclosed heating appliance needs an efficient and reliable ignition system. You cannot light the burner using a match because there's no point of access. On the other hand, as long as you have the heater serviced regularly, neither Piezo igniters nor electronic ignition systems are likely to give a problem.

Fan assistance

The idea of using a built-in electric fan to help distribute warm air from a space heater was developed in the 1980s. The air is usually sent along ducts and these enable you to heat a shower room and to control temperatures in other zones where heat is needed.

In most instances there are two main ducts emerging from the rear of heaters, which in turn serve the opposite ends of a caravan. However, on occasions you find that one end of a caravan stays rather cool whereas the other end seems to get hot. To adjust the balance, some Carver and Truma heaters have an output adjuster mounted on the back of the fan. The lever that alters air distribution is often below the fan unit and it's surprising how many caravan owners are unaware of its existence. This is partly because it is usually out of sight and rather difficult to reach. In fact it's often hidden away in the bottom of a wardrobe.

After the introduction of ducted systems and the idea of mounting a 12V fan on the rear of space heaters, manufacturers then decided that they would increase an owner's options by fitting a 230V mains heating element *within* the fan casing as well. The Carver Fanmaster introduced in 1994 is well known and means that you can provide mild heat to your caravan without using gas – as long as you're coupled to a mains hook-up. On models like the Mk 1 Fanmaster, however, you mustn't use gas and mains heating at the same time.

Then another strategy was followed in which heating elements were fitted inside the heater cabinet and adjacent to the heat exchanger. This system was followed in the Carver 4000 Fanmaster heater and also in the Truma Ultraheat. The Ultraheat appliance shown on page 294 offers 500W, 1,000W and 2,000W settings. An additional

Note
Chapter Twelve explains that hook-ups on sites can only provide a limited mains supply. So a Fanmaster fitted with both 1kW and 2kW heating elements, which draw 4.2 amps and 8.3 amps respectively, can easily exceed the hook-up capabilities of many sites. That's even without running any other mains appliances in your caravan.

The Truma Ultraheat has a 230V heating element with thermostatic output control, and its switch offers three different heat settings.

sophistication also allows it to be operated on gas and mains electricity *at the same time*.

Wet heating systems

A few of the more expensive caravans are fitted with a gas-fired central heating system that uses

Fan cut-out and reset switch

With a Carver Fanmaster model, where an electric element is mounted inside the casing of the fan unit, it's essential that at least one duct is left fully open whenever the heater is in operation. But even though one duct is usually installed without a closing device, it's still possible for this to be accidentally obscured, *eg* by a blanket that has fallen from a bed. So Carver fitted a safety cut-out switch on the fan casing to deal with overheating situations.

When this comes into operation, many owners presume that the heating system has broken. In reality you only need to carry out the following procedures:

1 Wait until the appliance has cooled down.
2 Open all the outlets.
3 Disconnect the mains supply at the consumer unit (see Chapter Twelve).
4 Reset the trip button by depressing the push switch on the side of the casing.

The accompanying photograph shows the reset switch, which is sometimes hard to locate. The fact that it's at the rear of the heater and often situated in the bottom part of a wardrobe can lead to some fumbling in the dark.

More recent models feature an automatic reset. So check the handbook, or if this is missing either seek the help of a caravan workshop or telephone the customer help-line at Truma (UK).

On the Carver Fanmaster, where the electrical element is situated in the fan housing, there's a reset button which is part of the over-heating safety cut-out.

If a space heater is wall-mounted under a wardrobe, the fan assembly can sometimes be accessed by lifting out a panel in the bottom of the clothing compartment.

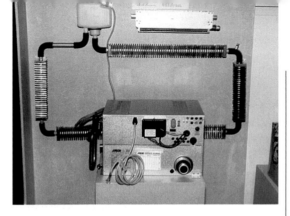

This display shows the Alde 3000 Compact heating system which uses radiators.

Spare parts
The names 'Carver' and 'Truma' have been associated with the manufacture of space and water heaters for a long time. In the mid-1980s the German company Truma supplied many components to Carver, which was based in Warwickshire. Later this joint venture was terminated, however, and the companies became wholly independent. Then, in the late 1990s, Truma took over the Carver product and subsequently opened a UK headquarters in Derbyshire. The supply of spare parts for Carver products was also taken over by Truma, albeit for a limited period.

radiators. The efficient 3000 Compact Alde system, for example, is highly regarded and has been fitted in some of the models made by Avondale, Bessacarr, Buccaneer and Vanmaster.

Diesel space heating

Space and water heaters that run on diesel fuel have been used for a number of years in boats, lorries and motor caravans. Recently a blown warm air system has been designed for caravans, too, and it can be retrofitted in both new and old models without too much disturbance. With a fuel consumption of around an eggcup-full of diesel fuel an hour, this system from Eberspächer is a worthy alternative to gas appliances. Its compact plastic fuel tank is easily mounted in an outside locker and the heater can be discreetly installed in a blanket box indoors. If the Eberspächer inline 230V electrical appliance is required, this can be added as well.

Diesel space heating from Eberspächer

A flat blue tank with surge baffles is easily installed in an external locker.

A heater the size of a shoebox is fitted where a wall heater once stood.

If required, a similar size 230V heater can be added in-line as well.

The controls include daily timing and a full seven-day schedule.

After the arrival of room-sealed gas appliances, touring caravan manufacturers ceased fitting instantaneous water heaters with exposed burners.

ⓘ Technical Tip

Draining down a water heater

With the onset of frosty weather, it is absolutely essential that you drain off the water from a heater. This is explained in Chapter Seventeen. Apart from that, few caravanners drain-down their water heater before taking to the road, in spite of the fact that its heavy contents take up a significant part of the permitted payload. For instance, a Carver Cascade holds nine litres (two gallons) thereby taking up 9kg (20lb) of a caravan's payload potential. Draining the contents is undoubtedly a strategy to consider if a caravan is loaded perilously close to its payload limit.

The drain-down point on a Carver Cascade water heater is found on its external flue cover. See page 317 for the release tap on a Truma water heater.

WATER HEATERS

Developmental features

Not long ago, a water heater was regarded as a luxury item and few caravanners complained about the need to boil a kettle to provide washing-up water. However, the arrival of caravan showers changed things for ever. Water heaters became commonplace and followed a similar evolutionary development to space heaters.

For example, heaters with exposed flames were deemed unacceptable more than a decade ago. In consequence, instantaneous water heaters like the Paloma or the Rinnai models are no longer fitted in British-built touring caravans. Instead, water-heating appliances that have a hot-water storage tank are the preferred choice. Since the stored water adds significant weight, some caravanning specialists advise that heaters are drained down before a 'van is towed. In practice, draining-down a tank that's full of hot water is rather wasteful so many owners disregard this suggestion.

Initially the water in an appliance's storage tanks was heated-up using a gas burner. Subsequent developments, however, saw tanks being fitted with a 230V immersion heater too. This meant that both gas and mains could be used – either as alternative

fuels or together to speed-up the heating time when starting from cold.

Although some water heaters are integrated with a space-heating appliance, others are stand-alone products that include:

1 The Carver Cascade (several versions since its debut in the mid-1980s).
2 The Maxol Malaga (also made bearing the Belling badge).
3 The Truma Ultrastore (in both 10- and 14-litre versions).
4 The Whale storage water heater (introduced in 2009).

Note: *Fully integrated space and water heaters are usually quite heavy and tend to be fitted more often in motor caravans. However, some touring caravans have been equipped with products like the Alde 3000 and the Truma 'Combi'.*

Storage water heaters

After it was first launched, the Carver Cascade underwent several changes. For instance, the original model has a very slow drain-down time due to air locks and it sometimes takes an hour before the last drops of water are released from the tank. The Cascade 2 Plus doesn't suffer from this problem because it has an air release point mounted at the top of its external wall plate.

In addition, the Cascade 2 Plus GE features a 660W mains heating element whereas the Cascade Rapide has an 830W heating element together with an overheat reset button situated behind a cover flap. Many British caravans have been fitted with a Carver Cascade water heater, and it has proved to be an excellent product. However, in 1999 Carver ceased manufacturing gas appliances for caravans.

Some years later a near replica product was launched called the Henry GE. Many of its spare parts can be fitted as replacement items on many of the Carver Cascade water heaters and the complete appliance is often installed in place of an old Cascade. It was no accident that the dimensions of a Henry GE are almost identical to those of a Carver Cascade.

Not that Carver's product was the only one on the market. For example, the Maxol Malaga and the Malaga E (with 230V heating element) have also been fitted into a number of caravans, including models in Fleetwood's 1995 range. Water heaters bearing the later name of the Belling Malaga were also fitted in the Bailey Hunter Lite range from 1997 onwards.

Solutions for Cascade water heater problems

When Carver ceased manufacturing the Cascade water heater, spares were sold for a limited period by Truma (UK). In addition a close replica of the Cascade was made independently and named the Henry GE. Many of its parts are interchangeable and the new product is available from your dealer via the wholesaler, Johnnie Longden of Poole, Dorset, *Tel* 01202 679121. Also noted for parts supply and the servicing of obsolete Carver Cascade water heaters is Arc Systems of Bradmore, Nottingham, NG11 6PF, *Tel* 0115 9213175.

A Belling water heater is fitted to some caravans such as the Bailey Hunter Lite which was made in the late 1990s.

Since the demise of Carver, many caravans like this Bailey Pegasus have been fitted with a Truma Ultrastore water heater.

At present the Truma Ultrastore is the product most often fitted in UK caravans. Like the Cascade and Malaga units, the Ultrastore is usually situated in a bed box with its intake and flue mounted on a side wall.

In 2009 Whale introduced a water heater that has an impressive cladding of insulation and a nominal tank capacity of 13 litres. Cold chamber testing also confirmed that it meets Grade III Classification of Thermal Insulation and Heating (EN1645-1). This product is being tested by manufacturers and is certain to be specified in caravans in the near future.

To operate these products correctly and safely you must check the manufacturer's instructions, which are usually repeated in the owner's user manual. Like any other gas appliance in a caravan, a water heater must also be serviced in accordance with its manufacturer's instructions.

SPACE AND WATER HEATER SERVICING

Helped by its angular shape, a Whale water heater fits neatly into confined spaces and is often installed in a caravan's blanket box.

The fact that caravan gas appliances are not used regularly throughout the year presents a problem.

Even a spider's web or other obstruction at a flue outlet can upset heater ignition. Periodic servicing by a qualified gas engineer is essential.

During storage periods it's not unusual for insects, moths and spiders to get into the air intakes or flues. In some instances this can upset the delicate air/gas balance; it can also interfere with the ignition process. For example, it's not unusual for a pilot flame to ignite on a space heater whereas the main burner subsequently fails to fire up. This is usually caused by obstructions – even a spider's web spun around the cowl on a roof-mounted flue has been known to upset heater ignition.

This is one of several reasons why routine and regular servicing of these appliances is essential.

BARBECUES

As a final comment, a few caravans have been manufactured with external gas connections mounted on a side wall. An example with its red control knob is shown on the Europa pictured on page 237.

These are intended for gas-operated barbecues which are permitted on many (though not all) caravan sites. Here is another pleasure of the caravanning experience although, once again, the vigilance about individual appliances mentioned earlier should be noted.

Thanks to gas couplings on some caravan walls, we can often enjoy the pleasures of al fresco meals.

CHAPTER SIXTEEN

SERVICING

Although car owners recognise that vehicles need servicing on a regular basis, some caravan owners are surprised to learn that caravans need servicing too. For example, brake assemblies need to be periodically inspected, cleaned, and adjusted. Moreover, it is important to monitor the condition of a caravan's tyres; if they fail to meet the required standard, the owner is committing an offence. Then there's the importance of arranging routine checks of gas appliances, gas supply systems, and electrical components.

Many workshops have elevating ramps to enable a service technician to have good access to brakes and running gear.

A caravan service involves several different areas of attention and the National Caravan Council advises that a standard operation would normally take four hours to carry out. The work helps ensure that a caravan is kept in good working order as a leisure home and that it's safe to use on the road. So how frequently should this operation be carried out?

SERVICE INTERVALS

With no mileometer in a caravan, there's no easy way of registering the distances it covers. Nor is it feasible to record the hours that a fridge or a cooker is in operation. As a rough guide, it is normally recommended that a caravan is serviced at least every 12 months, but more frequent inspections might be required if a caravan is used throughout the year. After all, the extremes of heat in summer and frost or snow in winter both take their toll.

It also seems that an increasing number of owners, especially those who have taken early retirement, are now spending several months of the year on touring trips – particularly in mainland Europe. With this pattern of frequent use, the recommendation of having a caravan serviced once a year is unlikely to be sufficient. All-important items like brakes are going to need checking and adjusting on a much more regular basis.

At the opposite extreme, the life of a caravan isn't helped if it stands unused for prolonged spells. For many mechanical components, remaining stationary is the worst thing possible. Even tyres deteriorate surprisingly quickly if the same part of the sidewalls remains flexed when a caravan is left parked and doesn't get moved. In reality, most caravans spend more time parked than being towed along the road.

Although it is generally recommended to have a caravan serviced annually, it is the owner who ultimately has to decide whether more regular attention is needed. However, don't presume that if it's seldom used, you could correspondingly *extend*

303

the period between service work. Lack of use can lead to problems like brake seizure, and if body leaks develop these need identifying at once. With that in mind, let's take a look at some of the jobs included within a standard service operation.

SERVICING JOBS

In a full service, around 50 jobs need to be carried out. Broadly speaking, these fall into the following areas of attention:

1 The chassis and running gear – which includes brake adjustment, wheel bearing checks, tyre checks, corner steady lubrication.

It is important to remove the brake drums in order to clean and lubricate moving parts in a brake mechanism.

2 Gas system and appliance checks – this would include a check for leaks in the supply system. Appliances will also be switched into action and the flame pattern inspected. Depending on accessibility, the work might also include cleaning gas burners on space heaters, water heaters and so on. However, where this involves elaborate dismantling work, the servicing of individual appliances is usually treated as an 'optional extra' and priced accordingly.

The gas supply pipes are being checked for leaks using air that is added at pressure from a purpose-made pump.

On recent caravans, the type of torque wrench needed to tighten the one-shot flanged nut holding a brake drum in place costs a three-figure sum.

Since the early 1990s, caravan brake drums have been held in place by a one-shot flanged nut; once it has been removed, a new one should then be fitted.

During a standard service, a new one-shot nut holding the drum in place is marked with a security paint to guard against tampering.

In this service operation, dust is being removed from around the burners in a Carver Cascade water heater before a flame check is carried out.

Many owners have a socket tester for checking a mains system; this is work included in a normal service.

3 Electrical check – to include road light operation, the safety of the mains supply system, operation of interior lights, etc.

4 Water system check – flushing through with purifying cleaner, checking operation of the water pump, filter changing, and tasks like lubricating the valve seal on a toilet.

5 Refrigerator operation check and service – in a standard service a technician will check to see that a refrigerator is achieving cooling when running on each of its three sources of power. If you want the full refrigerator service that is recommended by its manufacturer, this will include tasks like replacing the gas jet, realigning the igniter, and cleaning the gas burner and flue. To carry this out, a fridge normally has to be taken out of a caravan and transferred to a workbench. That's why most dealers offer a full refrigerator service as an optional extra.

6 Bodywork and general condition – this important checking operation should include: a damp test, a visual inspection of sealant condition, a window operation check and so on.

To check for damp in a caravan, an electrical meter is used and there are 30 to 40 points around the interior where a specialist will take readings.

7 Fire warning system check – to make certain that a smoke alarm is working and that a fire extinguisher is within its stated date life.

SERVICE SCHEDULE

As pointed out earlier, one of the aims of this book is to offer user guidance. It is not a DIY repair book, and readers who require more technical information about service operations are advised to consult its 'partner' publication, *The Caravan Manual*.

When the first edition of *The Caravan Manual* was published in 1993, a standardised service schedule was not in existence. To resolve this, the author added a proposed listing of key servicing jobs when the second edition was published in 1996. Many dealer workshops started to use this proposed schedule, and the industry's trade body – the National Caravan Council (NCC) – then held discussions with the author so that a fully recognised document could be formally approved.

As caravan specifications and equipment changes, so do service schedules. The latest to appear is given in Chapter Thirteen of the fourth edition of *The Caravan Manual*, which was published in 2009.

Working to a strict job list is important, and when arranging to have your 'van serviced you should ask to see the centre's service schedule before confirming the booking. Equally, when the work has been completed you should be given a copy of the schedule duly signed, stamped, and dated. This document should include guidance regarding the amount of wear on brake shoes, the tread left on the tyres, and so on.

This point is emphasised because some so-called 'service specialists' provide customers with no documentation at all about the work that they've carried out. Equally, there's no written advice on the condition of the brakes, tyres and so on, and no certification to verify the integrity of gas and electrical systems. Not only does this raise doubts about the thoroughness of an operation, but you also

Having your caravan serviced regularly is strongly recommended. However, there's a problem caused by primroses, daffodils, and the delightful 'rustle of Spring'. As Easter approaches, many eager owners plan their first post-winter holiday break – only to find that the local service centre is fully booked for weeks and weeks. Be ever-mindful of the seasonal nature of this leisure pursuit and take steps to book the caravan for servicing well in advance of your first trip of the year. This is also particularly relevant if your caravan's warranty requires that a service is carried out by a particular deadline.

have no written evidence to state that servicing work has been carried out. Needless to say, this kind of documentation is useful when you want to sell your caravan.

SERVICING PRIORITIES

When considering elements within a service operation, there's a difference between absolutely essential tasks, highly desirable work, and recommended jobs. For instance, keeping a caravan's brakes, tyres, suspension, and road lights in good order is absolutely essential. Equally important is the checking of a gas supply system and the safety of gas appliances. It's much the same with regard to electrical safety.

Rather less 'life-threatening' are issues like checking a water pump, and cleaning its grit filter. It might even be suggested that conducting a damp test on a caravan is not exactly a health and safety issue – although discerning caravanners wouldn't ignore this inspection.

Finally there are less important matters like repairing faulty cupboard catches, lubricating door hinges, adjusting spring mechanisms on roller blinds and so on.

On account of these differences, some service centres offer a basic brakes, chassis, and road light service. Many will also offer a damp test on its own, which you should have done whenever you suspect that a leak has developed unexpectedly.

Then there's the matter of receiving signed and dated certificates by:

1 A qualified electrician.
2 A qualified gas specialist.

Such documents verify the integrity of these supply systems, thereby providing peace of mind. In addition, gas and electrical certificates help when you

Mains electricity

To establish that a mains installation in a caravan meets current technical requirements, an inspection should be carried out by one of the following specialists:

Either An approved contractor of the National Inspection Council for Electrical Installation Contracting (NICEIC),

or a member of either the Electrical Contractors Association (ECA), or the Electrical Contractors Association of Scotland.

If there is no inspection certificate accompanying a pre-owned caravan, it is in the purchaser's interests to arrange for the 'van to be inspected before the mains system is put into service. To find your nearest NICEIC specialist telephone 01717 582 7746; to find an ECA member, telephone 0171 229 1266.

Gas

To undertake gas system work on non-business caravans, an operator must be deemed to be 'competent'. This can be achieved by passing relevant examinations such as ACS or ACoPs, and where the person has attended a recognised training course. Some caravan owners insist on repair work being undertaken by a CORGI engineer. (Note: CORGI stands for Council for Registered Gas Installers.) Registration was also a requirement for those who installed and maintained LPG installations as laid down in the Gas Safety (Installation & Use) Regulations 1994. However, CORGI has now lost the gas registration scheme rights and from 1 April 2009 the official industry stamp for gas safety is the Gas Safe Register.

decide to sell a caravan. In practice, many caravan workshops have to enlist the help of independent qualified specialists to carry out these checks and to issue approval certificates. That's why these elements are usually an 'optional addition' to a standard service, and an additional fee will be payable.

REFRIGERATOR SERVICE

It was pointed out earlier that where a refrigerator is concerned, a standard service is mainly only concerned with checking that it achieves cooling. However, manufacturers such as Dometic and

To carry out a full service on a refrigerator, an appliance usually needs to be removed and transferred to a workbench.

308

Thetford recommend a more elaborate annual service as described in the earlier chapter on refrigerators. This is also covered in more depth in *The Caravan Manual*, published by Haynes. Without doubt it is extremely inconvenient if a fridge lets you down during an important break. So a full refrigerator service makes good sense, even though many owners find their fridge works well for years and years without attention. However, that is no consolation if it eventually fails during a heat wave when you were enjoying a Mediterranean holiday.

MINOR REPAIRS AND AUTHORISATIONS

When a service is carried out, it's not unusual for a technician to find items that are faulty. Perhaps one of the interior lights needs a new bulb or a

(i) Technical Tip

Approved Caravan Workshops
An Approved Caravan Workshop is required to:
1 Display a detailed list of prices and labour rates.
2 Provide an estimate for any additional servicing or repair work over £150.
3 Give a realistic estimated time for completion and collection.
4 Use genuine spare parts when available.
5 Always provide a checklist of work done.
6 Start work *only* when given an owner's express authority.
7 Contact a customer for authority to continue if additional work is identified.
8 Notify an owner in writing of faults that are not rectified, with an honest assessment of the urgency of the repairs.

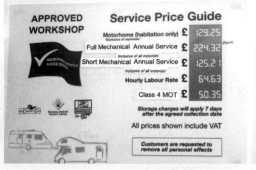

APPROVED WORKSHOP

Service Price Guide

Motorhome (habitation only) *'Exclusive of materials'*	£ 129.25
Full Mechanical Annual Service *'Inclusive of all materials'*	£ 224.32
Short Mechanical Annual Service *'Inclusive of all materials'*	£ 125.21
Hourly Labour Rate	£ 64.63
Class 4 MOT	£ 50.35

Storage charges will apply 7 days after the agreed collection date

All prices shown include VAT

Customers are requested to remove all personal effects

Touring and Motor Caravan Approved Workshops are required to display prices and labour rates in the Customer Reception area. (Photograph with permission of White Arches Caravans, Rushden.)

Many workshops have elevating ramps to enable a service technician to have good access to brakes and running gear.

replacement fluorescent tube. Many centres will replace small items like this without a further labour charge – as long as there's time to do the job within the allotted period for carrying out the service. The cost of the component, however, has to be borne by the customer.

This raises another point to consider when arranging a service. It obviously wouldn't make sense to re-book and return your caravan to a workshop for later replacements of inexpensive components like fuses or light bulbs. However, what would be the position if a new water pump was needed? This is something to discuss when booking a service – most owners like to be consulted before a technician embarks on more costly repairs. With that in mind you might want to agree a cost limit, so ask the service receptionist what procedure is followed if something serious emerges during the work.

CHOOSING A RELIABLE SERVICE SPECIALIST

If you own a caravan that is still under warranty, its manufacturer will stipulate that it must be serviced in accordance with information given in the owner's manual and the warranty conditions.

Failure to do this is likely to invalidate the warranty. To be absolutely sure that your local caravan service specialist is authorised to carry out the work, a call to the customer helpline of a caravan manufacturer is strongly recommended. Get the manufacturer's advisers to give their approval of your chosen service provider before making a booking.

Recognising that there have been examples of poor servicing in the past, an initiative by The Camping and Caravanning Club, The Caravan Club and The National Caravan Council led to the establishment of a nationwide chain of Approved Service Workshops.

This chain was instrumental in providing caravan owners with a list of reliable and accredited centres. The scheme was launched in 1999 and dealer-participation requirements have become increasingly demanding in subsequent revisions.

Part of the bid to improve the standard of servicing operations was the introduction of City & Guilds Examination 3941 Caravan Engineering (Touring Caravans and Motorhomes). This consists of two parts: 1. A written test relating to different aspects of servicing; and 2. A practical test in which a candidate is shadowed by an examiner while a standard caravan service is carried out.

Training regimes at Approved Workshops have thus been improved, with the result that a customer is assured that the technician attending to their caravan has the necessary competence to carry out the work.

Before being accepted into the scheme, service centre applicants also have to undergo a lengthy and elaborate independent inspection. However, it doesn't end there; a re-examination inspection is also conducted annually. Although most workshops undertaking service work are situated at dealerships, there are accredited mobile workshops too.

At the time of writing, there are over 200 Approved Workshops operating within the scheme and you can find your nearest centre by contacting one of the above agencies. Alternatively there is both a postcode and county search facility on the website www.approvedworkshops.co.uk, which informs enquirers of the distance to their nearest fixed or mobile facility. Equally there are free leaflets describing Approved Workshops, which are available from the National Caravan Council. The address of the NCC is given in the Appendix.

As a footnote, it should be added that there are other servicing workshops which are not members of this scheme. In some instances the standard of their workmanship is very good: in other cases it is open to conjecture.

During the practical part of a City and Guilds Examination, an assessor 'shadows' and checks the knowledge of candidates while they carry out a full servicing operation.

311

CHAPTER SEVENTEEN

WINTER LAY-UP AND SPRING PREPARATION

Modern caravans are so well heated and insulated that they can be used at any time of the year. However, circumstances might necessitate that your caravan is laid-up for winter, in which case there will be some pre-storage tasks to carry out. Equally, when you want to recommence your travels the following spring, there are some pre-season matters to consider as well.

Before the onset of cold weather, many owners transfer their caravan upholstery to a warm room indoors. That's also a deterrent to thieves, who seldom steal caravans whose cushions are missing.

As an alternative to setting-up a 230V domestic vacuum cleaner, some owners clean their caravan with a 12V rechargeable compact appliance.

Useful Tip

Fluff removal
In spite of work with a vacuum cleaner, fluff often remains around the perimeter of carpeted areas. Complete the job by putting on a rubber glove and wiping your finger around all the places that the vacuum cleaner didn't reach. The glove grips the fluff and pulls it away from a carpet pile.

Care needs to be taken when cleaning the stove-enamel surfaces of hobs and ovens.

In Chapter Four, the subject of storage was discussed in detail. Here are some jobs that need to be carried out before you turn the key in the door, fit anti-theft devices, and possibly add a caravan cover.

SPARE PARTS AND SERVICING

☐ **Spare parts:** Make a list of anything that was damaged during the season. If replacement items are needed, order them now. Anything from awning repairs to a light bulb should be arranged before the run-down to Christmas. Leave it until the spring and you may have to wait for weeks to receive delivery of the parts you need.

☐ **Servicing:** Book a service for next spring – even if it's still only October. The 'silly season' at dealer workshops starts in earnest in February or March. Servicing 'slots' are soon filled and it's 'first come, first served'. So think ahead and book in advance.

PRE LAY-UP JOBS

Indoor cleaning

☐ Start with a good clean inside using a domestic vacuum cleaner that you'll probably run via your caravan's 230V supply system. Alternatively, some 12V car cleaners and rechargeable products are effective alternatives. If there's room in your house to store caravan cushions and mattresses in a dry place, so much the better. Finding a caravan with its upholstery missing is also a deterrent to thieves.

☐ Use proprietary cleaners on the stove-enamel or stainless steel surfaces of your hob and oven.

Be careful what you use to clean a refrigerator food compartment. Refer to Chapter Eleven for details.

However, on plastic sinks and drainers, use the cleaning products recommended by the appliance manufacturer so that you don't abrade the surface.

☐ Put plugs in the sink, the wash basin, and the shower tray outlets, to prevent smells infiltrating the living space from stagnant water that might be held in the waste pipe.

☐ Clean out the inside of your refrigerator following the advice given in Chapter Eleven. Then leave the door slightly ajar so that the interior is kept ventilated.

Outside cleaning

☐ At the end of a season, it is always wise to give a caravan a good clean before putting it into store. However, busy owners and dark evenings often mean that it gets unceremoniously left. If possible, try to find time to remove the black streaks that form under external fittings. Products like Autoglym Caravan and Motorhome Cleaner are especially easy to use.

☐ Dealers often use a high-pressure hose to clean caravans, and experienced operators recognise where a forceful blast of water is likely to cause damage. Unfortunately there are inexperienced

Many caravanners purchase a soft cleaning brush with an extending telescopic pole. These are often sold at caravan exhibitions and outdoor shows.

Failure to put plugs into the sink, basin, and shower tray means that odours from waste water pipes can get into the living area.

315

Experienced users often clean a caravan with a high-pressure hose, but a powerful blast of water can sometimes introduce leaks, especially where body sealants are losing their flexibility.

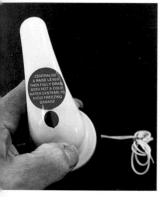

A crank-handled brush will help when cleaning less accessible areas.

On lever-operated mixer-taps keep the lever central so that both hot and cold feeds are opened up.

If your caravan has a drain-down tap, open it to drain off water and leave it open.

The air release stopper in a Carver water heater.

users who break plastic decals and introduce leaks – especially where sealants used under fittings and trim strips are starting to get brittle. Using a soft washer-brush on an extending pole is often considered a better way to clean a caravan.

☐ As regards the parts which are hard to reach, it's often easier to apply a cleaning treatment with the help of a crank-handled brush. These products are normally used for painting the back of domestic radiators and are sold by paint merchants. You'll find that they're particularly useful for removing dead flies from the front of a caravan's roof panel.

Protecting a water system from frost damage

☐ Before draining down a fresh water system, open all the taps and leave them open throughout the lay-up period. On lever-operated mixer taps like the Whale Elite models, it's most important to keep the lever central so that both hot and cold feeds are opened up.

☐ A few caravans are fitted with a drain-down tap. Open this to drain off water left in the pipes and leave it open. If there isn't a drain-down tap, you may have to disconnect one of the hose or pipe connections in order to drain residual water into a receptacle.

☐ After opening all the taps, drain down a Carver water heater by releasing the bottom stopper. It's meant to hang in place, but if it comes out completely, leave it in your sink as a reminder. Note that on the early heaters it can take an hour or more to release all the water from the unit. You then need to cover the hole so that spiders and insects don't get into the heater tank.

☐ Later Carver water heaters have an air release stopper on the top left-hand side of the casing. When this is undone, the drain-down operation proceeds much more rapidly.

☐ After the demise of Carver gas products, Truma

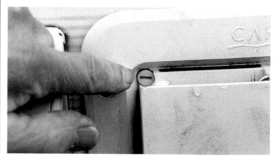

Avoiding frost damage

When water freezes in a pipe its volume increases by around 8.79%. If all the outlets are sealed – for instance, if none of the taps are left open – freezing water creates a serious pressure build-up in pipe sections that have not been completely emptied. Sometimes, flexible plastic hose can absorb this increase in volume without splitting but couplings and water-operated devices often get damaged; so do some of the components in water heaters.

With the increasing popularity of lever mixer taps, it has been found that if the lever is left open in the hot-water supply position, the cold water supply pipe may probably get damaged – and vice versa. So remember, if your caravan is fitted with this type of tap, make sure that its lever is lifted and left in its *midway* position. This precautionary measure means that both hot and cold feed pipes are then left open.

317

The drain-down stopper on a Carver water heater is at the bottom left of the outside plate.

water heaters have been fitted in many caravans instead. Once again, it is most important that these are also drained down before the frosts arrive.

☐ If your caravan is fitted with a Truma water heater, look for the yellow lift-up water release valve that drains off water from the unit.

☐ Submersible water pumps sometimes retain a small quantity of water. It's recommended to shake this out as well.

☐ If your water supply system is fitted with a taste filter, this is likely to retain some residual water. If that starts to freeze the expanding ice will often crack its casing. In Chapter Ten it was recommended that filters are removed before

Below left: The lift-up release valve on a Truma water heater is distinctively yellow.

Below: Shake the water from the casing of a submersible water pump. This particular pump is permanently attached to the caravan.

Winterban is imported from the USA and is a non-poisonous anti-freeze that's pumped into water systems prior to winter storage periods.

The flush water indicator tube on a Thetford bench-type cassette toilet is unclipped and used as a drain-down outlet.

Below: After repeated flushing operations, the last drops of unwanted water in a Thetford swivel-bowl toilet are emptied by removing a small rubber bung.

Below right: Draining the filling reservoir on a Thetford bench-type cassette toilet.

winter storage periods and that a replacement is purchased in readiness for your resumption of caravanning next season.

☐ To avoid drain-down operations, many boat owners and American RV (Recreational Vehicle) owners prefer to add potable anti-freeze to their fresh water supply systems. This is poured into a container, pumped into the system, and left during the lay-up period. The product is not poisonous – although you wouldn't want to drink it. Now the idea is catching-on in Britain and many motor caravan owners are already using Camco Potable Anti-freeze imported by ABP Accessories (see Appendix for the address). The water additive can also be used in stored caravans, although some water heater manufacturers, *eg* Truma, have not officially approved the use of anti-freeze in their appliances in case it reacts with seals and other components.

Toilet drain-down and preparation

A brief section on toilet lay-up procedures was given at the close of Chapter Ten. However, you should note these further points:

☐ Cassette toilets hold flushing water in their casing and bench-type Thetford units have a flush water indicator tube. You unclip this and angle it down into a bucket to drain off unwanted water. However, in a Thetford swivel-bowl version you empty the water by repeated flushing, followed by a collection of the last cupful or two of water by unplugging a rubber drain plug.

☐ The filling reservoir on a Thetford bench-type cassette toilet also holds a small quantity of water. The reservoir has its own plastic screw-cap for releasing the contents.

☐ Put cap covers over both your caravan's fresh water inlet and waste outlet. Ignoring this means

*Leave the release flap
open in your cassette
toilet so that it doesn't
stick in the closed position
during a long period in
storage.*

you are giving an open invitation to homeless
spiders.
☐ Leave the release flap in the bottom of a toilet
pan completely open during a storage period.
Even better, spray on some seal protecting fluid as
discussed in Chapter Ten.

Plug and socket protection

☐ The electrical coupling plug(s) on a caravan
and the equivalent socket(s) on a tow car need
spraying with a water-repellent product that
cannot damage their plastic casing. Some sprays
do cause damage. A particularly effective product
is Tri-flow, which combines PTFE with a complex
carrying agent; the author has found after many
years using this product that it keeps brass pins/
tubes clean and shiny for a long period after an
application. This industrial moisture repellent
lubricant is one of many treatment products in the
Ronseal range.

Gas cylinders

☐ The wisdom of transferring gas cylinders to a
safe, ventilated place was discussed in Chapter
Fourteen. It is also wise to tie a linen bag over
the end of a coupling hose or a cylinder-mounted
type of regulator to ensure that insects or spiders
cannot get into the supply system.

*Spray the plugs and
sockets with a water
repellent product that
doesn't damage their
plastic casing.*

*It is often wise to remove
gas cylinders from a
caravan before a lay-
up period, but refer to
Chapter Fourteen for
advice about storage
arrangements.*

It is often best to transfer a battery to a bench for periodic charging during a long lay-up period, as described in Chapter Thirteen.

Battery removal and charging

☐ It is most important to keep a caravan's leisure battery charged throughout an extended lay-up period. The subject of charging is discussed in Chapter Thirteen.

Tyres, suspension and brakes

☐ Always be aware that the walls of a tyre get damaged through lack of use. To avoid storage damage, fastidious owners mount their caravan on robust axle stands and remove the wheels. This relieves the suspension as well.

☐ Alternatively you can use 'Winter wheels', which are angle-steel structures fitted in place of the normal wheels. Sometimes called 'square wheels', these stands also act as security devices and the fact that you can then store your caravan's wheels in a garage means the tyres are rested and kept away from sunlight. However, 'Winter wheels' don't relieve the suspension – you need a pair of axle stands to achieve that objective. Note: 'Winter wheels' were originally made by PGR and similar products are now available from security specialists like Safe and Secure products.

☐ As long as a caravan is parked on level ground, the wheels are chocked, and there is no risk at all

If a caravan is left unmoved for an extended spell, cracks and general weakening can seriously affect the sidewalls of tyres.

of it running away, it's best to leave a hand-brake completely OFF. This means that any developing rust in the drum mechanisms won't leave the brakes well and truly ON.

Further measures

Other jobs may also be listed in your caravan owner's manual. Check this with care, because some of its appliances might be different from those discussed in this chapter. There is also a dilemma with regard to curtains and roller blinds. For example, it doesn't make sense to leave the interior of a stored caravan on view to passers-by, so many owners draw the curtains and close the roller blinds. This also helps prevent the interior fabrics from fading.

However, the manufacturers of roller blinds fitted with a recoil device point out that if they're left closed for extended periods, their recoil springs get weakened and lose their effectiveness. Although a 'tired' spring can be tightened, it is often difficult to reach its adjusting device. This might suggest that only the curtains should be drawn during a lay-up period – accepting that these might fade as well. All in all, owners have to make their own decision on the matter; some resolve the dilemma by purchasing a caravan cover instead.

If you can securely chock the wheels and there is no possibility of a caravan starting to move, it is beneficial to leave its handbrake off during a prolonged storage period.

Extending tyre life
If you do have to leave your caravan parked for a long period without putting it on axle stands, arrange to move it a foot or so (300mm) one way or the other every couple of months. This ensures that different parts of the tyre's sidewalls are placed under stress during the lay-up period.

During a long storage period it seems logical to close a caravan's roller blinds, but this often leads to a weakening of their recoil springs.

If a leak is suspected a plastic cover might give short-term protection, but condensation will form on the underside of impervious materials.

Caravans usually have several sharp projections that can cause a cover to tear. Good products are supplied with protective buffers and materials.

Plastic windows must be clean, but never apply a plastic 'cling film' like this. Its chemical might cause an acrylic pane to develop tiny 'crazing cracks'.

Caravan covers

If you park a caravan for a long period, it is certainly going to get dirty, especially if left near trees. There are also owners who suspect that leaks might be developing, and their response is to purchase a plastic cover sheet. This might offer a short-term solution pending proper repairs, but an impervious plastic 'tarpaulin' also seals in residual damp, and condensation subsequently forms on the underside.

This prompted the manufacture of tailor-made covers that are made from a 'breathable' fabric. Depending on the product these are reasonably waterproof, but there's often the possibility of rainwater seeping through their stitched seams. Also be aware that covers are effective at keeping a caravan roof free of dirt, bird droppings, and algae, although this might mean that a fabric's 'breathable pores' eventually get blocked with airborne dust.

Recognising that storing a caravan indoors is usually costly, a good quality, model-specific caravan cover is often a logical purchase. However, it should only be fitted to a dust-free, clean caravan otherwise the paintwork and windows will get abrasion damage as soon as there's a strong wind. Equally, any sharp projections need protecting before a cover is fitted. Secure straps are essential too. The accompanying illustrations draw attention to these issues.

This is not a job to tackle in breezy weather and a helper is usually needed. On many caravans a broomstick handle helps as well.

PRE-SEASON JOBS

Before setting off after a winter lay-up, you need to get everything working again.

323

After parking a caravan near trees a coating of green algae looks dreadful, but it can usually be removed with careful cleaning.

- [ ] When parked near trees, caravans often get covered with green algae. Don't be too distressed if you go to collect a caravan from an outdoor storage compound and find it stained and dirty.
- [ ] A good wash is usually needed and some owners do this using a high-pressure hose. However, as mentioned earlier, great care is needed. On its more powerful setting and used too close to a caravan, a pressure hose can blast away sealant from panel junctions, damage acrylic windows, and break brittle plastic decals.
- [ ] A soft hand brush is useful for removing spiders and their webs. There's also a purpose-made stiffened brush supplied by W4 accessories that cleans out awning channels too.
- [ ] A concerted effort to polish-up a caravan is a sure way to start things in style. If the acrylic windows sustained scratches through windy weather and nearby branches, Caravan Pride from Farécla,

Over-enthusiastic use of a high-pressure hose can damage brittle plastic decals.

Brush around trim strips with a soft brush.

Cleaning prior to the start of a new caravanning season.

A good polish will smarten up GRP body panels.

Seitz Acrylic Polish, and Fenwick's Windowize are products designed to reinstate their condition.

☐ Products like Mer polish will soon smarten up dull GRP ('fibreglass') body panels.

☐ Before reinstalling your leisure battery, give it a top-up if needed with de-ionised water as discussed in Chapter Thirteen.

☐ Underfloor spare wheel carriers often get rusted up and it's regrettable that a carrier's telescopic tubing is seldom checked and lubricated during a caravan service. This photograph shows pre-

Loosening up an under-floor spare wheel carrier.

Removing a water filter using a hardwood batten.

season loosening-up – a job that might need plenty of wire-brushing to remove rust, penetrating oil, and a quantity of grease to reinstate seized-up tubing.

☐ Fit a new water filter as described and illustrated in Chapter Ten. This one is being removed using a hardwood batten with a saw cut made in the end to grip the 'turn plate' on the cartridge. Trying to unscrew a cartridge manually by holding on to this plate often takes the finger strength of an Olympic wrestler.

☐ Then you'll want to set up the water system and try it out before leaving home.

☐ You'll also want to check fridge operation, the gas cooker and so on, especially if you couldn't get your caravan serviced because the local dealer was busy.

☐ Add to this a tyre-pressure check – not forgetting the spare – and you're well on the way.

As the summer season approaches once again, every best wish with your continuing caravanning adventures!

APPENDIX

A The national clubs for caravanners

The two principal caravan clubs have very large memberships and a long history. When they were formed around a hundred years ago, their activities and objectives were very different, but nowadays the services to members are much the same.

Membership benefits are wide-ranging and both clubs own and run some excellent sites. Some are for members only, whereas others admit non-members albeit with an additional surcharge. In addition, both clubs provide excellent guidebooks which list privately owned sites of all sizes, including hundreds of small venues licensed to accept no more than 5 caravans at a time.

Insurance schemes, holiday booking services, monthly magazines, technical advice, and popular towing and caravan ownership courses are offered by both clubs. Equally there are regional groups whose committees arrange local functions to supplement the clubs' national events.

So send for literature and decide if you'd prefer to join The Camping & Caravanning Club or The Caravan Club. Some owners cannot make up their mind so join both! The clubs' addresses are given in the accompanying list.

B Owners' clubs

At the time of writing, there are around 50 clubs devoted to particular makes of caravan, together with specialist associations like the Historic Caravan Club and other formally constituted bodies catering for particular groups of people. If you would like to learn more about these organisations, the addresses of club secretaries are periodically listed in caravanning magazines.

Needless to say, clubs catering for owners of particular makes of caravan are extremely valuable if you want spare parts and your 'van is no longer being manufactured. Members show great brand loyalty and usually arrange a programme of social events. Moreover, it's not unusual to find representatives occupying small stands provided by existing manufacturers at major indoor caravan exhibitions such as The Boat and Caravan Show held every February at the National Exhibition Centre, Birmingham.

C The National Caravan Council

The NCC, to use its well-known acronym is, '…the representative body for businesses trading in the UK caravan and motorhome industry.' (Annual Report & Accounts, 2005, P1.) Thus it represents the four sectors of the UK industry, namely: Touring Caravans, Motor Caravans, Caravan Holiday-Homes and Residential Park Homes. Whilst its main reason for existence is to serve its fee-paying trade members, the NCC runs many schemes which help individual caravanners.

In particular the NCC Approval Badge displayed on most UK-manufactured caravans confirms that the product complies with the relevant British or European Standards or Industry Code of Practice, together with UK laws. Other initiatives include The Approved Workshop Scheme, CRiS (Caravan Registration and Identification Scheme), *The Caravan Towing Guide* booklet, and the site guide entitled, *NCC Quality Graded Touring Parks.*

Information leaflets are available free of charge either from the NCC stands at major indoor exhibitions, or from the Association's headquarters. (See Address list.)

D Continental travel booking agencies

This handbook provides guidance about using a caravan and when read in conjunction with, *Driving Abroad* by Robert Davies (published by Haynes), it is immediately apparent that there's no reason why you should restrict your touring to the UK. In fact, taking your caravan around Europe is not as daunting as many imagine. Nevertheless, many caravanners find that to reduce the amount of pre-holiday 'paper-work', it's worthwhile entrusting the booking arrangements to one of the specialist agencies. Both the national clubs run ferry and site booking services, as well as specialists like: Eurocamp Independent, Select Sites Reservations, and The Alan Rogers' Booking Service.

These booking specialists provide helpful guidance as well as making ferry reservations and site bookings. Taking Select Sites Reservations as an example, this Company's Travel Pack includes a detailed *Holiday Guidebook*, a booklet on sites recommended for overnight stop-overs, a guide to your destination region, leaflets giving full information on your selected sites, Michelin Maps covering areas around your booked sites, and GB car and caravan stickers. It really does make the whole process easy.

If you decide to travel in Europe during the low season, there are also schemes whereby you can pre-purchase vouchers for use at participating sites at a considerable discount on the normal overnight fees. The Camping Cheque service is probably the best known of these off-season voucher discount schemes.

E Address list of key accessory suppliers

Please note: *This address list was correct at the time of going to press. It includes specialist suppliers and manufacturers whose products and services have been mentioned in this book. Several of the firms have web sites and these are easy to locate using search engines.*

Abbey and Ace Caravans - See The Swift Group

ABI Caravans Ltd,
(Ceased manufacturing touring caravans, in 2001)

ABP Accessories,
27 Nether End,
Great Dalby,
Leicestershire, LE14 2EY
Tel: 08700 115111
(Importer of Camco products)

Adria Concessionaires,
Hall Street,
Long Melford, Sudbury,
Suffolk, CO10 9JP
Tel: 0870 774 0007
(Adria caravans)

Alan Rogers' Guides,
Spelmonden Old Oast,
Goudhurst,
Kent, TN17 1HE
Tel: 01580 241000
(Guides listing inspected, high quality campsites)

Alde International (UK) Ltd,
14 Regent Park,
Booth Drive,
Park Farm South,
Wellingborough,
Northamptonshire, NN8 6GR
Tel: 01933 677765
(Central heating systems, Gas leak detector)

AL-KO Kober Ltd,
South Warwickshire Business Park,
Kineton Road, Southam,
Warwickshire, CV47 0AL
Tel: 01926 818500
(Chassis, running gear, security, stabilisers, wheel carriers)

Alpine Electronics, (UK)
Alpine House,
Fletchamstead Highway,
Coventry, CV4 9TW,
Tel: 0845 3131641
(Rearview cameras, mobile media products)

Approved Workshop scheme – See National Caravan Council

Aquaroll products – See F.L. Hitchman

Autoglym,
Works Road,
Letchworth,
Hertfordshire,
SG6 1LU
Tel: 01462-677766
(Caravan and car interior/exterior cleaning products)

Avondale Coachcraft Ltd,
(Ceased manufacturing caravans in 2008)

Bailey Caravans Ltd,
South Liberty Lane,
Bristol,
BS3 2SS
Tel: 0117 966 5967
(Manufacturer of Bailey caravans)

BCA Leisure Ltd,
Unit H8,
Premier Way,
Lowfields Business Park,
Elland,
North Yorkshire, HX5 9HF
Tel: 01422 376977
(Trade supplier of Powerpart mains kits, Powerpart Mobile and Smat towing mirrors; see Pennine Leisure)

Belling Appliances - See Glen Dimplex

Bessacarr Caravans – See The Swift Group

Blue Bio biological toilet fluid – See Sail and Trail

BP Gas Light – See Truma UK

BPW Ltd,
Legion Way,
Meridian Business Park,
Leicester, LE19 1UZ
Tel: 0116 281 6100
(BPW chassis and Winterhoff stabilizers)

Bolon Carpets for awnings – See Isabella International Camping

Brink UK Ltd,
Unit 7,
Centrovell Industrial Estate,
Caldwell Road,
Warwickshire, CV11 4NG
Tel: 01203 352353
(Towbars)

British Car Auctions
Tamworth Road, Measham,
Derbyshire, DE12 7DY,
Tel: 01530 270332
(Caravan auctions)

Brittania Specialist Fitting Services,
Unit 6, Wadehurst Industrial Park,
St. Philips Road,
St. Philips,
Bristol, Avon, BS2 0JE
Tel: 0117 955 1011
(Specialist installer of towbars and towing systems)

Buccaneer Caravans - See Elddis

Bulldog Security Products Ltd,
Units 2, 3, & 4,
Stretton Road,
Much Wenlock,
Shropshire, TF13 6DH
Tel: 01952-728171
(Bulldog stabilisers, SSK stabiliser importer, security devices)

C.A.K. Tanks – See Caravan Accessories

Calor Gas Ltd,
Athena Drive,
Tachbrook Park,
Warwick, CV34 6RL
Tel: 0800 626626
(Supplier of butane, propane and LPG appliances)

Calvers Caravan Storage,
Woodlands Park,
Bedford Road,
Clapham,
Bedford, MK41 6EJ
Tel: 01234 359584
(Indoor and outdoor caravan storage)

The Camping & Caravanning Club,
Greenfields House,
Westwood Way,
Coventry, CV4 8JH
Tel: 024 7647 5448

Camco Products - See ABP Accessories

Campingaz
Coleman UK Inc.,
Parish Wharf Estate,
Harbour Road,
Portishead,
Bristol, BS20 9DA
Tel: 01275 845024
(Supplier of Campingaz butane and LPG appliances)

Caravan Accessories (CAK Tanks) Ltd,
10 Princes Drive,
Kenilworth,
Warwickshire, CV8 2FD
Tel: 0844 414 2324
(Water, gas, and electrical accessories)

The Caravan Club
East Grinstead House,
East Grinstead,
West Sussex, RH19 1UA
Tel: 01342 326944

The Caravan Centre,
Unit 3A,
Gilchrist Thomas Industrial Estate,
Blaenavon,
NP4 9RL
Tel: 01495 792700
(Specialist breakers supplying caravan products)

The Caravan Seat Cover Centre,
Cater Business Park,
Bishopsworth,
Bristol,
BS13 7TW
Tel: 0117-941 0222
(Re-upholsterer, loose covers, and foam supplier)

Caravan Storage Site Owners' Association (CaSSOA),
Market Square House,
St James Street,
Nottingham,
NG1 6SG,
Tel: 0115 934 9826
(Register of approved caravan storage sites)

Carcoon Storage Systems Int. Ltd,
Orchard Mill,
2 Orchard Street,
Salford,
Manchester, M6 6FL
Tel: 0161 737 9690
(Trickle battery charger: Mail Order)

Carlight Caravans
(Ceased manufacturing caravans in 2004)

Carver Spares – See Miriad Products and Truma (UK)

CEC Plug-In-Systems,
(Contact your caravan dealer)

Ceuta Healthcare,
41 Richmond Hill,
Bournemouth,
Dorset, BH2 6H7
Tel: 0800 0975606
(Milton sterilising products and water treatment additives)

Clesse UK,
Unit 8,
Planetary Industrial Estate,
Wolverhampton, WV13 3XQ,
Tel: 01902 383233
(LP gas regulators and equipment)

Coachman Caravan Co Ltd,
Amsterdam Road,
Sutton Field Industrial Estate,
Hull, HU7 0XF
Tel: 01482 839737
(Manufacturers of Coachman caravans)

Compass Caravans Ltd – See Elddis

CRiS – See HPI

Crown Caravans - See Elddis

CTEK chargers – See RoadPro

B. Dixon-Bate Ltd,
Unit 45, First Avenue,
Deeside Industrial Park,
Deeside,
Clwyd, CH5 2LG
Tel: 01244 288925
(Towing accessories including cushioned towball units)

Dometic Group,
Dometic House,
The Brewery,
Blandford St Mary,
Dorset, DT11 9LS
Tel: 0844 626 0133
(Formerly Electrolux Leisure; amalgamated with WAECO in 2007: Air conditioners, refrigerators, Seitz windows, Cramer cookers)

Eberspacher UK,
10 Headlands Business Park,
Salisbury Road,
Ringwood,
Hampshire, BH24 3PB,
Tel: 01425 480151
(Diesel space heating systems for caravans)

EECO,
Exhaust Ejector Co Ltd,
Wade House Road,
Shelf, Nr. Halifax,
West Yorkshire, HX3 7PE
Tel: 01274 679524
(Replacement acrylic windows made to order)

Elddis Caravans, (Formerly the Explorer Group)
Delves Lane, Consett,
Co Durham, DH8 7PE
Tel: 01207 503477
(Manufacturer of Buccaneer, Crown, Elddis, and Compass models)

Elecsol Europe Ltd,
47 First Avenue,
Deeside Industrial Park,
Deeside,
Flintshire, CH5 2LG
Tel: 0800 163298
(Elecsol batteries)

Electrical Contractors Association (ECA),
ECA ECSA House,
34 Palace Court,
London, W2 4HY
Tel: 020 7313 4800
(Mains supply system inspection)

Electrolux Appliances – See Dometic Group

Elsan Ltd,
Elsan House, Bellbrook Park,
Uckfield,
East Sussex, TN22 1QF
Tel: 01825 748200
(Manufacturer of toilets and chemicals)

Exide Technologies Ltd,
6/7 Parkway Estate,
Longbridge Road,
Trafford Park,
Manchester, M17 1SN
Tel: 0161 786 3333
(Exide Gel and Lead/Acid Leisure Batteries)

Explorer Caravans – See Elddis

Farécla Products Ltd,
Broadmeads, Ware,
Hertfordshire, SG12 9HS
Tel: 01920 465041
(Caravan Pride acrylic window scratch remover and GRP surface renovator)

Federation of Automatic Transmission Engineers (FATE)
Tel: 07885 228 595
(Trade association for car transmissions)

Fenwick's,
Fir Tree Farm,
Chorley,
Cheshire, CW5 8JR
Tel: 01270 524111
(Caravan cleaning and care products)

Fiamma water pumps and water tanks – Contact your caravan dealer for Fiamma products.

Flavel Leisure,
Clarence Street,
Leamington Spa,
Warwickshire, CV31 2AD
Tel: 01926 427027
(Flavel cookers and hobs)

F.L. Hitchman,
46 The Trading Estate,
Ditton Priors,
Bridgnorth,
Shropshire,
WV16 6SS
Tel: 01746 712242
(Suppliers of portable water containers and cleaning chemicals)

Fleetwood Caravans
(Ceased manufacturing caravans in 2009)

FFC (Foam for Comfort) Ltd,
Unit 2,
Wyther Lane Trading Estate,
Kirkstall,
Leeds, LS5 3BT
Tel: 0845 345 8101
(New foam supplier, composite bonded foam specialist)

Forest Holidays,
(Organised through The Camping and Caravanning Club)
Tel: 0845 130 8224

Gaslow International,
Castle Business Park,
Pavilion Way,
Loughborough,
Leicestershire,
LE11 5GW
Tel: 0845 4000 600
(Refillable gas systems, Gaslow gauges, regulators, couplings and components)

Gas Safe Register™,
PO Box 6804,
Basingstoke,
RG24 4NB
Tel: 0800 408 5500
(The official industry stamp for gas safety, replacing CORGI)

GB-Sol,
Unit 2,
Glan-y-Llyn Industrial Estate,
Cardiff Road, Taffs Well,
Cardiff, CF15 7JD
Tel: 029 2082 0910
(Semi-flexible lightweight solar panels)

General Ecology Europe,
St Andrews House,
26 Brighton Road,
Crawley,
Sussex, RH10 6AA
Tel: 01293 400644
(Nature Pure Ultrafine water purifier)

GFL Caravan Panel Shop,
Unit 7,
Willacy Yard,
Bay Horse Lane,
Catforth,
Preston,
Lancashire, PR4 0JD
Tel: 01772 691929
(Replica caravan panels in GRP)

Glen Dimplex Home Appliances,
Stoney Lane,
Prestcot,
Merseyside, L35 2XW
Tel: 0871 22 22 503
(Belling, New World, Stoves, Vanette appliances)

Grade UK Ltd,
3 Central Court,
Finch Close,
Lenton Lane Industrial Estate,
Nottingham, NG7 2NN
Tel: 0115 986 7151
(Status TV aerials, Flat Screen TV and accessories)

Grangers International,
Grange Close,
Clover Nook Industrial Estate,
Alfreton,
Derbyshire, DE55 4QT
Tel: 01773 521521
(Awning proofing and cleaning products)

Grayston Engineering Ltd,
115 Roebuck Road,
Chessington,
Surrey, KT9 1JZ
Tel: 020 8974 1122
(Trade supplier of tow car spring assister kits)

Hawke House Marine Ltd,
Unit E1,
Heritage Business Park,
Heritage Way,
Gosport,
Hampshire, PO12 4BG
Tel: 02392 588588
(Cut-from-roll Vent Air-Mat; mattress anti-condensation underlay)

Hella Ltd,
Wildmere Industrial Estate,
Banbury,
Oxfordshire,
OX16 3JU
Tel: 01295 272233
(Hella towing electrical equipment)

Honda (UK),
Power Road,
London, W4 5YT
Tel: 020 8747 1400
(Portable leisure generators)

HPI,
Dolphin House,
New Street,
Salisbury,
Wiltshire, SP1 2PH
Tel: 01722 413434
(Caravan Registration & Identification Scheme)

International Tool Co Ltd,
Interlink Way South,
Bardon Hill,
Coalville,
Leicestershire, LE67 1PH
Tel: 08449 395910
(Mail Order, Dial-type tyre pressure gauges)

Isabella International Camping,
Isabella House,
Drakes Farm,
Drakes Drive,
Long Crendon,
Buckinghamshire, HP18 9BA
Tel: 01844 202099
(Awnings, Isabella product alteration service and reproofing)

Jenste,
The Stables,
Pashley Farm,
Ninfield Road,
Bexhill-on-Sea,
East Sussex,
TN39 5JS
Tel: 01424 893880
(RYD Live/neutral polarity changeover unit)

Jonic,
Unit 5, Woodgate Park,
White Lund Industrial Estate,
Morecombe,
Lancashire,
LA3 3PS
Tel: 01524 67074
(Memory foam, fitted sheets, mattress protectors, duvets)

Johnnie Longden Ltd,
Unit 24,
Dawkins Road Industrial Estate,
Poole,
Dorset, BH15 4JD
Tel: 01202 679121
(Caravan Accessories including components for older caravans)

Kenlowe Ltd,
Burchetts Green,
Maidenhead,
Berkshire, SL6 6QU
Tel: 01628 823303
(Radiator cooling fans and automatic transmission oil coolers)

Khyam Awnings,
Dealer listing via website
www.khyam.co.uk
(Quick-erect awnings)

Knott (UK) Ltd – See Miriad Products Ltd

Labcraft Ltd,
22B King Street,
Saffron Walden,
Essex, CB10 1ES
Tel: 01799 513434
(Lighting and 12V products)

Leisure Accessories Ltd,
Britannia Works,
Hurricane Way,
Airport Industrial Estate,
Norwich, NR6 6EY
Tel: 01603 414551
(Diaphragm pump repairs and POSIflow, FLOking sales)

Lunar Caravans Ltd,
6 Sherdley Road,
Lostock Hall,
Preston,
Lancashire,
PR5 5JF
Tel: 01772 337628
(Manufacturer of Lunar caravans)

Marlec Engineering Ltd,
Rutland House,
Trevithick Road,
Corby,
Northamptonshire, NN17 5XY
Tel: 01536 201588
(Wind and solar systems)

Magnum Mobiles and Caravan Surplus,
Unit 9A,
Cosalt Industrial Estate,
Convamore Road,
Grimsby,
DN32 9JL
Tel: 01472 353520
(Caravan surplus stock)

Maypole Ltd,
54 Kettles Wood Drive,
Woodgate Business Park,
Birmingham,
West Midlands,
B32 3DB
Tel: 0121 423 3011
(Towing accessories, electrical items)

Maxol heaters – See Propex

Maxview,
Common Lane,
Setchey,
King's Lynn,
Norfolk, PE33 0AT
Tel: 01553 813300
(Maxview TV dishes/aerials)

Merlin Equipment,
Unit 1, Hithercroft Court,
Lupton Road,
Wallingford,
Oxfordshire, OX10 9BT
Tel: 01491 824333
(PROwatt Inverters)

Mer Products,
12 Centrus,
Mead Lane,
Hertford,
Hertfordshire,
SG13 7GX
Tel: 01992 512698
(Caravan cleaners and polish)

Whitehead House,
120 Beddington Lane,
Croydon,
Surrey, CR0 4TD
Tel: 020 8401 0002
(Distributor of Mer Car Care products)

Milton Steriliser – See Ceuta Healthcare

Miriad Products Ltd,
Park Lane,
Dove Valley Park,
Foston,
South Derbyshire,
DE65 5BG
Tel: 01283 586060
(Accessories; UK distributor of Knott running gear & BPW chassis)

Morco Products Ltd,
Morco House,
Riverview Road,
Beverley,
HU17 0LD
Tel: 01482 325456
(Instantaneous Water Heaters)

Munster Simms Engineering Ltd,
277 -279 Old Belfast Road,
Bangor,
Co Down,
BT19 1LT
Northern Ireland.
Tel: 028 9127 0531
(Whale water products and semi-rigid pipe)

The National Caravan Council,
Catherine House,
Victoria Road,
Aldershot,
Hampshire,
GU11 1SS
Tel: 01252 318251

National Inspection Council for Electrical Installation Contracting,
(NICEIC)
Warwick House,
Houghton Hall Park,
Houghton Regis,
Dunstable, LU5 5ZX
Tel: 01582 539000
(Independent voluntary body for electrical installation matters)

National Trailer and Towing Association,
1 Alveston Place,
Leamington Spa,
Warwickshire, CV32 4SN
Tel: 01926 335445
(Trade Association for all aspects of towing and equipment)

The Natural Mat Company,
99 Talbot Road,
London, W11 2AT
Tel: 020 7985 0474
(Anti-condensation mattress underlay)

Nikwax,
Unit F,
Durgates Industrial Estate,
Wadhurst,
East Sussex, TN5 6DF
Tel: 01892 786400
(Awning proofing products)

NICEIC,
Tel: 01717 5827746
(Professional trade association for electrical contractors)

PCT,
Holbrook Industrial Estate,
Holbrook,
Sheffield, S20 3GH
Tel: 0845 123 1111
(Towbar manufacturers and towing electrics)

Pennine Leisure Supplies,
Unit G9,
Lock View,
Elland,
West Yorkshire, HX5 9HD
Tel: 01422 313 455
(Wholesaler of Accessories and BCA Powerpart products)

PGR Products Ltd,
Unit16 Allenby Business Village,
Crofton Road,
Lincoln,
Lincolnshire, LN3 4NL
Tel: 01522 534538
(Sectional TV mast, security, winter wheels)

Plug-In-Systems,
(Contact your caravan dealer)

Powerpart electrical accessories
– See Pennine Leisure

Powrwheel Ltd,
6 Priory Industrial Estate,
Airspeed Road,
Christchurch,
Hampshire, BH23 4HD
Tel: 01425 283293
(Caravan motorised movers)

Propex Heatsource Ltd,
Unit 5,
Second Avenue Business Park,
Millbrook,
Southampton, SO15 0LP
Tel: 023 8052 8555
(Space heaters and Malaga Water heaters)

Pro-Tec Covers,
202 Leeds Road,
Bradford,
West Yorkshire, BD3 9PS
Tel: 01274 780088
(Breathable, model specific caravan covers)

Pyramid Products Ltd,
Byron Avenue,
Lowmoor Road Industrial Estate,
Kirkby in Ashfield,
Nottinghamshire, NG17 7LA
Tel: 01623 754567
(Awnings and caravanning accessories)

Remis UK,
(Caravan blinds – Order through dealer)

Reich UK,
91 Hednesford Road,
Cannock,
Staffordshire, WS12 5HL
Tel: 01543 459243
(Importer of motorised movers and accessories)

Right Connections UK Ltd,
7 Churchill Buildings,
Queen Street,
Wellington,
Telford,
Shropshire, TF1 1HT
Tel: 0871 226 2030
(Towbar vehicle-specific wiring kits)

Ring Automotive Ltd,
Gelderd Road,
Leeds, LS12 6NA
Tel: 0113 213 7389
(Vehicle lighting, towing and general accessories)

RoadPro Ltd,
Stephenson Close,
Drayton Fields Industrial Estate,
Daventry,
Northamptonshire, NN1 5RF
Tel: 01327 312233
(Suppliers of chargers, inverters, satellite TV systems, electrical accessories)

Ronseal Ltd,
Thorncliffe Park,
Chapeltown,
Sheffield,
South Yorkshire, S35 2YP
Tel: 0114 246 7171
(For suppliers of Tri-Flow penetrating lubricant with Teflon®)

RYD Live/neutral polarity
changeover unit – See Jenste

Sail and Trail,
The Old Barn,
Main Street,
Newton,
Nottingham,
NG13 8HN
Tel: 0845 3960620
(Mail Order: Blue BIO toilet fluids and leisure products)

Sargent Electrical Services Ltd,
Unit 39,
Tokenspire Business Park,
Woodmansey,
Beverley,
Hull, HU17 0TB
Tel: 01482 881655
(Electrical control systems and low voltage panels)

Seitz products – See Dometic

**Selmar Guardian Chargers
Tadmod Ltd,**
Galliford Road,
Malden,
Essex, CM9 4XD
Tel: 0161 859444
(Selmar stage chargers, from marine specialists)

Sew 'n' So's,
42 Claudette Avenue,
Spalding,
Lincolnshire, PE11 1HU
Tel: 01775 767 633
(Bespoke awnings, cover systems, bags and generator covers)

SF Detection,
4 Stinsford Road,
Nuffield Industrial Estate,
Poole,
Dorset,
BH17 0RZ
Tel: 01202 645577
(SF350 Carbon monoxide detectors)

Ship Shape Bedding,
Turners Farm,
Crowgate Street,
Tunstead,
Norfolk,
NR12 8RD
Tel: 08704 464233
(Cut-from-roll DRY Mat™ Anti condensation mattress underlay)

Shurflo Ltd,
5 Sterling Park,
Gatwick Road,
Crawley,
West Sussex,
RH10 9QT
Tel: 01293 424000
(Shurflo diaphragm water pumps)

Smat towing mirrors – See BCA
Leisure

**The Society of Motor
Manufacturers and Traders,**
Trade Sections Department,
Forbes House,
Halkin Street,
London, SW1X 7DS
Tel: 020 7235 7000
(Publishers of SMMT booklet Towing and the Law)

Solar Solutions,
Stepnell Reach, Unit 1,
541 Blandford Road,
Poole,
Dorset, BH16 5BW
Tel: 01202 632488
(Solar panel accessories)

Sold Secure Trust,
5c Great Central Way,
Woodford Halse,
Daventry,
Northamptonshire, NN11 3PZ
Tel: 01327 264687
(Test house conducting security device testing)

Specialised Accessories,
1-2 Riverdale House,
Dockfield Road,
Shipley,
West Yorkshire, BD17 7AD
Tel: 01943 864828
(Breathable, model specific caravan covers)

Spinflo cooking appliances – See
Thetford

The Stabiliser Clinic,
Holme Grove,
Bypass Road,
Garstang,
Preston,
Lancashire, PR3 1NA
Tel: 01995 603745
(Stabiliser testing and overhaul service)

Stoves plc – See Glen Dimplex

Swift Group Ltd,
Dunswell Road,
Cottingham,
Hull, HU16 4JX
Tel: 01482 847332
(Manufacturer of Abbey, Bessacarr, Sprite, Sterling & Swift caravans)

The 12Volt Shop,
9 Lostwood Road,
St Austell,
Cornwall, PL25 4JN
Tel: 01726 69102
(Mail order of twelve volt electrical components)

Thetford (UK) Spinflo,
4-10 Welland Close,
Parkwood Industrial Estate,
Rutland Road,
Sheffield, S3 9QY
Tel: 01142 738157
(Norcold refrigerators, toilets and treatments, Spinflo cooking appliances)

Towing Electrics Ltd,
Unit 3F, Moss Industrial Estate,
Woodbine Street East,
Rochdale,
Lancashire, OL16 5LB
Tel: 01706 638065
(Caravan and Towing relays)

Towsure Products Ltd,
151-183 Holme Lane,
Hillsborough,
Sheffield, S6 4JR
Tel: 0870 60 900 70
(Accessory supplier and towbar manufacturer)

Towing Solutions Ltd,
The Old Dyehouse,
London Road Terrace,
Macclesfield,
Cheshire, SK11 7RN
Tel: 01625 433251
(Complete towing installation service, Publisher of 'How to Pass the Towing Test: B+E explained')

Trav-L-Cool water-evaporative air conditioner – See CAK

Tri-Flow Suppliers – See Ronseal

Truma UK,
Park Lane,
Dove Valley Park, Foston,
South Derbyshire, DE65 5BG
Tel: 01283 586050
(Space and water heating systems, gas components, water systems, caravan mover, Carver spares)

Tyron UK,
Castle Business Park,
Pavilion Way,
Loughborough,
Leicestershire,
LE11 5GW
Tel: 0845 4000 600
(Tyron Safety Bands)

VanMaster Touring Homes Ltd,
Unit S32,
Standish Court,
Bradley Hall,
Bradley Lane,
Standish,
Wigan,
WN6 0XQ
Tel: 01942 212194
(VanMaster caravans)

Vanroyce Caravans,
(No longer in manufacture)

Varta Automotive Batteries Ltd
Broadwater Park,
North Orbital Road,
Denham,
Uxbridge,
Middlesex,
UB9 5HR
Tel: 01895 838989
(Gel-type, non-spill leisure batteries)

Ventair mattress underlay – See Hawke House Marine

Ventura caravan awnings – See Isabella International Camping

V & G Caravans,
107 Benwick Road,
Whittlesey,
Peterborough,
Cambridgeshire,
PE7 2HD
Tel: 01733 350580
(Replacement replica panels in GRP)

W4 Ltd,
Unit B, Ford Lane Industrial Estate,
Arundel,
West Sussex,
BN18 0DF
Tel: 01243 553355
(Suppliers of 230V kits, socket testers, and ribbon sealants)

WAECO International,
(Battery chargers, inverters and electrical accessories)
See Dometic

Watling Engineers Ltd,
88 Park Street Village,
St. Albans,
Hertfordshire,
AL2 2LR
Tel: 01727 873661
(Designer/manufacturer/fitter of towing brackets)

Webasto Products UK,
White Rose Way,
Doncaster Carr,
South Yorkshire,
DN4 5JH
Tel: 01302 322232
(Water evaporative air conditioners)

Whale Products - See Munster Simms Engineering Ltd,

Winterhoff coupling head stabilisers - See Miriad Products Ltd and BPW Ltd

Witter Towbars,
Drome Road,
Deeside Industrial Park,
Deeside, CH5 2NY
Tel: 01244 284500
(Towbar systems and cycle carriers)

ZIG Electronics Ltd,
Saxon Business Park,
Hanbury Road,
Stoke Prior,
Bromsgrove,
Worcestershire,
B60 4AD
Tel: 01527 556715
(Low voltage control components, chargers, and gauges)

Zippo UK Ltd,
Unit 27,
Grand Union Centre,
336B Ladbroke Grove,
London,
W105AS
Tel: 020 8964 0666
(General purpose large-size gas lighters)

INDEX

333

334

335

W

Wall vents 43
Warranties 14, 17, 19, 21, 46, 127, 307, 310
Water evaporative cooling units 117
Water heaters 49-50, 175, 295-299, 305
   draining down 296-297, 316-317
   immersion 296
Water ingress 19, 46, 127
Water pumps 177, 185, 307
   diaphragm 184, 189-190
   electric 49, 177, 186-187, 189-191, 242, 244, 259
   hand or foot-operated 175, 185-186
   submersible 184, 187-189, 317
   switching 190-191
Water systems 175-197, 316-317
   combined manual and electric systems 186-187

containers 97, 105, 169, 172, 176-177, 179-180, 183
direct coupling 178
draining down 58, 316
filters and purifiers 183-184, 307, 317, 325
fresh water points 175, 178
fresh water systems 177-179, 182-183, 185
in transit 176
non-return valve 186
pipes 181-183
sterilising systems 181-182
system checking/cleaning/sterilising 305, 325
tanks 296
taps 191, 316-317
waste water system 177-178, 182-183
winter strategies 180
Weighbridges 73-76, 98, 119, 123, 138
Weight distribution 39, 94
   checking 73, 75, 98
   ratio 72, 81

Weight terminologies 70-71
   actual laden weight (ALW) 71, 73-74, 76-77
   gross train weight (GTW) 70, 74, 76
   MRO (Kerbweight) 70-71, 73, 75
   MTPLM 71, 75-77, 98, 119, 123
Wheel bearings 303
Wheel brace 98, 102
Wheel spats 36-37
Wheels 320-321
   13in 50, 99
   14in 50, 99
   alloy 107
   required tightness 102
   roadside changing 101-103
   steel 107
Winches 54
Wind generators 241, 256
Windows 23, 37-38, 45, 48, 143, 153, 305, 322-323
   cracked 38
'Winter wheels' 320